# The Boo

## Builders of
# Dunham
# Massey

The Hall and moat

# David Eastwood

# The story of five generations of the Booths of Dunham Massey

Old Sir George fought doughtily in the Civil War, built a fine house and piece by piece put together a large and rich estate before dying at a great age.

His son William, from the little we know, enlarged the estate, but had he not died young, might have fatally alienated his tenants with his ambitions of grandeur.

Young Sir George inherited a rich estate almost without entails. Loyal to his principles, he tried to bring about the restoration of parliamentary government, was lucky to escape with his life and his estates intact, and then proceeded to neglect them.

His son Henry inherited large debts and made them much worse. Suicidally foolhardy and brave, his Presbyterian principles almost led to a shameful death before he, with a few others, brought about a dramatic change of regime, so far-reaching in its effects that our monarchy of today would not exist in its present form without it.

And lastly, the third George Booth, second Earl of Warrington. He inherited an enormously debt-ridden estate and a neglected house. Judging by any modern standards, he was bankrupt. But when he died sixty five years later, he left behind a rich estate, a fine modern house and unrivalled collections. Dunham Massey is the envy of many other great houses and cared for in perpetuity, should remain so for ever.

The second Earl of Warrington could not have imagined the vast social changes that have taken place since he died, but at least he would have been glad that much of his wealth remains intact as a source of pleasure to those who visit the house that he would still recognise.

**CHURNET VALLEY BOOKS**
1 King Street, Leek, Staffordshire.ST13 5NW  01538 399033
www.thebookshopleek.co.uk

(C) David Eastwood &Churnet Valley Books 2004
ISBN 1 904546 16 1
Printed in England by the Bath Press

# Preface & Acknowledgements

As a voluntary Room Steward and, latterly, Tour Guide at Dunham Massey Hall, I began to realise that no one had done detailed research on the Booth family who had built the Hall and were influential, to say the least, in the Civil War and the revolution of 1688. Gradually I began to fill in the gaps for my own interest. Then some colleagues said "Why don't you write a book?" This is it, and my thanks go to them. My thanks go also to past and present staff of the National Trust at Dunham Massey for their support and encouragement, in particular Mrs Margaret Stone for her help on several occasions in allowing me access to an invaluable account book of the second Earl of Warrington. Mr James Rothwell, National Trust Historic Buildings Adviser, read much of my first typescript and made many valuable suggestions. I am delighted that my research made partial recompense to him in his latest edition of the Dunham Massey Guide Book.

Archivists and librarians have been unfailingly generous in their efficient help. First among them must come the staff of the John Rylands University Library of Manchester (JRULM), home of the Dunham Massey papers and the Tatton of Wythenshawe papers. I hope the other staff there will forgive my singling out Mr John Hodgson, who not only read much of my TS and made many valuable suggestions, but put my decades-old Latin to shame with his masterly translation of the first Earl of Warrington's stately verse.

Trafford's Local History Unit staff got used to my monopolising their space; the City of Manchester Social Sciences Library were rarely defeated by even the most obscure requests for books from the depths of their basements; their archives have some surprising treasures. The staffs of Chester City Archives and Cheshire County Record Office (now happily amalgamated) are founts of knowledge and I owe them much for their patient help with the Earwaker Papers and deciphering important words in the dreadful handwriting of Sir William Brereton's secretaries. The National Library of Wales provided several inexpensive inches of photocopies and supplied over the counter within a very few seconds many documents from John Oldbury's papers.

I must also pay tribute to Hazel Rollans, who while trying to find a portrait of Mary Oldbury, by chance found a pointer to the existence of the Oldbury papers and shared the knowledge with me. The British Library in London could not have been more helpful on a day when time was a severe constraint. And the Bodleian Library's photocopies opened an entirely new window on old Sir George Booth after the Civil War.

My thanks to his Grace, the Duke of Beaufort, for permission to use papers from his archives; the previously unknown details they give of Lord Warrington's unhappy marriage are fascinating. My thanks to the National Trust at Tatton Hall for allowing me to consult John Bruston's rare book on the Vale Royal.

I need hardly say that all errors are entirely my own and that I beg forgiveness if I have failed to properly credit any of the illustrations.

*And the last shall be first and the first shall be last....* Most of all to my dear wife Mary for her unflagging support, advice and companionship; for the sustaining coffee passed through embrasures in my ever-growing wall of books and files; and for uncomplainingly sharing our house for many years with the shades of five long-dead gentlemen. *Greater love hath.....*

# Genealogical Table of the House of Dunham.

**ROBERT DEL BOOTH or BOTHE, yr Son of John Booth of Barton, Lancashire, d. 1460, m. Douce, yr dau. and coheiress of Sir Wm. Venables, d. 1453.**

1 WILLIAM BOOTH, Son and Heir, d. 1442 Mar. 1, dau. of John Dutton, of Dutton, Esquire.
2 Raufe m. Margaret, dau. of Thomas Sibell, of Sandwich, Co. Kent.
3 Geffrey.
4 Hamond or Hamon, Clerk, LL.D.
5 Lucy, m. to John Chantler, of Bache.
6 Ellen, m. to Robt. Legh, of Adlington.
7 Alice, m. to Robt. Hesketh, of Rixton.
8 Joan, m. to Hamon Massey, of Rixton.
9 Margery, m. to James Scareb ick.
10 John Bishop, of Exeter, warden of Manchester College, d. 1478.
11 Robert, Dean of York.
12 Edward or Edmond, Archdeacon of [Stow.
13 Peter.

1 GEORGE BOOTH, Son and Heir, b. 1445, d. May 25th, 1484. Mar. Katherine, dau. of Robt. Montfort, Lord of Bescott, Staff. and Monkspath, Warwickshire.
2 Richard.
3 Lawrence.
4 John.
5 William.
6 Douce, m. to Thomas Legh, Westhall, High Legh, 1461.
7 Anne, m. to John Legh, of Booths, after to Geffery Shakerley, of Shakerley, Lanc.
8 Ellen, m. to Sir John Legh, of Bagiley, 1466.
9 Margery, m. to John Hyde, of Haghton, Lanc.
10 Alice, m. to John Ashley, of Ashley.
11 Elizabeth, m. to Thomas Fitton, of Pownall.
12 Joan, m. to William Holt, of Lanc.

1 WILLIAM, Son and Heir, b. 1473. d. 1519. Mar. first, Margaret, coheiress of Sir Thomas Ashton, Ashton-under-Lyne. Mar. second, Ellen, dau. of Sir John Montgomery, Throwley, Staff.
2 Lawrence.
3 Roger.
4 Alice, otherwise Anne, m. William Massey, of Denfield Rostherne.
5 Ellen, m. Thomas Vawdrey, afterwards Trafford, of Bridge Trafford, in Cheshire.

1 GEORGE, Son and Heir, b. 1490. d. 1531. Mar. Elizabeth, dau. of Sir Thomas Butler of Bewsey, nr. Warrington.
2 John Booth.
1 William.
2 Hamnett.
3 Edward, from whom the Booths of Twamlow, Cheshire.
4 Henry.
5 Andrew.
6 Jane, m. to Hugh Dutton, son and heir of Sir Piers Dutton, of Hatton and Dutton (1520), afterwards to Thos. Holford, of Holford, nr. Nether Tabley, esq.
7 Dorothy, m. to Edward Warren, son and heir of Laurence Warren, of Pointon, esquire 15(?).
8 Anne, m. to Sir William Brereton, of Brereton.

GEORGE, Son and Heir, b. 1515, d. 1543. m. Elizabeth, dau. of Sir Edmund Trafford, of Trafford, esquire.
2 John.
3 Robert.
4 Ellen, m. to John, son and heir of John Carrington, of Carrington, esquire (1537).
5 Anne, m. to Wm. Massy, of Podington, Wirrall, esquire.
6 Margaret, m. to Sir Wm. Davenport, of Bramhall.
7 Elizabeth, m. Richard Sutton, of Sutton, esq. (1561).
8 Dorothy, m Robert Tatton, of Wythenshawe, esquire.
9 Alice, m. Peter Daniel, of Over Tabley (1550).
10 Ciceley died without issue.

WILLIAM, Son and Heir, b. 1540, d. 1579. m. Elizabeth, d. of Sir John Warburton, of Arley.
2 Elizabeth, m. Sir William Chantrell, of Bache.
3 Mary, m. Randle Davenport, of Henbury.
4 Anne, m. — Wentworth, of Yorkshire.

GEORGE, Son and Heir, b. 1556, d. 1652. m. firstly Jane, daughter of John Carrington – (no issue.) m. secondly Katherine, daughter of Sir Edmund Anderson, d. 1638.
Edmund, second son, a lawyer, died without issue.
John, m. a daughter of – Prestwich, of Hulme, Manchester, d. 1644.
Robert, b. 1570, was a soldier in Holland.
Peter, b. April 1576, d. September 1576.
Richard, b. 1578, m. — Massy, of Cogshall.
William, d. 1572.
Mary, eldest daughter.
Elizabeth, second daughter, twice married.
Dorothy, m. Rafe Buningham, of Barrowcock, Derbyshire.
Alice, m. one Panton.
Elinour or Elinor, b. 1573.
Susan, b. 1577, twice married.

WILLIAM, d. 1636. m. Vere, d. and co-heiress of Sir Thomas Egerton.
Francis, b. 1603, d. 1616.
Thomas b. 1604, d. 1632.
Edmund b. 1608, d. 1617.
John, knighted 1660.
Mary died unmarried.
Alice m. George Vernon, of Haslington, esquire, d. 1663.
Francis d. 1669.
Susan m. Sir William Brereton, of Hondford or Handford, died 1637.
Katherine unmarried.
Ciceley died young.
Elizabeth, second wife of Richard, Lord Byron, of Newstead. (No issue.)

GEORGE BOOTH, Knt. and Bart., b. 1620, d. Aug. 8th, 1684, m. firstly Katherine, dau of Theophilus Fiennes, Earl of Lincoln.

— m. secondly Elizabeth, daughter of Henry Grey, Earl of Stamford and Baron Bonville and [Harrington, d. 1690.

1 Thomas, b. 1620, d. 1632.

Vere, died unmarried 1717.

2 HENRY LORD DELAMER, created Earl of Warrington April 17th, 1690, d. 1693, aged 42. m. Mary, d. of Sir James Langham.

1 Wm. Booth, b. 1648, d. 1661-2.
3 Charles d. in France unmarried.
4 George Booth d. in 1726, having had issue by his wife Lucy, dau. of Robert, Lord Viscount Bodmin, Charles Henry, who died unmarried.
5 Cecil Booth d. unmarried 1711.
6 Neville Booth d. unmarried 1685.

5 Robert Booth, Rector of Thornton and Archdeacon of Durham 1691, Dean of Bristol 1708, d. Aug. 8th, 1730, m. first Anne. d. of Sir Robt. Booth, of Salford, Knt., by whom Henry d. an infant; m. secondly Mary, dau., of Thomas Hales, of Howlets, co. Kent, by whom Mary, who died unmarried, Elizabeth, wife of Charlton Thrupp, esquire, and Vere, wife of George Tyndale, of Bathford, esquire, Robert, George and Edward, and Nathaniel Booth, of Hampstead, esquire, who succeeded to the title of Lord Delamere, in 1758, d. Jan. 9th, 1770

Elizabeth, wife of Edward Conway, Earl of Conway. (d. 1645)
Anne died young.
Jane died young.
Diana, wife of Sir Ralph Delavel, of Seaton Delavel, co. Northumberland, afterwards of Sir Edward Blackett, of Newby, co. York.
Sophia died young.

1 James died an infant.

2 GEORGE BOOTH, Earl of Warrington, b. at Mere Hall, May 2nd, 1675, d. Aug. 2nd, 1758, m. Mary, eldest dau. and coheiress of John Oldbury.

3 Langham Booth, Groom of the Bedchamber to King George II., M.P. co. Chester, 4 and 7 Anne, and 1st George I., b. 1684, died (unmarried) 1724.
4 Henry Booth, b. 1687, d. at Rotterdam, 1726.

Elizabeth, wife of Thomas, eldest son of Sir Thomas Delves, Dodington, Bart., d. 1697.
Mary, wife of Hon. Russel Robartes, d. 1741.

MARY, b. 1703, d. Dec. 1772, m. May 1736, to HARRY GREY, fourth Earl of Stamford, d. May 1768, buried at Enville.

GEORGE HARRY, b. 1737, M.P. co. Staff. 1761, succeeded as fifth Earl of Stamford, &c., May 1768, Lord Lieutenant of the County of Chester, 1783, created Baron Delamer of Dunham Massey and Earl of Warrington April 20th, 1796, d. 1819, m. 1763 to Henrietta Cavendish Bentinck, second daughter of William second Duke of Portland, b. 1736, d. 1827.

Booth Grey, b. 1740, M.P. for Leicester, 1768, d. 1802, m. 1782 Elizabeth, daughter of Charles Mainwaring, of Bromborough, esquire. She died in 1823.

John Grey, b. 1743, d. 1802, m. 1773 Susanna, fourth dau. of Ralph Leycester, of Toft.

Mary b. 1739, d. 1783, m. 1764 to George West, second son of George Earl of Delawarr.
Anne b. 1741-2, d. 1743.

GEORGE HARRY, Sixth Earl, b. 1765, d. April 26, 1845, m. 1797 to Henrietta Charlotte Elizabeth Charteris, eldest dau. of Francis, Lord Elcho, b. 1773, d. 1838.

William Booth Grey b. 1773, d. 1852, m. first, 1802, Annie, only dau. and heiress of Thomas Pryce, of Duffryn, co. Glamorgan—she died in 1737; m. secondly, 1838, Frances Somerville, sister of Lord Somerville.
Anchitel Grey b. 1774, d. a bachelor 1873, Prebendary of Durham.
Henry Grey, Captain R.N., b. 1776, d. 1799, being shipwrecked on board the Weasel in Barnstaple bay.

Henrietta b. 1764, d. 1826, m. 1785 Sir John Chetwode, Bart., of Oakley Hall, Staffordshire.
Maria b. Nov 2nd, 1767, d. Nov. 21st, 1767.
Maria b. 1769, d. 1838, m. 1794 to John Cotes, of Woodcote, co. Salop.
Louisa b. 1771, d. a spinster 1830.

Sophia b. 1777, d. 1849, m. 1809, Booth Grey, of Ashton Hayes.
Amelia b. 1779, d. 1849, m. 1800 to John Lister Kaye, of Grange, near Wakefield, esquire.

GEORGE HARRY BOOTH GREY, b. 1802, d. 1835, summoned to Parliament as Lord Grey of Groby, 1832, m. Katherine, fourth dau. of Francis, 7th Earl of Wemyss.

Maria b. 1800.
Jane b. 1804, m. 1825 Sir John Benn Walsh.

Henry Booth Grey b. 1807, d. 1857, an officer in the army.
Henrietta Charlotte b. 1798, d. 1866, m. 1820 the Rev. Jas. T. Law, son of the Hon. Dr. Law, Bishop of Bath and Wells.

Booth Grey, of Ashton Hayes, b. 1783, d. 1850, m. Sophia Grey, dau. of George fifth Earl of Stamford.
Elizabeth Kynaston b. 1786, d. 1853, m. 1828 Rev. Chas. Mytton, who assumed the name of Thornycroft.

GEORGE HARRY GREY b. 1827, succeeded In 1845 as seventh Earl of Stamford and Warrington, &c., m. first Elizabeth, dau. of Mr. John Billige, of Wincarton - she died Oct. 1854; also to Catherine, dau. of Mr. Henry Cocks, Aug. 29th, 1855.

Margaret Henrietta, Maria m. 1846 to Henry John, son of Mark Millbank, esquire, and died March 7th, 1852.

Harry Grey, in holy orders, b. 1783, d. 1866, m. first Frances Elizabeth, dau. of Hugh Ellis, of Carnarvon, esquire ; secondly to Mary Hervey—by latter no issue.

1 Henrietta b. 1775, m. 1802 to Chas. Mytton, M.A., afterwards Thornycroft, Rector of Eccleston.
2 Mary b. 1778.
3 Emma b. 1782, d. 1851, m. to Thomas William Tatton, of Wythenshawe, esquire.
4 Anna Maria b. 1791, d. 1827, m. Rev. T. Clarke.

Dunham, 1697, the Jacobean Hall. Lord Warrington had begun the formal planting of the park.

Dunham Massey Hall in 1750, after Lord Warrington's rebuilding. By John Harris.
*Both pictures courtesy of The Stamford Collection (The National Trust) Photographic Survey, Courtauld Institute of Art.*

# Contents

'Old' Sir George Booth 1566-1652.

OLD GEORGE BOOTH
|
WILLIAM BOOTH
|
YOUNG GEORGE BOOTH
|
HENRY BOOTH
|
GEORGE BOOTH

# Chapter One
## The First Sir George Booth

Sir George Booth, the builder of Dunham Massey Hall, was, for much of his immensely long life, one of the most important and influential gentlemen in the whole county of Cheshire. He spent the first 76 years of his life in peace and plenty, a leader of society, a Deputy Lieutenant of the county, a High Sheriff, a Justice of the Peace, and a man of great power and influence in local affairs. In spite of his high positions, he never sought a place at Court where he might increase his power and wealth.

However, the even tenor of his ways was swept away in England's Civil Wars, and for much of Booth's last ten years of his life (he died at the great age of 86) he was compelled against his will and inclination to take an active part in the struggle. He was lucky to enjoy excellent health apparently until very shortly before his death, and in spite of the turbulence of those last years, his estates at his death were much larger and richer than those he had inherited so long before.

George Booth was born in 1566, the second son of Sir William Booth and his wife Elizabeth, daughter of Sir John Warburton of Arley, neighbouring Dunham. His father was 26 years old at the time, the eleventh in a line stretching back to the beginning of the 14th century, and the third of his name to be knighted. The Booths inherited the manor of Dunham Massey in 1435. It is likely that they did not live there but at one of their other properties, perhaps at Bollin Hall or less likely at Styal. There was a dwelling on or near the site of the present house but almost nothing is known of it. Ancient tradition says that Hamo de Massey held the land in 1080 under the Earl of Chester and built a motte and bailey there, but if he did no trace of it has ever been discovered. Sir William served as Justice of the Peace for Cheshire, but only one of his cases is quoted in the Quarter Sessions Abstracts published by the Lancashire and Cheshire Record Society. It is a certificate signed by him and Peter Warburton in 1575 that Rafe Lytler of Barnton had been appointed to serve in the Irish wars under Captain Malbe.

Sir William Booth died in 1579, leaving a widow and no less than eleven children, a remarkably high survival rate for those days, although his eldest son died in infancy. In such times of high infant mortality, it was most unusual that the other ten all seem to have survived to get at least some benefit from the estate. Sir William was only 39 years old when he died, and the death seems to have been sudden and unexpected, because he left no will. As he was a Tenant-in-Chief, an Inquisition Post Mortem had to be held.

The Inquisition Jury found that he held over 2,000 acres of arable and heath land in Sinderland, Bowdon, Partington, Dunham, Sale and Timperley, extending as far as Wilmslow, Dean Row, Pownall Fee and Styal, and even out to Staley (now Staleybridge). This holding included four manors and 58 messuages (dwelling houses) and was rich by itself. But in addition there were reversions (where relatives had benefits which reverted to the owner on their death or moving away) totalling over 3,000 acres, with another 38 messuages, so in all the estates comprised almost 5,400 acres of cultivated land and heath.

George, his heir, was only 13 years old at the time, and could not therefore take up his inheritance, even though he was already married!  He was only eleven when he married - or was married to - Jane Carrington, the daughter of another local landowner and four years older than her husband.  In any case George was too young to manage the estates in his own right and someone else had to do it on his behalf until he came of age.

The question was who?  The Booths were among the leading gentry of Cheshire, but did not have quite the same pre-eminent position that they came to enjoy in the next century.  Nevertheless they were conscious of their relative importance and they wanted upward mobility.  Young George was technically a Ward of the Crown, and as such the selection of his Guardian was the responsibility of Queen Elizabeth herself.

Wardship was not primarily concerned with the welfare of a minor.  Mediaeval land tenure enabled the title holder (in this case the Queen) to demand rent in lieu of knight service.  The sovereign could not act personally as guardian to all wards, and since the wardships were valuable, they were granted or sold, often to the highest bidder.

The Queen's choice fell upon her favourite, Robert Dudley, created Earl of Leicester in 1564 and for many years the most powerful and influential courtier in England.  The Queen showered him with gifts and honours and he became fabulously wealthy.  He virtually dominated North Wales and among his positions was that of Chamberlain of the County Palatine of Chester.  This made him ideally suited to be young George Booth's Guardian.  It was in fact to the potential advantage of both parties.  If George's period of wardship proceeded satisfactorily and he grew up on good terms with Leicester, the door might be open for him to receive great riches and advancement.  From Leicester's point of view, a wealthy guardianship was always useful; it tended to increase his local influence and it gave him almost unlimited powers over his ward's estate.  There was no control over his wardship, certainly no obligation to produce annual accounts.  An unscrupulous guardian had freedom to plunder his ward's estate without let or hindrance, to enrich himself entirely at the expense of the young person for whom he was nominally responsible to the Queen.  Fortunately there is no indication that Leicester tried anything of the sort with young Booth and his estates.

On the contrary they seem to have developed a friendly relationship by the time Booth came of age, the proof of which can be seen in a campaign in Europe.  Protestant England and Catholic Spain had been at loggerheads since the marriage of Queen Mary Tudor and Philip of Spain in 1554.  Spain was extremely rich and powerful and her influence was strong.  In addition to the support of their Catholic co-religionists in France, they ruled the coastal Netherlands.  Spain was far enough away not to pose an immediate threat to England, but Spanish colonies just across the North Sea were another matter.  By the 1570s Queen Elizabeth and her advisers had begun to appreciate the potential danger which was made more imminent by the signing of a formal alliance between Spain and France. The Netherlands appealed to Elizabeth for help and a detachment of English soldiers, commanded by Sir John Norris, was already on the Continent.  Eventually Elizabeth, prodded by Leicester and Lord Burghley, agreed to send a sizeable army of 400 cavalry and 4,000 foot soldiers to join Norris.

Later that year Leicester himself was appointed Commander-in-Chief of the combined opposition to the Spanish forces, and George Booth, still not quite twenty years old, accompanied him. The English army placed garrisons in several towns in the event of their being attacked by the Duke of Parma's Spanish troops and Leicester's young staff officers, including Booth, found themselves being used in various capacities - trusted messengers, secretaries, commanders of small detachments - and otherwise being trained for higher command. Potentially they were in no little danger but the Queen ordered that the lives of *"the younger gentry should not be risked in dangerous ventures"*.

Leicester and his retinue eventually returned to England in 1587, roughly coinciding with Booth's coming of age. Booth received the Queen's "livery" (permission) to enter his estates, and when he took formal possession from Leicester there would have traditionally been great celebrations among his own tenantry and grand formal gatherings among the gentry of Cheshire. No record of them survives, but as it is clear that Booth came of age to a rich inheritance it may be assumed that Leicester, helped no doubt by Lady Elizabeth, George's mother, and the estate steward, George Parker of Altrincham, had looked after his inheritance well.

After a few years, during which Booth learned how to manage his estates, he began a series of property acquisitions that made him one of the chief landowners in Cheshire and one of the leaders of the County's gentry. Rapidly he became a man of great influence and authority, particularly in his home ground in the north of the county. The lands he inherited in Dunham and Sinderland, neighbouring Dunham, gave him a rent of £554 a year, and he also had Bollin Hall and property at Wilmslow, a distant estate at Thornton le Moors on the Wirral, and the extensive Carrington estate.

He enjoyed a good and comfortable income; it allowed him to take his place among Cheshire's gentry, but was not enough for excessive ostentation. It did allow him to begin a series of land purchases that lasted forty years. When he came of age, his expenses were initially rather heavy, because he had four brothers and five sisters to provide for. Settling them satisfactorily took about eight years. Each brother was given a £20 annuity and each sister was given a portion of £600 for her future marriage prospects.

Booth began to expand seriously in 1595 by acquiring property in Sale, for which he paid William Chauntrell the large sum of £1,000. He beat this two years later when he enlarged his Bollin Hall property by buying land at Norcliffe for £1,150, a year that also saw him appointed Sheriff of Chester. However his permanent advancement came in 1599 when he was knighted like his father and at least four other Booth ancestors. Small land purchases followed in the next few years, including expansion in Dunham, then in 1605 he bought half of Ashton under Lyne from Sir Richard Hoghton of Hoghton Towers, which cost the vast sum of £5,500.

Superficially, at least, only one of these purchases seems to have been an adequate investment in terms of annual rental received. Only one of them gave a return of more than 2% a year, and that, more land in Sale with 13 tenants, was one of the cheaper acquisitions. The others show a return on paper of between 1% and 2% on the investment and the Dunham Massey land, which was bought from an absentee landlord living in Shropshire, was less than 1%. Even the expensive purchase of half of Ashton-under-Lyne only returned 1¼% and it eventually cost Sir George much more than the agreed price. He had to borrow £600 from Lady Elizabeth Egerton, his daughter-in-law's mother. Unfortunately for him, she denied that he ever made the yearly repayments and charged him interest on the interest, so the original £600 ended by costing him over £1600!

But to judge the value of a property by means of a simple cost/income comparison does not tell the whole story by any means. The actual receipts from the tenants could be, and often were, considerably more than the nominally agreed rent, depending on the kindness or the rapacity of the landlord. Fines, heriots and other feudal dues were commonly exacted, and if they were not too onerous, tenants did not object because they expected them in any case. A common example is that frequently a holding was let out on the basis of three lives, the lives of the tenant himself, his son, and his grandson. When the tenant died, his tenancy would pass automatically to his son, and of course one life would have been used. However, it was normal for the three lives to continue to roll, that is the son's grandson would become the third 'life' and so on - a new third life would be added. The practice was popular among landowners and their tenants; for the former it saved trouble finding suitable tenants - he would always have a good idea of the ability of the families, or his steward would; and for the latter, because the practice gave welcome security and stability. But the transfer was not without expense for the tenant. The successor was expected to pay a 'fine' to the landowner, which could be twice or three times the agreed annual rent. This being occasional, rather than annual, would not show on the rental value of the property. According to Sir George's son William, the 'three lives' agreement was the usual custom on the Booth estates.

Nor would the fines for small misdemeanours show on the value, when they were awarded by the local Manorial Court. Obstruction of a right of way, damming or diverting the course of a stream, or interfering in some way with a neighbour's work, were minor nuisances but could easily escalate if left unchecked, so they were duly punished by small fines. Once again the landlord would profit, but so would the community as a whole, since then as now, it was better to nip petty problems in the bud than to let them get too important and difficult to resolve.

A third example is that of waste land. Inevitably there were almost always odd corners that were not worth incorporating into a larger holding, deemed too small and unprofitable or too barren. If however there was a surplus of manpower locally, a man might risk building a little cottage and trying to work that patch to make some sort of living from it. If he was hardworking and lucky with the weather, he might in due course begin to make a go of it. All this time, a tolerant landlord would turn a blind eye to the illegal occupation, but if it began to be successful, he might officially notice the patch of waste land had been settled. It could then begin to yield a modest rent.

Mills were also extremely profitable. The farmer paid rent for his land but he had also to pay the miller to grind his corn. He then had to pay the landlord a percentage of what he paid the miller - who in turn also had to pay rent to the landlord! The tenants were compelled to have their corn ground only in the estate's mill! So for little or no effort the landowner's actual income from his property was considerably greater than the stated annual rental; and if he was not too greedy there would be no problems.

Not enough estate papers from the period have survived to enable a direct judgement about Booth as a landlord, whether he was kind or grasping, whether he was popular or disliked, or just accepted philosophically by his tenants. However the Court Leet papers indicate that he was fair-minded. In 1618 for example, an unnamed tenant asked to ease the entrance into Broome Field, Carrington. Many landlords would have insisted on the tenant paying for this privilege, but Booth gave the man a note to John Carrington, the steward, stating that no fine was to be levied in this case.

Ten years after receiving his knighthood, Sir George had the opportunity of unexpected promotion. James I conceived the idea of creating a new type of honour, the baronet. Knighthoods could not be inherited, unlike the five grades of the peerage, which were all hereditary until life peerages came into being in recent times. James realised that he could extract money from suitable knights by creating a sort of hereditary knighthood, whereby the title could be inherited by the eldest surviving son. Income was generated by charging a fee for the honour - and also if the proposed recipient refused! Sir George Booth was honoured by being included in the very first ten baronetcies created, which proved that, although he was no more than a provincial squire when seen from the perspective of Court life, he was a man of much importance in his own sphere.

The newly elevated Sir George Booth, Bart. conceived the idea of moving his seat from Bollin Hall to Dunham at about this time. It is likely that Bollin Hall was too mediaeval in style and too old-fashioned to suit him, and he decided to build a new mansion within the park at Dunham. His concept was an open square, with no frontage on the south side. The main entrance would therefore have been direct to the Great Hall, itself an interesting relic of mediaeval thought. No records survive of the construction, but in about 1615 he *"builded three parts of Dunham house, all his barnes, Milles, gardenes and Stables and at every other demaine house putt some parte thereof in reasonable repair, and built his Courte houses and Marled at Dunham fiftie Eight acres and at Carrington twentie acres."*

When he was settled in his new house, further property acquisitions followed. He had already bought the tithes of Bowdon from Robert Tatton esq for £4,000. They realised an income from 300 tenants of £300 a year, which seemed a remarkably good investment. He had increased his holdings at Thornton le Moors, and his colleague on the Bench, Sir Urian Legh of Adlington, had sold him land in Hattersley. By 1620 he had bought a small area of land in Bollington from William Legh, more land in Altrincham from Oswald Moslie, William Rowcrofte and John Carrington, a few tenancies in Sale from John Bryan, and Bank Meadow in Hale from Edward Vaudrey of Riddings in Timperley. The most expensive of these purchases, a reasonable £400, was eclipsed in 1620 when he bought a house in Chester and the tithes of Mottram in Longdendale for a combined cost of £1,450. The Chester house was to provide a pied-a-terre when he was required to be in the city on county business as a Justice of the Peace.

The 1620s passed with only one minor land purchase, some land in Hale belonging to Ralph Barlow, Booth bought for £70. In the 1630s however, when Booth was getting quite elderly, two acquisitions gave him a great deal of trouble, and only one of them was of his own making. His eldest son William was determined to carve out his own career as a landed gentleman and the chance of buying a large estate in Warrington came his way. The landowner was Thomas Ireland of Bewsey and the negotiations began in 1627 when William Booth offered £6,900 for the land. Ireland refused and the matter went into abeyance for nearly a year, until November 1628, when Booth increased his offer slightly. The following month the two gentlemen agreed on a price of £7,300 for the property. Unfortunately, it was far too much for William's means and even for his father's. They could raise about £5,000 between them, so William was forced to look elsewhere for the finances. The method he chose was not calculated to endear him to the tenants of the estates, either in the old properties or in Warrington itself, and although old Sir George went along with it, he certainly regretted doing so later. William wrote to his stewards, John Carrington and William Rowcrofte, giving them precise instructions:

"I would wish you to call the tenantes all together and to signifie unto them that my father and I have gone thorow with Mr Ireland for Warrington, and the summe wee are to give is above £7,000; that this was done makeing noe doubt but that towardes it every one of them being tenantes would by their assistaunce enable us to finish it.

"That it is such an opportunity for them to shew their loves unto us and to gaine our respectes unto them, as the like is never in probability to bee againe.

"That the whole countrey observes to see by this what respectful tenantes they are to their Maister, who ever hath bene more favoureable to them, than most other landlordes have bene to others."

Then came the bad news followed by the unconcealed threat.

"That the desire now made unto them is for three years rent; which if they will give, my father and I would have you to assure them from us both that during our two lives noe more rentes nor guiftes shall be required.

"On the other side if they faile us in this, they may provoke us to sharpe courses, especially mee, who have had a purpose to take the third part of every liveing as it falles, letting the tenant enjoye two parts only without fine......"

William tried to justify himself by claiming that other landlords had been demanding three years rent just for spending money, which was readily granted "if not for love yet for feare" - and it did no more than allow the landlord to enjoy enhanced prestige among his neighbours. The Warrington purchase was so exceptional that such an opportunity would probably never come again. It would be disgraceful if the deal should fall through just because of the recalcitrance of the tenants; it would be common knowledge that the Booths could not afford the deal without help and the tenants would not give it. William was even determined that the tenants would have little or no opportunity to refuse. The unfortunate stewards had to speak to them in public, "to the end their affections may be wroghte uppon if it may bee: after, I think it fitt, those who.... have promised, bee called publikely before all the rest to know what they will doe...."

William knew human nature; it would be a brave man indeed to refuse his demands after such a public meeting. But he had another trick up his sleeve just in case anyone did. They would have to explain themselves to his father, no less. It would be a braver man yet who could stand up to the redoubtable old Sir George Booth, well into his sixties, who had served a term as High Sheriff, a Justice of the Peace for forty years already, and a Deputy Lieutenant of both Cheshire and Lancashire.

*"Such as peevishly denye deale with them in their kyndes and commaund them at a certaine daye to attend my father and give their answere to my father themselves; this I would not have done till you have finished all others, because roughnes being used to any before you have all their answeres may incense some crabbed spirits...."*

The arrangements were that the tenants should pay in three instalments, a total of £500 in each of the first two and £1,500 in the third, with other unspecified means. For individual tenants, the contributions would range between 30 shillings and £30. This still left about £4,800 of the total cost of Warrington to find, and William decided to borrow it from his mother-in-law, but without her knowledge. Lady Elizabeth Egerton, the mother of Vere who had married William in 1610, had in 1625 or before appointed him to collect money owed to her on her behalf *"...for which hee gave her his owne bondes & use for many yeares, whereuppon the great sommes of money ....did multiply and arise due to her."* In the period 1625-27 he collected nearly £3,200 for her and this source of temporary wealth seemed ideal for his purpose. He 'borrowed' what he needed and gave her his bond for it.

He did of course repay various amounts to her, with interest and arrears of interest, but he still owed large sums when he died prematurely in 1636. His mother-in-law began proceedings against his estate in the Court of Common Pleas at Westminster. Old Sir George had to assume responsibility for the debts and to pay them off to Lady Elizabeth, and altogether he had to pay her over £7,300, plus interest of £589 a year. There were other lesser debts and heavy funeral expenses as well. The Warrington estates were yielding less than £300 a year and William's personal estate was no more than £595 in total. The purchase of the Warrington estate must have seemed originally an excellent investment, but thanks to his own improvidence and embezzlement they proved to be very unwise. As well as the natural grief at losing his eldest son, William' death caused Sir George huge expenses over the next few years.

William's other investment was interesting, but also quite expensive. In 1633 Christopher Anderson had the lease from William Bowdon of Altrincham of 2 acres of land in Dunham Massey near the River Bollin, with salt springs, brine springs, salt water and salt pits. In 1635 he assigned the residue of the lease to William for £1,700, to which he added two more brine seeths at Bollington and Agden for £600. Sir William Brereton, William's brother-in-law, much admired them. They were just like the salt works he had seen at Newcastle on Tyne a few years before, which he described in minute detail:

*"In the breadth whereof is placed 6 ranke of panns, 4 pans in a rank. Att either outside the furnaces are placed in the same manner as are my brother Boothes, under the grate of which furnaces the ashes fall....These 24 pans have only 12 furnaces and 12 fires...they are placed by two and two together one against the other. The 6 pans in the highest ranke, the bottom equal with the top of the lower....*

*"The highest pans are thrice filled, and boiled till itt begin to draw towards salt, then a spiggott beeing pulled out, the brian (Brine) thus prepared, runnes into the lower pans, which brings itt to a larger proportion of salt, then otherwise, gaines time and saves fire, because itt must bee longer boiled in the other pans, and would spend fire, which is saved by reason of the heate which derives from the furnace of the upper pan, which by a*

*passage is conveyed under the lower pan."*

The salt produced was in hard black lumps, which were sent to Colchester for further refining *"to make salt upon salt, which are sold for a greater price than the rest, because without these at Colchester, they cannot make any salt."*

The lease of the salt works remained with the Booths until 1655, when young Sir George, who had bought the freehold, sold it back to William Bowdon, the original owner.

William' death, on 26 April 1636, was sudden and he did not leave a will. The Inquisition Post Mortem said that his assets were the manor of Stayley, areas of meadow, pasture and heath in Tintwistle and bits and pieces of land in Dunham Massey and Hale. The Inquisition Jury listed the Warrington estates as 66 messuages and 152 cottages, a mill and over 750 acres of meadow, pasture and heathland. However his financial state was so chaotic that he had sold Stayley Hall and much of its land a few months before his death and mortgaged the rest, together with Warrington, to Richard Brereton of Ashley.

As if all that were not bad enough, Sir George was left to bring up William's children, particularly George, William's eldest surviving son (Thomas, the first-born, had died in 1632 aged twelve). George became heir to the whole estates when his father died, but was still a minor aged thirteen and Charles I granted the wardship of young George to his grandfather, who, at the age of 69, became his legal guardian. By the time young George came of age in 1643, old Sir George had paid £4,000 to the Crown to formally end the wardship, and £1,500 in Chief Rents. He gave George £600 a year maintenance and when George married Katherine Clinton, the daughter of the Earl of Lincoln, the young couple were given £200 a year extra. George's coming-of-age present was the profits of the Warrington estate, at roughly £600 a year.

In 1633 Sir William Brereton married Old Sir George's third daughter, Susan Booth, but she died after only four years of marriage. Sir William and Sir George served together as magistrates of the Quarter Sessions and remained on good terms until the Civil War. In 1635 Sir George was on the Magistrates' Bench when Richard Massie of Sale appeared before him, brought by Brereton. He had overtaken Brereton on the road and a dispute arose between them. Massie admitted that he *"did use some provoking gesture and words to the said Sir William, affirming myself to be as good a gentleman as he and as well born and bred.... and did in other particulars wrong the said Sir William and undeservedly enter into comparisons with him...."* Brereton had taken grave offence but had wisely refrained from making matters worse. He contented himself by taking Massie to court and demanding an apology. Massie reluctantly grovelled *"...I do hereby promise and declare that the same was a rash and unadvised attempt and that I did both abuse myself and wrong him, who is much better than myself, for which I am very heartily sorry... and for the future I will demesne myself towards him with that respect which his worth and place require...."*

Sir George Booth's first wife, Jane Carrington, had died young. He had then married Katherine, the daughter of Sir Edmund Anderson, the Chief Justice of England, who gave him altogether six sons and six daughters and lived until 1638. During her lifetime she received an allowance of £100 a year from her husband. William's brothers were Francis, who died aged 13 in 1616, Thomas, Edmund, John and another Francis of whom nothing is known.  Edmund also died young, aged eight, and in 1632 Thomas *"riding desperately, fell off his horse and broke his neck"* at the age of 28.  This left only John surviving and Sir George provided for him with an annuity of £160 and many capital gifts of land and property.  Lady Katherine also gave Sir George six daughters. Alice and Cicely died young.  Little is known of Mary, Katherine and Elizabeth, but Susan made the important marriage to Sir William Brereton of Handforth.  Sir George gave each daughter an annuity of £80 a year.

## Sir William Brereton and the Great Duck Decoy

In 1631 Sir William Brereton gave his future father-in-law the chance of investing in an unusual enterprise.  He owned a piece of land in Saltney Marsh, south west of Chester, which was rich in wildfowl every year, and he conceived the idea of constructing a duck decoy.  The ducks and other wildfowl would then be sold in the local markets and, with a small capital expenditure, should make a tidy profit.  Would Sir George like to go half shares with the costs and profits?  He would, and in May 1631 he and Brereton signed Articles of Agreement to build a decoy *"with what convenient speed may be upon land of the said Sir William Brereton."*

Sir William and Sir George would share equally the costs of building the decoy and a cottage for the keeper and the annual running costs.  The keeper would have to enter sureties of £200.  The two partners would each be entitled to half the fowl taken during the lifetime of Lady Brereton, but if she happened to die before Sir George had recouped his initial outlay, Sir William would recompense him for the remainder.

Further agreements clarified other related matters; Sir George had the right to withdraw from the enterprise at any time, in which case Sir William would take over totally; the initial outlay was estimated to be just over £330; it was expected to bring in not less than £100 a year, but if it was less Sir George would abate his £50 share in proportion and if more he would receive more again in due proportion.

Altogether it was a friendly gentlemen's agreement between an elderly aristocrat and his future son-in-law and the decoy was built and operating by the summer of 1631.  If they had had any idea of the problems that the decoy would create and the hard work it would cause them, they would surely have abandoned the scheme before it even started.

Sir William and Sir George had not taken into account the temptations that the decoy would pose to the local poachers, who very quickly realised that they no longer had to do the hard work of stalking their prey but merely needed to collect the birds when the keeper was looking the other way.

But what remedy did the partners have in law?  They were not quite sure, so Sir George decided to petition the King and his Privy Council.  They had *"built at great charge a coy adjoining Chester and near the sea. whereof the counties thereabouts may be furnished thereof at easier rates and in a more plentiful manner than formerlie.... Many dissolute persons.... make it their continuall imployment to shoot and to kill and destroy foule contrary to the laws of the land."*  They therefore asked the King's authority to restrain and punish the offenders and enclosed a Certificate from the inhabitants of Chester that they considered the decoy *"to be a publique good and verie advantageous to the Countie by reason that Wee and our Marketts about us have beene ....furnished in a larger proportion with fowle than formerlie..."*

The King agreed that it was *"very fitting that such disorders be prevented"*. If Sir George and his partner found *"any persons to use any gunnes, dogges, netts, Lyme or other unlawful engines to destroy the said wildfowle or to hunt or destroy the young ducks within five miles,"* they could impound the hunting equipment and send the names of the offenders to the Privy Council. Justices of the Peace were commanded to give the partners all possible help (Booth and Brereton were of course JPs themselves) and offenders were to be bound over until the next Sessions, or committed to prison if they refused bond. One William Ithell was described as *"a principal offender."*

In March and April 1633, Booth and Brereton reported to Sir John Coke, a Principal Secretary to the King. They requested that if there was any attempt by other persons (they mentioned in particular Lord Strange) to have their grant revoked, they wanted the chance to defend it in person. Lord Strange and his solicitor Mr Winn were petitioning against the decoy and trying to get signatures from as far as Lancaster Assizes, sixty miles away. Sir George was very stately in his language *"If the chief actors therein were but called to yield an account why my son Brereton may not employ his own inheritance to his best advantage, as well as the rest of the owners of Coyes in England do, I am confident however, they may mask themselves under the pretence of public grievance, yet they cannot make it appear to be of any other quality than the rest of the Coyes in this kingdom."*

The vandalism began again, but this time the culprits were identified and Booth and Brereton named them to the Privy Council. According to them the decoy had been invaded by Richard Langford, Thomas Jenkins, Randle Eaton and Rees Edwards, all of Denbigh. They had come armed with guns, pistols and staves to drive the birds away from the decoy to where the gang of four could trap or shoot them in areas they had always used quite legally before the decoy was built.

On this occasion they were met by Richard Finlow, the parish constable, helped by Thomas Clough and Thomas Hurlbutt, who demanded *"in quiet and peaceable manner"* that the guns and staves be handed over in the King's name. Langford and the others refused and *"demanded who durst take and attempt to take the same." "They did thereupon assault, stricke and wound and grievouslie beate"* the constable and his men *"violentlie assaulting them... knocking downe and hurting another in the arme that hee is yet disabled to follow his calling."* In a brief struggle the constable managed to disarm one of them but they grabbed the pistol back again and fired it twice, swearing they would burn the decoy and kill anyone who tried to take their guns.

The Privy Council shrugged off the matter by authorising Sir John Bridgeman, Chief Justice of Chester, to send for the gang and bind them over *"by such means as you shall find best"* to which Bridgeman wrote to the Justices of the Peace instructing them to use *"all dilligence for the p'vention of all Ryotous assemblies and violent attempts."* He also ordered Richard Arshone of his staff to execute a warrant on Langford, but the criminals detained it and would not give it back or obey it.

Meanwhile the decoy was attacked again and Thomas Hurlbutt and Richard Woodworth of Doddlestone were assaulted as before *"in a dangerous maner to the greate effusion of there blood and apparent danger of death."* Woodworth had demanded that everyone should keep the peace and report to the next Sessions and had allowed the malcontents to take away their guns unmolested - not that he had much choice in the matter.

At the next Knutsford Quarter Sessions, the JPs (who included Booth and Brereton - a blatant conflict of interests!) notified all constables that there had been many and violent attempts to disturb the decoy. The laws were not being properly obeyed, even to the extent that gentlemen were ordering their servants to shoot the wildfowl. As for the servants, they *"habituate themselves in a Course of Idleness against the Lawes of this Land."* The constables were to be informed to present all offenders at Quarter Sessions.

This was easier said than done, because the decoy was not by any means universally well received. A petition from *"noblemen, gentlemen and others of Cheshire, Lancaster, Flintshire and Denbighshire"* landed on the King's desk, claiming that from time out of mind they had bred duck and other fowl for eating and hunting as allowed by the laws. The new decoy had *"destroyed them in such abundance that it is apparent that within a short time, it will not onlie be the better destruction of all fowle in theise parts but already your petitioners are altogether deprived of there wonted passion and recreation."* Sir William Brereton, they said, was developing a monopoly and selling the birds at excessive prices. As for Sir George Booth, his great name was being used to add a spurious legality to the decoy. It ought to stop operating for three months during the nesting season.

Rather wearily, Brereton and Booth compiled a defence of the decoy. Its opponents they said might be keen falconers as they claimed, but they had no ponds or moats in their own lands, so wildfowling was impossible for them. It was quite untrue that prices of duck in the markets had increased and the contrary would be proved on oath. The decoy keeper, John Peeterson, was a Dutchman and knew well the habits of migrant birds. All the birds trapped were well fed, and Sir William Brereton would not object at all to neighbours scaring them off their own land. However the King's injunction against other people shooting the birds *"hath beene most contemptuouslie beene (sic) disobeyed"* and there were certain unspecified whispering insinuations of undue influence. Brereton and Booth therefore requested a hearing by the Privy Council to establish themselves in His Majesty's good opinion.

In due course both parties with their counsels were called to the Star Chamber to explain their points of view in person. The opponents repeated their claims that the decoy was harmful to the wildlife, its existence was a restraint to their lawful inheritances and it increased prices for duck and fowl in markets. Sir William Brereton flatly denied infringing any liberties other than indicting some *"dissolute persons"* and provided a certificate that the fowl were actually more numerous than formerly.

Their Lordships of the Privy Council were not amused at having their valuable time wasted by such a petty squabble and announced that they would not get involved again with the controversy. Both parties could continue to enjoy any liberty they were permitted by law, but *"dissolute persons should (not) be suffered purposelie and maliciouslie to destroy the Fowl."*

Sir John Bridgeman issued warrants to the sheriffs of Flint, Denbigh and

Montgomery for the arrest of the Denbighshire Four, who duly appeared before the magistrates (excluding Brereton and Booth this time!) and each had to answer the same set of questions. Their responses varied greatly. Eaton and Jenkins were virtually monosyllabic. They had never heard of Brereton and Booth, Jenkins did not even know about the decoy, they did not know that shooting the sitting birds was unlawful, they did not know of the King's involvement, they had not assaulted anyone, they did not know that they had been indicted, they had not been given any money. The only substantial difference in their stories was that Eaton knew about Bridgeman's warrant and claimed that it had been detained by Langford. Someone he did not know had actually hit Finlow and knocked him down. Although it was only in self-defence, they were scared they had killed him and they ran away. Edwards was more co-operative. He knew of Booth and Brereton and the decoy, but nothing of the King's grant and warrant. There was a plot with Eaton to do some shooting, and here Edwards introduced a complication - it was on the orders of Sir Richard Crewe, but without promise of any reward. Eaton had let off a couple of pistol shots to frighten the birds, and when someone they did not recognise ordered them to stop, they obediently did. There was no fighting or even any threats made, even when they were ordered to hand over their guns. He knew Richard Finlow and had heard of Bridgeman's arrest warrant, but had not taken it from Arshone.

As for Langford, he was positively voluble. Yes he knew of Brereton and Booth and of the decoy. On the evening in question he had visited Finlow with the other defendants and had spent a quiet evening chatting with Finlow's servants and left peacefully. His only weapon was *"a little staff about a yard long."* He did not shoot in or near the decoy and there was no fighting. Arshone had come to him very drunk and said he would not serve the warrant on him officially for £40! Eventually it had ended up in the hands of Sir John Crewe, who had *"conceived some unkindness to Sir William Brereton concerning an horse bought of him..."* Being in Finlow's house all evening, he, Langford, saw no fighting or shooting, but assumed that if there was any, Eaton and Edwards must be the culprits. He was completely innocent of anything, and denied absolutely all *"Riotts, routs, unlawful assemblie, contempts, and all and every other the Misdemeanours in the said Bill of Contempt."* As for financial help, Sir John Crewe had suggested going to London and offered to lend him a horse but he had not taken the offer.

Other important witnesses were called. John Peeterson had been the keeper of the decoy for two and a half years and said that when the waters were high in winter, birds were plentiful and the markets were well supplied. In summer, however, at low water, it was easy to scare the birds away. George Manley lived at the house nearest the decoy and had seen the effects of shooting. He agreed that the markets were well furnished and did not think that the decoy would destroy all the birds. Nicholas Heginbotham, a 32 year old gentleman and lawyer, brought up a new name, that of William Echell who had done some shooting. Bernard Bradshaw of Hawarden had also seen Echell with yet another man, Alex Harvey. There had been random firing and he had seen the gunsmoke. Peeterson, recalled, agreed that Echell and Harvey had been firing.

The case rumbled on for months and it seems that Sir George became tired of the whole matter, because although his name is often mentioned as being an original partner with Brereton, he never appeared in person again except as a magistrate from time to time. At the end of 1634 one Peter Bennett claimed in front of the Grand Jury to have been ordered by Lord Strange to shoot the wildfowl and, being a servant, he had to obey. Brereton grumbled that if Lord Strange had really wanted duck to eat, he should have asked, and Brereton would have happily given him a dish of them.

Another aristocrat, Sir Richard Trevor, made his appearance, claiming that the Denbighshire Four had only fired at the ducks in the decoy on his explicit orders. This instantly caused Brereton to take proceedings against him, with lawyers acting on each side. During the proceedings, which took place before Sir George Booth, witnesses for both sides retold their own versions of events. A parade of witnesses confirmed various parts of the story. All on Sir William Brereton's side - doubtless well drilled - affirmed that the birds were far more plentiful since the decoy had been put up and that market prices were much lower than before, which was, of course, all to the benefit of ordinary people. However if they were indiscriminately shot at, they would certainly desert the area and things would be worse than ever.

Unfortunately the story of the Great Duck Decoy stops in the middle of Brereton's Letter Book without any indication of the outcome.

## Justice of the Peace

The case of the bird decoy has been treated in some detail because it illustrates well the duties of the Justices of the Peace and their occasional complexity. To serve as a Justice of the Peace was a very important part of the civic responsibilities of the gentry. They were not, for the most part, qualified lawyers, but had to undertake administrative and financial duties as well as trying judicial cases. They were responsible for supervising the collection of taxes, subsidies, forced loans and Ship Money, in addition to the everyday administration of justice. The Quarter Sessions had in addition to its judicial function many of the responsibilities of a modern county council, an important function that called for experience and the application of common sense.

How often an individual attended on the bench was a matter for him alone. There were four sessions a year, held at Epiphany, Easter, Midsummer and Michaelmas and at Chester, Knutsford, Middlewich, Nantwich, and in rotation at Northwich. Sir George Booth served as a JP for over sixty years and was one of the more conscientious attenders. In fact of the forty or so who were on the Commission at any one time, only three JPs, Sir George, Sir William Brereton and Henry Mainwaring, averaged more than twice a year.

Their work was vitally important, because justice at all levels had to be seen to be done, but nevertheless it was fairly routine and not always with any detailed knowledge of the law. Examples have been published by the Record Society of Lancashire and Cheshire and many include the work of Sir George Booth. Analysing the papers listed by the Record Society during his service shows that bridge maintenance and poor relief constituted the bulk of the Sessions work. At least 19 bridges needed repair or rebuilding and there were another nine cases of road maintenance.

Poor relief of one kind or another was also a major burden to the justices; no fewer than 24 men petitioned them for the restitution of pensions formerly granted, and 17 were applications for first relief. The plague caused four more applications in 1605 alone and bastardy was the consideration in five cases during the period. Squabbles between tenants, an education grant, orders concerning recusants, drunken brawling in church, common assault, vagrancies, the duties of constables and alehouse licences were all dealt with.

Applications to erect cottages on waste land were common and in 1620 Booth supported Thomas Webster, a mason, who wanted to live near his quarry so that he could earn a better living and do good for others. The application was duly granted. And many years later, when William Ratcliffe tried to have Nathaniel Higginbottom's cottage pulled down, not only did Booth confirm Higginbottom's permission, he also had Ratcliffe bound over to keep the peace until the next Sessions!

In 1605, Sir George was one of the Justices of the Peace when the plague broke out in Chester. The Privy Council authorised a collection for the relief of the victims, but it was not enough and Sir George and 19 of his colleagues on the Bench agreed that another collection should be made throughout the whole county. Finally no less than four collections were authorised to relieve suffering from the plague in Chester alone that year.

In 1610 a quarrel broke out between Mr Maire and Mr Alexander Hulme, both of Mere. Before it got out of hand, Sir George and his *"uncle Warburton of Arley"* managed to effect a reconciliation between the gentlemen to their satisfaction, but just in case it broke out again they ordered them to sign recognizances against any further breach of the peace. Unfortunately the clerk of the court was away. Sir George, concerned that Messrs Maire and Hulme would be unfairly fined for not having provided sureties, wrote to the clerk accordingly: *"Upon sight you will give order for the free discharging of the gents from any penalty."*

A few years later he was unable to attend the Nantwich Sessions for the appointment of a High Constable for Bucklow Hundred. Henry Hough of Knutsford had been proposed, but Sir George had doubts, and he wrote to the Sessions:

*"I have informed myself (upon complaint of his unfitness for the place) of his estate, and I find his freehold of land is exceeding small, so small as suits not to bear that office, and the more unnecessary for him in regard his best means is by trading in commodities, being a shopkeeper. I desire you will make known unto the Justices at the Sessions that some other fitter man be chosen for this service.*

G. Bouthe, Dunham Massey, 9 October 1614"

This letter is proof that Booth was concerned not only for the efficiency of the service, but also for the individual. Either Hough would suffer through not being able to devote enough time to his shop or the constable's office would suffer if he continued with his normal life.

A year or two later, Booth set free Robert Davie of Wilmslow, who had been put in prison because he could not find sureties for good behaviour for misdemeanours against Booth himself. At the same time Booth submitted a recognisance against John Heyward of Carrington *"my tenant, who is so disordered being a common drunkard and haunter of ale houses as I cannot rule him."* This was an untypically harsh judgement and Sir George must have been tried beyond endurance.

In 1624 for instance, John Worrall of Nantwich, an old soldier, asked to have his military pension restored and for arrears to be paid. It had been reduced because the kitty was a fixed amount and there were too many old pensioners. Sir George and Sir William Brereton on the Bench heard evidence that a number of the old soldiers had died and there was money available again, so they were pleased to restore Worrall's pension. "Bully" Kent was another soldier pensioner. He had received his pension promptly for three years, but had then gone to sea for three years. He had now returned, and applied to have his pension reinstated please? Yes he could, said Booth and Sir John Savage.

In 1633 Robert Malbon found himself short of funds and recalled a period ten years before when he *"did undertake the buying of his Maties composicion oxen"* to the satisfaction of the King's Clerks of the Green Cloth. Although he had been granted an allowance, the great price of oxen meant that he was £20 a year out of pocket, so he applied to be reimbursed. Very similar was the case of George Smith. He had been responsible for buying oxen for the King in 1635 and was allowed £7-10/- each but had lost money on the deal because the King's officers had refused many of them and insisted that he should buy better animals at £9 each. Only the personal intervention of Sir William Brereton prevented his total ruin. He petitioned the Chester Quarter Sessions for reimbursement and Booth and Brereton personally examined his accounts. It was clear to them that Smith was an honest man and had been hard dealt with by the King's purchasers and they were quick to certify as much to their fellow Justices. In their opinion Smith's allowance of £7-10s per ox was too low. He should be allowed at least £8-10/- per animal and be repaid £20 for the losses he had already incurred.

Sir George again demonstrated in 1639 that he was always willing to listen to tales of hardship and to relieve them if he could. Thomas Haumeire of Little Neston admitted that he was *"of mean condition"* but had friends in Malton in Yorkshire who would help him. However the parish constables en route would arrest him on sight as a vagrant if he had no pass. Sir George kindly wrote out a pass in his own hand acknowledging to *"all Justices of the Peace, maiors, Bayliffes, Constables and all other his Maties officers"* that Haumeire and his son Peter were travelling lawfully with permission. This may seem a little matter, but Sir George's attitude should be compared with many other JPs who could and perhaps would have dismissed Haumeire without further ado.

Thomas Marbury let Sir George know of the activities of two confidence tricksters, Cuthbert Cartington and Richard Curteis. Their *"foul offences"* were that they *"under color for purveyors for his Ma'ty's navie, enter into men's houses and offer to take their victuals at half worth, which if any poor man deny then they amerse him in £5 for the King's use and threaten poor men with great punishment in the Star Chamber..."* Mr Daniell of Daresbury had caught them and John Williamson the constable of Over would bring them to the next sessions. There it was proved that their alleged commission from the King was forged, and Cartington was sent to London for examination before being committed for trial at the next Assizes. Curteis was lucky, in that Sir George Booth found that he had no *"forward hand"* in the crime and he was freed on his own recognizances.

Several inhabitants of Rostherne petitioned for relief for one Jane Lance, *"a poor old woman.... hath always lived in the parish and by great pains takeing maintained herself honestly without being burdensome to her neighbours and also found someone who would give her lodging for such labour or payment as she was able to yield."* Unfortunately Jane was grown too old to do any work and had been thrown out of her lodgings. One wonders why one among the six petitioners did not give shelter to poor Jane, but Sir George without further enquiry ordered the churchwardens and overseers of the poor to house her and give her relief.

He showed similar compassion for Ellen French, a *"poor aged woman"* of Great Budworth. A fire had destroyed her barn and its contents and she had nothing to live on. Booth allowed her a collection in all the churches in Bucklow Hundred.

Davenham was another parish reluctant to give relief. One Brock was executed at Chester Assizes in 1635, leaving a widow Anne and six children, all utterly destitute. She had twice petitioned the Quarter Sessions and each time they had instructed Davenham to give help. The overseers of the poor were still employing delaying tactics, claiming that the family had moved around several parishes, which should all contribute. Great Budworth were however giving relief for the youngest child who was born there. They were even getting Lord Savage to press their case. Booth was having none of that. Anne Brock was desperate and *"All that she hath is gone and the cold winter approacheth."* Booth spelt out his order with unmistakable clarity, confirming the previous order and instructing Davenham to maintain the family *"as the law in that case hath ordained."*

In 1629 he received a letter from Thomas Legh concerning the death of his servant John Greene. The Coroner's Jury had no doubt that it was murder and that the culprit was one John Ward, who had been put in close confinement. Legh was concerned that the matter might be dealt with *"suddenly and secretly"* and asked Sir George to ensure that Ward should be *"presented to the public view of the Bench to receive condign punishment for the capital crime, to satisfy the law in due season."* (He did not appear)

Another serious case was that of Richard Hunt of Nether Walton. He had seduced a girl called Christiana Sotherne and promised to marry her. She became pregnant but Hunt deserted her, denied the baby and married another woman, also pregnant by him. Christian was adamant that Hunt was her seducer and the father of her child. Even worse her parents had thrown her out and she had nothing. Nether Walton was responsible for giving relief, but Hunt was *"a man of good abilitie and well able to maintain the bastard child"*, so they saw no reason why they should. Booth and Brereton agreed. *"Richard Hunt upon sight hereof shall take and keep the child with meat, drink, lodging and apparel for the term of twelve years, or until it shall be able to get its own living."* The only concession was that Christian was to contribute ten shillings a year for the child's keep.

The maintenance of roads and bridges was a common bone of contention. Frodsham Bridge was ordered for repair and monies collected, and the work was in progress when the money ran out. Sir Thomas Aston and Sir John Savage complained that Francis Newton, the Head Constable of Bucklow Hundred, was sitting on the remainder of the cash and refusing on some pretext to hand it over. Aston wanted him sacked or at least fined, but Booth looked deeper into the matter. Newton confirmed that he did have some of the money, but many people had refused their assessment. Booth therefore instructed him to go to the village constables with orders that anyone who had refused their contribution was to appear before the Judges at the next Assize to answer their contempt.

In 1630 one Lawrence Bressie of Wybunbury obstructed an ancient right of way to the village church and Sir Thomas Delves helped his tenants prefer an indictment against him. Bressie was an awkward man with *"a desire to be troublesome"*.

By 1642 Warrington Bridge was in a very poor state of repair but the problem was compounded by the fact that half of it was in Cheshire and the other half in Lancashire. Fortunately the Lancashire justices agreed to pay £150, the cost of mending their half and the fact that some materials could be shared would reduce the cost to Cheshire. The work was considered too important to wait until a full meeting of the justices could be arranged, so Sir George Booth agreed, on his own authority, that £120 should be spent.

Another case involved Anne Brereton who lived near Buglawton. A bridge on a vital road had been destroyed by a flood but she could not afford to rebuild it. However, if the County agreed to pay the cost of rebuilding, she would be willing to maintain it. Sir George Booth, then 83 years old, was typically concise in his instructions. *"I desire my fellow Justices in my absence to order the matter conteyned in this letter according to the Judge's Order herewith sent."*

New taxation by Charles I automatically caused more hardship and therefore more applications for relief. Stockport in 1640 was a case in point. The Churchwardens and Overseers for the Poor were desperately trying to be fair but were seriously over-stretched. They had 80 families already on relief and had collected £80, but when they asked for another £50 they were met with a general refusal to pay any more. At their wits end, they petitioned Sir George, Sir Richard Wilbraham and Sir William Brereton for *"such order in and concerning every branch of this their petition as you shall conceive to be just."* The fact that they did not petition for anything specific shows clearly the straits they were in. The three wise men agreed to assess fines on all those who were harbouring paupers, perhaps using them as slave labour.

Stockport remained in Sir George's mind two years later, in spite of the approach of the Civil War. He received a complaint about the conduct of the Overseers of the Poor in Stockport and after investigation established that they were retaining large sums of money collected for the poor and refusing to give accounts for it. On his authority, all village constables were to apprehend the named overseers on sight and bring them before the next Sessions to answer for their conduct.

The Civil War created new difficulties and a large increase in work for Sir George and his colleagues. Nantwich had petitioned the Committee of Parliament for Plundered Ministers, and the Committee had ordered them to pay £50 from the estate of Henry Mainwaring to the Dean and Chapter of Chester. They objected, believing that the money should be devoted to Nantwich instead. However they found that Sir George was not necessarily a soft touch, as he refused to consider the matter; it was not, he thought, a proper matter for the JPs.

One Ciceley Travis, a widow, caused Sir George much work as a direct result of the war. She and her husband Thomas were tenants of Yieldhouse, the property of the Collegiate Church of Manchester. Thomas had unfortunately been one of the 300 killed at the Battle of Atherton Moor, near Wakefield, and she had been evicted by Canon

Duncalfe and George Romiley. The legal case was extremely complex. The tenement was held for three lives, of which the deceased Thomas was the second. However Thomas had been cast into prison and had released his rights to his father George, who leased it to his younger son, also George, and leased his own half to three other gentlemen. Thomas was married at the time to one Elizabeth and the two of them continued to live in part of the property, while George Travis senior lived in another part! It appeared, however, that Thomas had no right to dispose of the lease in the first instance. Only George senior had that right, so any further disposals were null and void. Sir George Booth was drawn into the matter by Thomas's second wife Ciceley and contacted the Justices of the Peace of Lancashire, suggesting a meeting of the interested parties which he would attend. There was no answer, so Sir George wrote again. *"....Richard Hoult with some 3 or fouer more with armes and weapons did forcibly out her of the possession thereof to the utter overthrow of her.... and her said small children. She hath bene with me and brought a draught of her case and an approved opinion thereof which I have seene and appointed her to shew unto you. For my own part I conceive the widowes claime just and that she hath suffered much wrong and damage."* As her Deputy Lieutenant, Sir George commended the matter to his Lancashire colleagues, but kept a careful note of all the circumstances. He made no secret of the fact that the law and common practice were both on Widow Travis's side.

Only a few months later, Henry Mainwaring himself made a request of Sir George. Thomas Beckett had been chosen to be Constable of Goostrey but had refused to take the oath. There was no good reason, as he was fit, he lived in the village and his wife had a reasonable estate. Only the previous year in fact, Beckett had paid a labourer to do some work rather than do it himself, so he was obviously well able to afford the expense of being constable. It is not clear whether Mainwaring's letter to Sir George was approved.

The work of the Justice of the Peace was mainly at the lowest level. For a conscientious man such as Sir George Booth, it was onerous and took up as much of his time as he cared to devote to it - and that was a great deal, even in his old age. The work of the Deputy Lieutenant of the County was much less time-consuming and in general terms did not impinge much on the lives of ordinary people; that is until the start of the Civil War in 1642, when the decisions and actions of the Deputy Lieutenants began to exert considerable influence on virtually every household in the county. Until then the duties had been largely nominal and ceremonial, with the exception of responsibilities in respect of the county militia and as Commissioner for the collection of revenue for the government. Sir George was Collector of Loans for Cheshire in 1612 and had to report that some people either could not or would not pay the loans. He was having to approach private money lenders and would appreciate being sent some blank Privy Seal documents to regularise the transactions. In 1625 the King appointed him as Collector of the forced *"loan"* of £10, *"which few men would deny a friend"* as a *"testimony of good affection"* and which was supposed to be repaid by the King within eighteen months.

In 1626 he reported having sent nearly £900, but had received only £50 or so in the previous two months, plus a lot of excuses. His friend Richard Egerton of Ridley thanked him for his forbearance regarding dues in his area. He had collected various sums and would send them immediately to Booth's agent in London.  At the same time, Egerton asked for Booth's lenience towards one Widow Alport.  The unfortunate lady had hoped for reasonable expectations from her late husband, but his estate was in such danger that she had no assets.  Egerton hoped that the kindly Booth would overlook Mrs Alport on this occasion.

In spite of these problems, Sir George was re-appointed Collector in succeeding years.  In 1631, the Privy Council decided that the King had an absolute right to levy fines on gentry who refused knighthoods, in addition to those who did accept, and Sir George was appointed Collector to Lords Derby, Savage and Strange, the Commissioners.

The earliest example surviving of Sir George's responsibilities with the militia comes from 1614, when the Earl of Derby, Lord Lieutenant of Cheshire, commanded in the King's name a muster of the militia.  Booth, newly appointed Custos Rotulorum of Cheshire, and his colleague, Sir John Savage, wrote to William Aldersey, Mayor of Chester.  He was to arrange with all the constables of the city's wards for all the trained militia to assemble on the Roodee for inspection by Sir George and Sir John, together with all their arms and equipment.

Exactly the same happened seven years later.  The Privy Council had decided to reinforce the army in Ireland and wished to levy 100 men from the county and city of Chester.  Sir George *"intreated"* the Mayor to assemble the fittest men possible, with the exception of the Trained Bands, to be reviewed and mustered for the King's service. Interestingly, Booth uses the word "intreated" rather than the more usual "commanded", and this may indicate that he was personally opposed in principle to the uprooting of men from their homes without warning, recompense or training, for dangerous service which some would not survive.

The Mayor of Chester felt the same way and protested vigorously.  He had, he said, a parchment *"under the hand and Signett Manuall"* of Henry VIII exempting the inhabitants of Chester from providing soldiers for any service whatsoever until the command should be revoked by him. Whatever Sir George Booth may have felt personally about the iniquity of taking men from their homes for military service, he clearly considered that the Mayor's excuse was too flimsy to be taken too seriously.  He knew perfectly well the steps that such a letter should have been through before being properly authenticated, and if in modern times we may feel strangled by red tape, the civil servants of four centuries ago had already invented it.  Booth consulted Sir William Brereton and they explained exactly why in their reply to Lord Derby:

*"We are of opinion that the said deed doth not bynde the king's heires and successors because the graunt is not passed under the great seale of England nor the seale of the Countie Palatine, neither doth it appear by the Maior's list that the said deed was graunted to the Maior of Chester and his successors but onely to the Maior that then was... so that the said graunt was void upon the removal of the said Maior. Moreover it is certaine that the graunts made to maiors of corporations and to their successors are first passed under the hand and signett manuall of the kinge and are then brought to the lord privie seale, who then causeth the said graunts to be written out again in parchment and then putteth thereto the privie seale and keepeth the graunts under the king's hand*

*and signett with him for the warrant and then the graunts under the privie seale are to be brought unto the Lord Chancellor or Lord Keeper of the Great Seale or Chamberlayne of the Countie Palatine of Chester, who likewise causeth the said graunts under the privie seale to be written over in parchment verbatim and then sealeth them with the Great Seale of England or Seale of the Countie Palatyne, and keepeth with him the said graunts under the privie seale with him for his warrant."*

If the document had not gone through all these tortuous processes, Booth and Brereton thought that it would have been valid only during the lifetimes of Henry VIII and the then Mayor. In the circumstances they proposed to continue with the command of Charles I. Nevertheless they considered that the demand for 100 men was excessive. The Mayor was being unreasonable in their opinion in trying to gain a general exemption for his men, but the two Deputy Lieutenants were not wholly unsympathetic to his attempt. In their opinion neither the city of Chester nor the county as a whole could raise the 100 demanded. In fact they could manage no more than 20 at most and so far only seven had been actually chosen, though they were in process of assembling more, so that only the seven most able would eventually be selected. Meanwhile would Lord Derby be kind enough to decide whether he wished the Mayor to send his alleged Deed to the Privy Council for their further consideration? There is nothing further surviving, but it is most unlikely that the Mayor succeeded in his claim.

All militia needed to be trained, and the King needed to be satisfied that they were properly trained. The Privy Council sent Mr Philip Cotton and Mr Arthur Humberstone in 1626 *"to signify his Majesty's gracious pleasure concerning the instructing and exercising of the Trained Bands....."* The Deputy Lieutenants had to report to the Council on the efficiency of the two trainers, and Sir George Booth and five of his colleagues expressed themselves satisfied. *"They have took extraordinary pains in bringing the soldiers to perfection and knowledge in the use of their arms, according to the modern forms of discipline.... these gentlemen's endeavours have corresponded with his Majesty's royal commands, and they have not misspent the time they had allotted them for their stay here...."*

## The Civil War

The year 1642 was climactic in the history of England. It was the year that the Civil War broke out and determined over succeeding generations whether England would be an autocratic or a democratic monarchy. This is not the place to go into the detail of the causes and the progress of the war, which had actually been brewing for some years, but a few words will suffice to set the background for Sir George's declining years, during which he saw more action than in the whole of his already long life beforehand. Luckily for him he remained in excellent health and physical fitness, certainly with all his mental faculties, throughout the war and for some years afterwards, and his influence on the conduct of the struggle in Cheshire was probably second only to that of his son in-law Sir William Brereton.

Even before the war broke out the contending factions were beginning to form. The moderates were coming to be known as the "Popular Patriots" and Thomas Marsden of

Chester referred to Sir George as such just before the elections of 1640, the so-called 'Long Parliament': *"Sir William Brereton and Sir Thomas Ashton were both lately with me and both of them are pretty confident and full of reproaches against the two popular patriots Sir G... B... and Sir R*(ichard) *W*(ilbraham)*, neither of whom will appear at the election it is said, or if they do, they are sure to be boldly accused in the face of their country as adversaries to the peace of it."*

This was a slur on Sir George's philosophy. Within a short time, he would prove that far from being a war-monger, he was prepared to go to some lengths to preserve peace in his beloved Cheshire. The fact that he was unsuccessful does not matter; he did his best to prevent his county from being embroiled in the war.

Charles I believed completely in his divine right to reign as an autocrat. Parliaments were useless in his opinion. They served merely to obstruct his prerogative to raise the subsidies essential for his rule, and from 1629 to 1640 he called no Parliaments. Instead, he split the country in two important ways, firstly by insisting on a unified Book of Common Prayer. This smacked of Popery to many people and aroused the opposition of Puritans such as Sir William Brereton, and Presbyterians such as Sir George Booth. Secondly Charles created a new national tax, the so-called 'Ship Money'.

For centuries the coastal counties had been accustomed to paying extra taxes to build warships in times of national emergency and this had never caused any problems, because the protection of the coast was in the best interests of the seaboard counties. This was the situation in Cheshire, because Chester was of course an important port for the traffic in the Irish Sea. However it had always been understood that this taxation would only be levied if absolutely necessary.

The King, unable to receive subsidies because he refused to call Parliaments, began to levy Ship Money every year from 1634, and not only that, imposed it for the first time in history on inland counties, with predictable unpopularity. The people realised very well that there was no emergency and that the King was imposing the tax simply as a substitute for parliamentary subsidies. Moreover the tax bore more heavily on some than on others and even Sir Thomas Aston, a convinced Royalist and the Sheriff of Cheshire, felt obliged to complain *"that some townships pay 30s where others of the like rent and extent pay not 2s."*

Similarly, Sir Thomas Powell, Sheriff of Cheshire in 1639/40, complained to the House of Lords that he had done his best to get *"a good round sum of the Ship-Money out of his bailiwick"* but had failed. Soon after, he grumbled about his own invidious position. If he did not collect the tax quickly, the Lords would think him inefficient. If he was too good at it however, he would be deemed *"too officious and a pick-thank if I inform against those of my neighbours and countrymen here, who are much to blame for their backwardness in paying, and for persuading others by word or example."* Powell even reported one George Vernon of Whatcroft, who threatened his village constable, that if he was pestered again about his non-payment, he would *"whett his knife in his guts!"* He was supported by the county's Justices of the Peacc and Deputy Lieutenants as a group, who were all very unhappy about Ship-Money and included it in a petition of grievances drafted by Sir Richard Wilbraham to the Earl of Derby, the Lord Lieutenant, who was not actually a Cheshire resident.

They also demanded that the county militia should be preserved from service in the King's Scottish wars (the first and second Bishops' Wars) on the reasonable grounds that if the Trained Bands were taken, others would have to be trained at great expense in their places. They specifically asked that all the 500 militia should not be assembled to be exercised with men of the King's armies *"lest they fall to be mutinous and disordered which we may have cause to fear from a late experience we had..."* It seemed that 180 men had been sent out of the county, but on their return they nearly mutinied in Chester City itself. Sir George Booth whole-heartedly agreed with the petition and was responsible for collecting the signatures of those Justices who lived in the north of Cheshire - *"There be left a convenient place for the noble men of the country to write their names."*

In the name of religion, the King also wanted to impose his new Prayer Book in Scotland, where Calvinism was particularly strong, and the result was armed rebellion and the first Bishops' War of 1639. It ended with the Pacification of Berwick in June of that year, but threatened to break out again in 1640. This time the King was forced reluctantly to summon a Parliament, but they refused any subsidy unless he redressed their grievances, namely his undue use of royal prerogative and his failure to call regular parliaments. The King refused to listen to their grievances and dismissed the Parliament after only three weeks. However his position had been seriously weakened and when the second Bishops' War broke out, the Scots soundly thrashed the King's army, short of money and supplies as it was. By November 1640 the King was compelled to summon another parliament, the Long Parliament, which was to last twenty years. The members for Cheshire were Peter Venables, a royalist, and Sir George's son in law, Sir William Brereton, who thus expanded his national influence.

1641 saw the storm clouds of war beginning to gather. The Commons and the King were set on a collision course and Charles was reluctantly compelled to agree to a series of measures designed to reduce his authority. They included the abolition of the prerogative courts he had established, the making illegal of the financial devices of the previous eleven years and the Triennial Act which required that Parliament would automatically sit every three years if not summoned by the Crown.

Although the King agreed to these measures, he did so with bad grace and the question still remained, what would happen if he simply ignored them and recommenced ruling without Parliament? Furthermore, they did not go far enough for many members in reducing the King's powers. The result was long discussions within the Commons on more extreme measures and finally the Grand Remonstrance of November 1641. This was a lengthy and comprehensive criticism of the King's policies in State and Church and how these policies were threatening to create an unbridgeable gap between him and his people, led of course by the Commons. It was drawn up by John Pym, an extremist member of Parliament and one of its leaders, who had been a Member since 1614 The Grand Remonstrance listed the reforms that the Long Parliament had already achieved, but demanded more action to resolve more outstanding grievances.

The King was allegedly being led astray by *"evil counsellors"*, some of whom it alleged were in the pockets of foreign princes and were maintaining continual differences between the King and his people for their own ends. Others, claimed the Remonstrance, wanted the return of Roman Catholicism. The Jesuits in particular hated the laws as obstacles to the changes which they so much desired. The peril should be averted by replacing the *"evil counsellors"* with ministers who had the approval of the Commons - which would of course place the King firmly under the thumb of the MPs. As for the church itself, it was riddled with corruption and patronage and many reforms were needed. The best way of achieving these reforms was to curb the power of the bishops by making them subservient to a synod of Protestant churchmen.

Altogether the Grand Remonstrance listed over 200 major and minor criticisms of the King and his actions, all of which would be overcome with the reforms that the Commons desired. The compilers of the Remonstrance were careful not to blame the King directly, however, and insisted on referring to *"the King in Parliament"* as the ideal form of Government.

If the King could be brought to agree with these *"reforms"*, the dispute between himself and his Parliament would have been avoided at least for the time being. But he did nothing. If he was angry at the studied insult of being unable to choose trustworthy and sensible advisers, he showed no sign of it. In fact he ignored it completely. He knew that the Grand Remonstrance had squeaked through the Commons after an all-night sitting with a wafer-thin majority of eleven and felt that he was still safe for the time being. Only when it was formally presented to him did he acknowledge its existence, and then only agreed to read it in due course.

Sir Thomas Aston who had complained about Ship-Money still remained a dedicated Royalist and he tried to encourage the King with a petition in defence of the episcopacy, violently attacking Puritanism. He claimed to have the support of no less than 6000 nobles, gentry, clergy and freeholders of Cheshire, but when he asked Sir George Booth to endorse it, the old gentleman refused indignantly. It did however provoke a reply from some anonymous Puritans, probably not in Cheshire, which Aston in turn answered with another anti-Puritan petition, allegedly in the name of the county.

Aston's second petition stung Sir George into an "Attestation" organised by him and his friends Sir Richard Wilbraham and Sir Thomas Delves. They were supported by over 40 of their colleagues in the Deputy Lieutenancy and Commission of the Peace in criticising Aston but at the same time disassociating themselves from the over-radical Puritans. As Presbyterians they were essentially moderate and wanted no more than an overhaul of the church and the simplification of its episcopal command structure. In their opinion the demands of some of the more extreme Puritans went too far and they wanted no part of it. However the 48 gentry who signed the Attestation were almost exactly counter-balanced by the 43 who rallied to Aston's side by signing an open letter of support to him. It must therefore have been clear to Charles and his advisers that Cheshire at least was split down the middle and that he could not count on the full support of its people by any means.

Sir George Booth's anger was also roused by other matters. The rebellion by Irish Catholics who sensed the weakness of the King broke out in October 1641, and Charles was compelled to send forces to crush the outbreak. The King's armies crossed the Irish Sea via Chester and en route through Cheshire their appallingly undisciplined behaviour of looting and arbitrary taxation caused Sir George to petition Parliament in protest.

Booth was still desperately anxious to preserve the peace, although the tension in the country was stretching to breaking point. As one of the Deputy Lieutenants of Lancashire, he had considerable influence there, and helped to organise a petition that just might bring the King to reason. Its most important aims were to reduce corruption in the church by the institution of a national synod, the appointment of more preachers and more equitable distribution of its income. More controversial was the request that all non-Protestants should be dismissed from the King's councils. Predictably, His Majesty ignored the petition.

In January 1642 Charles took a fatal step by forcing his way into the House of Commons in a foolhardy attempt to arrest John Pym, Denzil Holles, John Hampden, Sir Arthur Haselrig and William Strode, the famous 'Five Members'. Warned of his coming, they took refuge in the City of London,. Meanwhile, Charles, thwarted, left his capital city for Hampton Court and then Windsor Castle.

By May of 1642, the battle lines were drawn. The Commons declared that all military forces, including the local militias, were under the control of Parliament, and that the King seemed bent on making war. The King, who had established his Court in York, retorted furiously that anyone who obeyed the Militia Ordinance was automatically guilty of High Treason and only two weeks later issued his Commission of Array, a general call to arms which was virtually a declaration of war. Parliament replied that anyone in Leicester, Lincoln or Cheshire who did not obey the Militia Ordinance or tried to publish the King's Commission of Array would automatically be proclaimed a "delinquent." During the following two months, minor skirmishes took place, but the crucial moment came on 22 August when the King raised his battle standard at Nottingham Castle.

Even at this eleventh hour Sir George Booth was still determined on moderation. It was probably, though not certainly, he who wrote to Lord Strange, son and heir of the invalid Earl of Derby, Lord Lieutenant of Cheshire, calling for moderate mediation between King and Parliament and desiring a truce in the meantime. To ensure peace in Cheshire, he wanted the suspension of both the Royalist Commission of Array and the Parliamentary Militia Ordinance and a guarantee that no troops of either side would enter the county. The county's militia should be controlled by the magistrates, effectively himself and others of like mind; those of both sides who had already offended against the peace should be pardoned.

His keynote was moderation and he believed that the county as a whole agreed with him: *"The whole county shall rise against them which are enemies against the peace,"* he declared and sent one John Bretland of Thorncliffe to see Thomas Leigh of Adlington, who was known to be a royalist, to persuade him either to disband or to use his troops as neutral against anyone raising forces for one side or the other. Bretland was out of luck. Not only was he unsuccessful, but he was himself later suspected of delinquency and his estates sequestered. It took him years to prove his innocence. Witnesses testified that Bretland was often used by Booth and other Deputy Lieutenants *"in matters of public concernment for the Parliament",* but it was not until 1655 that Bretland finally managed to convince the Committee for Compounding of his zeal for the Parliamentary cause.

Unsuccessful with Lord Strange, Booth led five of his friends, Sir Richard Wilbraham, Sir Thomas and Henry Delves, Philip Mainwaring and William Marbury in petitioning Parliament direct: *"...we declare and profess ourselves enemies to all those.... that shall be discovered to be agents in making our wounds deeper by fostering and fomenting the unfortunate mistakes and fearful jealousies betwixt head and body, his Majesty and his Parliament...."*

Within a month of the formal outbreak of hostilities, the King came to Cheshire to drum up support and summoned all the known neutralists and moderates to meet him for a conference. The city of Chester was worried that the King might decide to remain there as his stronghold but they gave him and the Prince of Wales all possible honours, a sword and £200 in gold to him and £100 in gold to the young Prince. Sir George Booth had been seriously concerned about the conduct of the King's forces and the damage and destruction they were causing, and he refused to attend. He was lucky in this decision, because the King, outraged at the lack of co-operation he was receiving, virtually kidnapped three of his friends, Wilbraham, Mainwaring and Thomas Delves. Sir William Brereton disappeared to London.

This was the first time that Booth, justifiably outraged, openly sided with Parliament. Moderate, peaceful and neutralist though he was, if necessary he would support the Parliamentary side as far as possible and was already taking steps to enlist and arm his tenants. His grandson George was also busy recruiting and telling everyone how vehement he was against the King.

Charles pretended to be deeply hurt. In fact even before the formal outbreak of hostilities he was aware that Booth was unlikely to help the Royalists and he had made a last appeal to Booth's conscience and patriotism. He and his father had both had experience of Booth's fidelity, and was *"a little troubled to hear that you should be an active agent for such as without any legall authoritie take upon them to arm our people contrarie to our express commande.... Yett wee being confident such actes cannot proceed from any disaffection to us under whome you have soe long discharged offices of trust with commendable integritie, but rather that you have been deluded by those plausible Artifices of our Adversaries... that upon the first notice given us by our Servant Sir Thomas Aston that you have conformed yourself to the obedience of our legall Authoritie... Wee shall retourne both to yourself and your Grandchild Our ffree and Generall pardon for all by past and shall willingly retain you both in our good opinion and still repose in you our wonted confidence of yr Loyall affection to us...."*

It was far too late for such an appeal. Perhaps a waverer might have been persuaded back to the fold, but Sir George Booth was too strong a character and also too old to be swayed. He had already nailed his colours to the mast in Manchester the previous month, when he and other Deputy Lieutenants of Lancashire, first of all reviewed an estimated 7,000 or 8,000 militia and then held an emergency meeting to discuss ways and means of preserving Manchester and the area for Parliament. Parliament ordered Lord Strange to surrender all the arms and powder in the town, but when the Deputy Lieutenants refused, he attacked and there were casualties on both sides.

The death of Richard Parcevall, a linen weaver, was said to be the first fatal casualty of the whole Civil War. An anonymous chronicler of the events wrote *"This is the beginning of Civil Warre, being the first stroke that hath been struck, and the first Bullet that hath been shot.... Many thousands I doubt will loose their lives, before that this Kingdom will be settled in peace and unity as it hath bin formerly; for noe man knoweth the Cruelty of War but those that have felt and tried it; for when that time cometh, many a child will be Fatherlesse, and many a poor wife Husbandlesse."*

Manchester was by and large fortunate in avoiding much involvement in the war after September 1642. However the early signs were not good. On Sunday 25 September, while the bulk of the Royalist forces were contesting Worcester, Lord Strange (who had succeeded to the Earldom of Derby on his father's death) made the first of several attempts to capture Manchester. The church bells rang the alarm and the men abandoned the sermons to collect their pikes, halberds and muskets. The attack was unexpected and there was no overall command.

However there were six officers in the town, each with his own men, including Colonel John Booth, Sir George's surviving son, who commanded a detachment of men, mostly tenants of the Booth estates at Millgate. He and three other local commanders realised their relative weakness and wrote overnight to Richard Shuttleworth and John Starkie at Haslingden, asking for urgent help. Their urgency was underlined when Strange attacked several times during Sunday, Monday and Monday night, in foul weather, but made no impression on the defenders and gave up after losing perhaps 150 men. Meanwhile the defenders, numbering less than 200 altogether, suffered only a handful of casualties, but their prospects of help were not good. The reply from Lancashire was disappointing. They badly needed to keep troops near the Royalist stronghold of Lathom House, a large quantity of arms and ammunition had been captured, and *"for aid from the Parliament forces or any other ways, we have no hope of any."*

The need to maintain constant vigilance placed Manchester in a difficult position. Booth and his colleagues knew that there were at least 1,400 Royalist troops billeted within striking distance of the town. Richard Holland, Booth and four other gentlemen therefore wrote again to the Lancashire Parliamentary committee for help. *"It is apparent our charge and loss is great, which if you would help to support, the advancement for money upon the propositions etc for maintenance, and the sending us some 200 musketeers for a week or two, for our assistance, might much extenuate and lighten it...."*

At this stage, John Booth and the other gentry in the area were not in favour of a difficult and prolonged war. There were widespread arguments in favour of a negotiated solution and John was one of several gentlemen who signed a letter to the Earl of Derby, the Lord Lieutenant, containing proposals for a plan of pacification that they hoped would be acceptable to Parliament. Under the plan, Manchester would effectively become an open town. No more fortifications would be constructed, all arms would be given up and all the gentry of Lancashire and Cheshire would *"be free and secure from all attempts against Manchester."* Furthermore *"...what they shall expect to be*

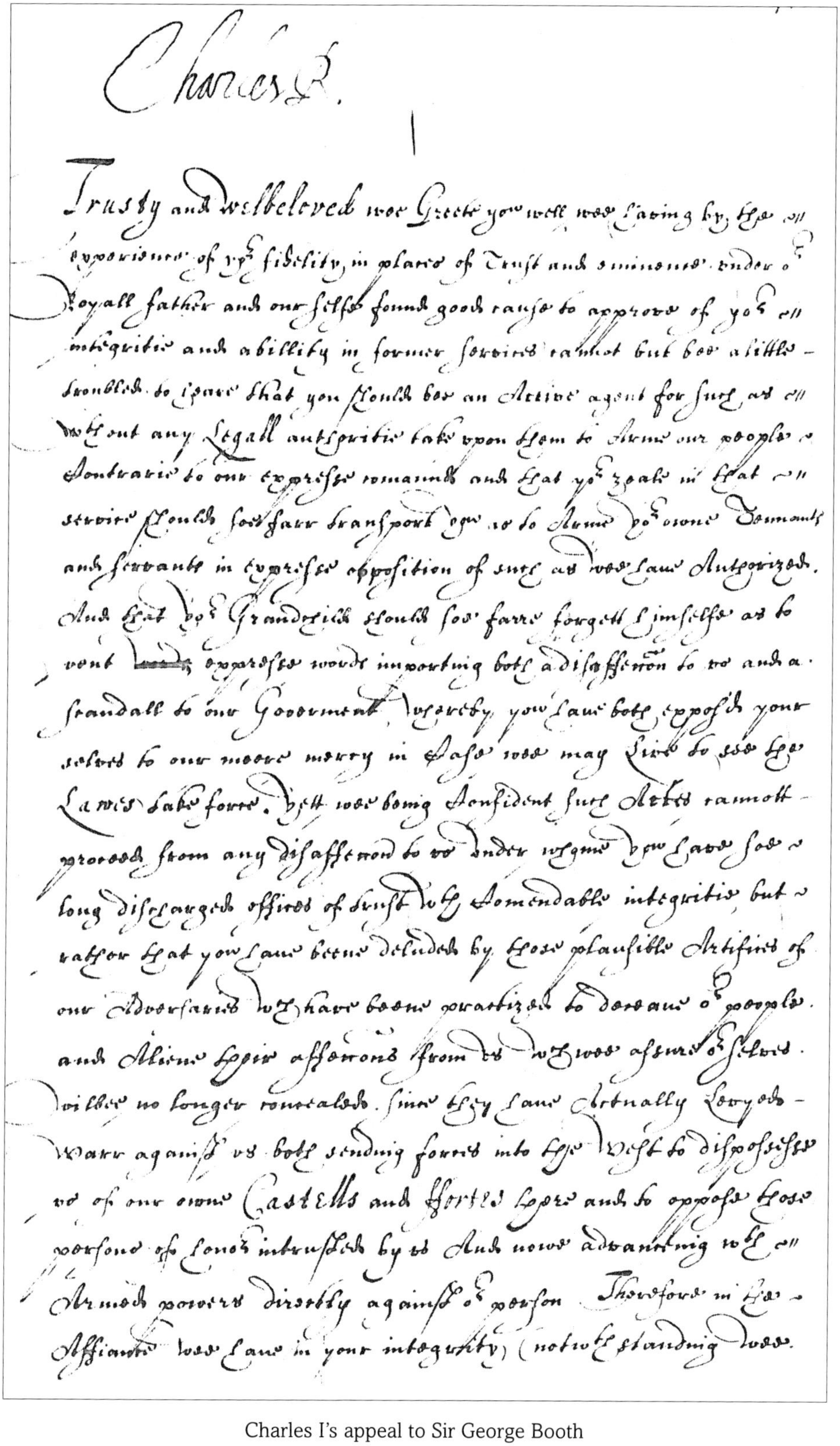

Charles R.

Trusty and welbeloved wee Greete you well wee having by the experience of yor fidelity in places of Trust and eminence under or Royall father and our selfes found good cause to approve of yor integritie and abillity in former services cannot but bee a little troubled to heare that you should bee an Active agent for such as without any Legall authoritie take upon them to Arme our people contrarie to our expresse commands and that yor zeale in that service should soe farre transport you as to Arme yor owne Tenants and servants in expresse opposition of such as wee have Authorized. And that yor Grandchild should soe farre forgett himselfe as to vent expresse words importing both a disaffection to us and a scandall to our Government whereby you have both exposed your selves to our meere mercy in case wee may live to see the Lawes take force. Yett wee being Confident such Actes cannot proceed from any disaffection to us under whome you have soe long discharged offices of trust with commendable integritie but rather that you have beene deluded by those plausible Artifices of our Adversaries which have beene practized to deceave or people and Alien their affections from us which wee assure or selves will bee no longer concealed since they have actually levyed warr against us both sending forces into the West to dispossesse us of our owne Castells and fortes there and to oppose those persons of honor intrusted by us And nowe advancing with Armed power directly against or person Therefore in the Affiance wee have in your integrity (notwithstanding wee

Charles I's appeal to Sir George Booth

*performed towards them in way of peace, the same they are to perform unto and towards both the counties; not offending the counties, not to be offended by them. And this is the only real intent."*

These were noble aims indeed and the reply from the Royalists was reasonably conciliatory and was to the effect that any proposals approved by Lord Derby would be forwarded to Parliament without delay for their consideration, but meanwhile there would be no relaxation in preparations.

The chief signatory was that of Lord Wharton, the Lord Lieutenant appointed by Parliament but not of course ratified by the King. He had been in post only a few days and his influence must have been slight. The whole tone - moderate Presbyterianism, improve the church, rid it of its excesses - is that of Sir George Booth. Only Sir Thomas Stanley of the other four signatories might have had the standing to draft the petition, but although Booth was ordinarily much less active in Lancashire than in Cheshire, this is surely one case in which he stood up to be counted. In the event, Parliament and the King were both set on war. The hotheads had won the day and there was no chance for peace.

John Booth distinguished himself in February 1643 at the battle for the control of Preston, a Royalist stronghold. A captain at the time, he was in a force of about 1,600 men who carried out a surprise dawn attack on the town. Their prospects were not good, because many of the attackers were armed only with bill-hooks and halberds, excellent for close-quarter combat but no use otherwise. Moreover Preston was well fortified, with inner and outer walls. Booth and Captain Holland led their companies but were beaten back three times. Finally a breach was made and Booth led the first wave of attackers. Seeing that the assault was not going well, he scaled the walls and shouted to his men either to follow him or to leave him to fight and die. His brave example was good enough: they followed him, overwhelmed the defenders and captured the town. In the official report to Parliament, Booth received a well-deserved mention in despatches, he *"behaving himself most bravely."*

Cheshire however was a different sort of problem for both sides. Only the City of Chester itself was of great strategic importance, because of its effective control over the Irish Sea, and therefore over any reinforcements from Ireland. Brereton rather rashly attempted to drum up support for Parliament, but the Mayor stabbed his sword through the drum and arrested Brereton's supporters. Serious disturbances occurred and only simmered down when Brereton was driven out of the city in shame by an angry mob.

The castle was firmly in Royalist hands. Nantwich was the only other town of any strategic importance. Public opinion in the rest of the county generally favoured the Parliamentary side, but there were very few hotheads of either party. The leading gentry much preferred if possible to refrain from any hostilities, which could only bring damage and destruction probably without any determining influence on the war as a whole.

Sir George helped to make a second attempt to preserve Cheshire from the evils of war. This took place at a meeting of the moderates at Bunbury in December 1642. Their aim was to make Cheshire a de-militarised county. All fighting within the county was to cease immediately, with no resumption without the consent of the King and both Houses of Parliament or in self-defence; both sides were to disband except for nominal forces of

200 men a side; no reinforcements were to be brought in from outside, all prisoners were to be released without pre-conditions and all fortifications were to be dismantled; all property that had been captured during the period of hostilities was to be returned to its owners forthwith; the Commissioners of Array were to procure a promise from the King that he would send no troops into Cheshire; and the Deputy Lieutenants would not put into execution the Ordinance of Militia. Lastly, *"all the said Parties do agree and promise each to other on the word of a Gentleman... that as well themselves, as also their Friends, Tenants, Servants, and all others in whom they have any interest, shall, as much as in them lies, perform the Agreement; And it is further desired, that all the Parties joyn in a Petition to his Majesty and both Houses of Parliament, for putting an end to the great Distractions and Miseries fallen upon this Kingdom by making a speedy Peace..."*

All the nobility and gentry of the county, with the obvious exception of those who were already active, were to sign the Treaty immediately, and Sir George was deputed to obtain the signatures of the gentry from the north of the county. If the Treaty of Bunbury had been permitted to come into force, it might well have influenced other counties and had a salutary effect on the whole conduct of the war. However, Parliament refused to countenance it at all. The hotheads condemned it without reservation. *"Things of the neuter gender are without life"* they said, and they would not tolerate any compounding with the *"delinquents"* on the Royalist side.

This second rejection by the firebrands in the Commons must have been a grave disappointment to Sir George Booth. At 76 years of age he must have felt that he was really too old for the battles that he knew were soon to take place, especially as he was the de facto second-in-command to the man who was effectively in command of the county's forces, his own son-in-law, Sir William Brereton of Handforth Hall. Brereton, like Booth, was a Justice of the Peace and a Deputy Lieutenant of the county, but he was also a Member of Parliament, active in the Commons and more radical than most of the gentry who took Parliament's side in the war. Moreover he was only 43 years old, widely travelled and in the opinion of his Commons colleagues, ideally suited to lead Cheshire's military. Fiercely ambitious, he did nothing to disillusion them.

Brereton had already received his instructions from Parliament in London before the formal outbreak of war. The King was still under the influence of *"wicked Counsell"* and might draw together *"the Knights, Gentlemen, freeholders and inhabitants of the Countie of Chester"* to form a guard for himself. Brereton, or in his absence the other Deputy Lieutenants, was therefore to ensure that the provisions of the Militia Ordinance were to be strictly observed. If anyone tried to sway the Militia to the King's side, his name was to be reported to the Speaker of the House of Commons. However Parliament remained anxious, they said, to provide for the King's safety and knew of no threat to him. The greatest danger was that *"furtive, disaffected and malignant persons, obnoxious for their bad counsels"* might raise support against the authority of Parliament. Brereton was to ensure the safety of the post, confine Catholics to their homes, and most importantly, collect the arms and ammunition in the county.

Cheshire as a whole was lucky to escape serious bloodshed in the early days and months of the war. Even so, Nantwich was almost the site of a major battle even before the King raised his standard at Nottingham, when Sir William Brereton and his Deputy Lieutenants encountered by chance a body of the King's Commissioners of Array only a mile from the town. Fortunately for the town, both sides agreed that it was pointless to open hostilities, and with moderation from two local gentlemen, a compromise was reached.

Edmund Jodrell of Yearsley was a friend of old Sir George and was required to provide a pikeman for the levy. This man was not ready and Jodrell asked Sir George to be excused on this occasion, giving some money instead. Sir George was ready to oblige and suggested to his grandson that perhaps Dennis Bocking of his own tenants could serve in the absent pikeman's place - *"...he comes to you on Mareback with a Cogell to the end you may send him back...."* One George Hollingworth was also possible and not much good for anything else. *"....and make him serve with a muskett that doth live so Idly and lewdly."* Flimsy material indeed for an army.

Jodrell was grateful and sent a donation of £20. The Deputy Lieutenants led by Sir George seized on this and promptly asked him to increase it to £100 *"which we may desire may come cheerfully and willingly from you as it has come from divers others..."*

Jodrell unwisely ignored the demand, and Sir George wrote rather more brusquely a few weeks later. *"We not doubting of your forwardness and pensiveness shall forbear to press you, only desiring your answer to this may be sent to Dunham.... so we may know whether to send to receive your moneys...."*

Again Jodrell ignored the demand, and this time the Cheshire Council of War, excluding Sir George, politely requested £300! This time Jodrell did answer in some slight panic. He mentioned his gift of £20 and claimed that his finances were nothing like as great as some people supposed, so he could not afford anything more. The storm clouds gathered above his head and prison threatened. Sir George did his best to help and suggested that Jodrell should be allowed to speak in his own defence. It was not enough and Jodrell was confined with other gentlemen prisoners in Nantwich in March 1643 and remained there for more than four months while his house was looted of almost £100 of goods and property. (He claimed £150 at the least!) His first petition for release was unsuccessful and after seven months in captivity he petitioned Sir William Brereton personally. This time he was luckier and was released pending payment of *"any reasonable sum ...which Mr Jodrell is well able & ought by the Ordinance of Parliament to advance..."* and was even given a letter signed by Brereton, Booth and three other Deputy Lieutenants as a protection against any more plundering.

The Commons sent their Militia Ordinance to Brereton and Booth early in January. The King, it said, was *"seduced by wicked Counsell, hath raised War against the Parliament"*, and Brereton and Booth were empowered to raise and train militia forces against any invaders. They had to search suspicious people and seize all arms and ammunition. They had sweeping powers to recruit militia officers, to imprison *"Popish recusants"*, to liaise with neighbouring counties for mutual defence and to raise money from taxes. And running like a refrain through these Rules of Engagement was the repeated injunction to obey any instructions from Parliament. It was a declaration of Martial Law.

Nantwich remained a town for Parliament, but not for long. Just a few days before the Battle of Edgehill, a large troop of Royalist cavalry appeared. Although Nantwich was well-provisioned, it faced a superior number of troops which could call on reinforcements from the King's army near Shrewsbury. Sensibly they decided on discretion and surrendered the town without a shot. The town temporarily fell into Royalist hands, governed by Brereton's old colleague in the Short Parliament, Sir Thomas Aston.

The autumn and early winter of 1642/43 saw a lull in the fighting in Cheshire. It was broken at the end of January 1643 when Brereton, with a force of no more than about 500 men, advanced on Nantwich to organise its parliamentary sympathisers. His advance guard met Aston's own cavalry and there was confused skirmishing in the darkness until one soldier, more clear-headed than others, managed to load and fire a small cannon. It did no damage but caused panic in the Royalist ranks, who thought they were facing very superior forces and fled in disarray. Aston himself ran for three miles according to contemporary accounts before getting a horse to Whitchurch. Brereton was so elated with his success that he claimed that Aston had been shot in the buttocks, but this picturesque but painful detail was later proved to be false.

Another skirmish took place four months later, when a Royalist force under Lord Capel mounted a particularly incompetent assault. They suffered a few casualties from defensive musket fire and withdrew ingloriously, having killed an unfortunate calf! With the end of the battle, Brereton realised that he badly needed reinforcements. They arrived quickly, including the Mainwarings, Thomas Marbury, Edward Hyde and Robert Duckenfield with their men. Brereton was busy fortifying and provisioning Nantwich against another attack. We do not know if any of the Booth family were able to join in time for the next clash at Tarporley, but old Sir George and his grandson were definitely at the Battle of Middlewich, if not before. In any case they would certainly have joined as soon as they heard of the outbreak of hostilities and young George Booth's troops of horse would have been particularly welcome. The cavalry were vitally important, not only as shock troops in battle but as fast reconnaissance units, able to traverse the countryside and get the intelligence back to headquarters far faster than on foot.

Brereton sent out for all able-bodied men between 16 and 60 to meet him at Tarporley. Aston heard of the arrangement, sent a message to prepare for battle there and was fortunate to get the advantage of high ground. Once again the conflict was indecisive, although the Royalists had heavy guns and Brereton had none. Casualties on both sides were light because there was virtually no close-quarter fighting and the long-range artillery was inaccurate.

Neither side was in any hurry to fight. It was a month between Nantwich and Tarporley, and another month between Tarporley and Middlewich. Brereton camped at Northwich, Aston plundered the country for supplies in the area of Over and Weaverham, and not until 13 March did either feel ready for another battle. Aston showed his military inexperience by garrisoning Middlewich, a town with no defences at all. His strength was in numbers of troops - he had over 1,000 in all - and in having three cannons, while the Parliamentary forces had none. Brereton did however have better cavalry and they had the advantage of being outside the town, while the Royalist horse were hemmed in by the town's narrow streets.  Brereton was also expecting reinforcements in forced marches from Nantwich.

The battle began early in the morning of 13 March.  Young Colonel George Booth, with his troops of horse, was a mile or so to the west of the town, facing hostile fire from Aston's guns and musketeers who lined the hedgerows.  His task was to prevent a Royalist breakout while Brereton waited for the Nantwich forces approaching from the south and began to probe the defences.  The Royalists held him off easily but he was in considerable danger, under constant enemy fire.  A good commander, he would not show any concern he may have felt.  On one occasion a cannon ball pitched just in front of him and bounced clean over the front ranks of his troops, and soon after that another round pitched in deep mud and soaked Booth and two of his officers with the splash.

If the ground had been hard in that spot, or if the guns had been raised a fraction, the course of the day might well have been different.  Narrow escapes indeed, but they had the effect of distracting the attention from the enemy of the Nantwich men approaching along Booth's Lane.  Aston's men did not see them until too late, and they were too inexperienced to change front to meet this fresh attack.  The musketeers fired a volley but had no time to reload and retreated rapidly.  The horses could not manoeuvre in the narrow streets and had no choice but to retire.  The absence of any effective command was now too much for the Royalists; some fled to the east without waiting to see what was happening and others barricaded themselves up in the church from which they were soon persuaded to surrender when Major Lothian, a professional soldier, blew the door in.  Aston never recovered from the disaster.  He managed to escape, but eventually reached Chester without any of the troops under his command!

Brereton, flushed with success in three battles, went to London and was officially appointed commander of Cheshire's forces. His power continued to increase. He also gained control of the committees for sequestration of delinquents, the advancement of money and the examination of ministers. It was from this time that the antagonism between him and the Booth family began.  Brereton was proud of his appointment and never missed any opportunity of demonstrating his importance. Until then, communications from London had always been addressed to *"the Deputy Lieutenants"*, or to *"Sir William Brereton, Sir George Booth or other the Deputy Lieutenants"*, recognising that Brereton and his fellow Deputy Lieutenants were co-equal.  However from then on, Parliament relegated Sir George to no more than Brereton's deputy whenever Brereton was away, and Booth felt it keenly.  He was after all senior to Brereton in age and status, he was his father-in-law, he was still active in mind and body in spite of his great age, and he felt that he was entitled in every way to be the commander. His own authority was technically limited to the committee controlling the finances needed for the siege of Chester and the administration and collection of the monthly assessments to pay the troops.

The relationship between Brereton and his father-in-law, his nephew and his brother-in-law turned frosty.  They continued to address each other in terms of punctilious courtesy - *"your very loving father-in-law"*, *"your assured faithful son-in-law to serve you"* - and their aim to serve Parliament was the same, but they were never again on such friendly terms.  John Booth in particular was always quick to take offence.  In 1645 he was criticised by the County Committee for failing to send enough men and money to help in the siege of Chester, and answered *"which I cannot perceive by your answer was any otherwise accepted than with slight."*

Replies such as that were hardly likely to endear him to haughty high commanders and caused his brother-in-law, Brereton, to suspect him of disloyalty.  Brereton disliked his fellow Deputy Lieutenants, who as a body objected to his use of Cheshire's troops outside the county and begged *"that the small forces belonging to this countie may.... be confined to the defence thereof."*  Such a request, which would tend to reduce Brereton's powers, was guaranteed to arouse his fierce opposition.

The struggle during the rest of that summer was complicated, with no pitched battles but a large number of skirmishes led by Brereton's troops of horse, mixed with occasional sorties out of the county to help the Militia in Staffordshire or the Lancastrians.  Successes and failures balanced each other, but the fall of Warrington into Parliament's hands was especially important and the town remained in their possession for the rest of the war.

For Old Sir George, it was very satisfying.  He was Lord of the Manor of Warrington, since he and his son William had bought it years before and he had the honour of riding into the town at the head of the Parliament forces on Trinity Sunday, 27 May 1643, after a siege of only six days.  He appointed his son, John, Governor of the town, and he remained so for four years.

Sir William Brereton was not of course totally successful.  Shortly after his triumph at Middlewich he was defeated at the Battle of Hopton Heath by the Earl of Northampton, and in November 1643 the Royalists received reinforcements from Ireland.  Brereton and Booth were anxious not to do battle with them and wrote a conciliatory letter, hoping that they *"may not now through mistakes or misinformation be divided and we under the brand of rebels be made enemies."*  Brereton and Booth recognised that the army had been sent to Ireland to fight for the Protestant religion and said it seemed strange that they should be called upon to fight Protestants in England. *"For this reason we have tendered our respects to you... and we doubt not but to procure satisfaction from the Parliament for the service you have done in Ireland, with the like preferment here, and show yourselves as real here for the Protestant religion as you did there, which will engage us all to remain your affectionate and faithful friends."*  Would a parley be possible, to avoid bloodshed?  The reply from Colonel Sir Michael Ernely was courteous but curt: *"We were not engaged in the service of Ireland other ways than by the King's Commission... If you can shew the like Commission from the King for the Arms you carry, we shall willingly treat with you; otherwise you must give us leave to carry ourselves like soldiers and Loyal Subjects."*

With the lost opportunity to attack the Royalist reinforcements as they landed, Brereton's Lancashire men abandoned him and returned home and he had to retreat hastily.  The Royalists triumphantly proclaimed that he had received such a welcome that he dared not show his face in Nantwich!  He put garrisons into Hawarden Castle and Nantwich, but he could not prevent them from besieging Hawarden, which eventually surrendered and became a Royalist fortress.  Brereton retreated further into North

Cheshire, leaving Sir George Booth as Governor of Nantwich and young George Booth as commander of the garrison.

The prospects for the Booths did not look good. Old Sir George, in his seventy eighth year, was besieged in a small and poorly fortified town; his grandson was young and inexperienced, and his troops were outnumbered by Lord Byron, an experienced and highly professional soldier with 1,000 cavalry. The Parliament forces suffered a series of setbacks. Byron captured Beeston Castle and took prisoner Major Lothian, Booth's chief military adviser, and Sir William Brereton suffered another defeat at Middlewich. The future of Nantwich as a Parliamentary stronghold looked gloomy indeed.

Lord Byron, justifiably confident, set up his cannon round the town and made sure the defenders knew about them, but before actually beginning hostilities he gave them a chance to surrender. They were to deliver up all their arms, guns and ammunition for the King's use, and in return he promised pardon and safe conduct to any who promised to return to their homes. Failing that, he would *"by God's help use other means for the recoverie of his Majesties right and vindicating of his and the Country's wrongs; whereby if you, and those many good people, who are forced to bee among you, shall perish, both your owne blood and theirs shall rest on you own heads."* Byron would await Sir George Booth's reply and if none came within two hours he would start the bombardment.

Booth did not deign to write to Byron, but sent a messenger with his answer that Nantwich was being kept for God and the King, and he would hold it against Byron *"so long as it pleased God to enable us."* Booth showed his powers of leadership by ensuring that his own troops heard his message of defiance and they responded by cheering him to the echo. As for Byron, he opened fire on the town in accordance with his threat and continued for several days. On 17 January alone his cannon fired at least 100 rounds into Nantwich, but without causing much damage or many casualties and he began to realise that Booth was never going to surrender just through artillery fire.

Rumours began to spread about the fate of the town and its people when it would eventually fall. Byron indignantly denied in public that he had any plans to massacre all its inhabitants. *"I have therefore thought fit once more to send unto you, that the minds of the people with you, may be dispossest of that false and wicked slander.... And I do charge you... that you will impart and publish the said Summons I sent to the people with you, and that you yeeld up the town of Namptwich into my hands for his Majesties use and submit yourselves to his Majesties mercy, which I am willing to offer unto you."*

Sir George's written reply was typically proud and defiant. *"We have received your last Summons, and do returne this answer, that wee never reported, or caused to be reported, that your Lordship, or the Armie, intended any such crueltie, wee thinking it impossible for Gentlemen and Souldiers so much to forget humanitie: and if any have informed you otherwise, it is their own conceit, and no reulnle. Concerning the publishing of your former Summons, it was publikely read amongst the Souldiers and Townesmen, as your Trumpeter can witness, and since that time multitudes of coppies of it have been dispersed among the Townsmen and others, and from none hath it been concealed and detained. For the deliverie of this town, wee may not with our consciences, credits, or reputations, betray that trust reposed in us, for the maintaining and defending this towne, as long as any enemy shall appear to offend it. Though we be termed Traytours and Hypocrites, yet we hope and are confident, God will evidence and make knowne to the world in his due time (though for the present we should suffer) our zeale for his glorie, our unfained and unspotted loyalty towards his Majestie, and sinceritie in all our professions."*

In spite of his defiance, Booth must have known that his situation was perilous. Byron's army held all the strong points around the town. He had no idea from where or when any relief might come. However he took heart from the courage of his defenders when Byron finally launched a frontal assault, which was repelled with an estimated 500 casualties including his Master Gunner, Captain Sandford and several other officers.

Help was on its way, although he could not have known it, and on 21 January a large army under the command of Sir Thomas Fairfax left Manchester southwards. They joined forces with Brereton, who had been summoning up reinforcements from wherever possible, including a regiment from Lancashire commanded by Colonel John Booth. The opposing armies met a mile or so to the north west of Nantwich near Acton Church on 25 January. At first neither side seemed at all sure how best to proceed. The Parliamentary horse could not charge because of the broken countryside and hedges, and the Royalist cavalry stayed completely static. At the same time the Royalist centre was undecided, but their wings were pressing hard against Fairfax's infantry, led by regiments commanded by Colonels Holland and, predictably in the thick of it, John Booth.

At this crucial moment, young George Booth launched a surprise sally from Nantwich. He and his defenders knew nothing of the approach of Fairfax's relieving force or of Brereton's army, so the start of the fighting must have been a complete surprise to them. Moreover, Booth had as we have seen lost his chief military adviser, Major Lothian. The fact that he was able to appreciate the situation and launch a perfectly timed assault shows that he had a shrewd grasp of military tactics. As it was, a Royalist regiment guarding the western exits from the town was swept aside by the sudden attack by up to 1,000 determined men just when they least expected it, and the centre of Byron's army collapsed.

As Fairfax explained in his report to the Earl of Essex: *"yet it pleased God, after two hours fight they were forced by both wings to retreat to the Church, where they were caught as in a trap."* The wings were thus left isolated and only one regiment, that of Robert Byron, Lord Byron's brother, managed to escape in some sort of order. They marched off to Chester with their colours flying, but the rest of Byron's army surrendered with little or no resistance. Of the senior commanders, only Lord Byron and his brother escaped. The Parliamentary victory was total, and they dominated all the county except Chester itself.

Their domination was in some doubt elsewhere in the area. The Earl of Denbigh was the Lord Lieutenant, on the Parliamentary side, of four counties including Shropshire, where the Royalist army was threatening, and in March 1644 he asked for help from Cheshire and Lancashire. John Booth and Richard Holland answered that their regiments could not help in the relief of Wem because they were down to a total of only 600 men, due to *"sickness, diseases, and other disasters of war"*, and the survivors were in poor morale through irregular pay, worn-out clothing and *"evil accommodation of diet and lodging."* Old Sir George took up the matter and tried to find out the strength of the King's forces in the area and where they were, so that he could be prepared for any emergency.

It was a critical period for the King, who sent out the brave and dashing Prince Rupert in May 1644. With a large army, he had instant successes. When he reached south Cheshire, he received reinforcements from Byron and captured Stockport, Bolton and Liverpool in quick succession. There remained Manchester, Warrington and Nantwich, the last two of which were, as we have seen, Booth strongholds. Colonel John Booth was unable to send reinforcements to his father, because his men were urgently needed for the siege of the Royalist stronghold of Lathom House and his and Colonel Holland's regiments were no stronger than they had been two months before.

It was to be a false dawn of hope for the King, whose army of 17,500 men was decisively defeated by Fairfax and Cromwell at the Battle of Marston Moor in July, perhaps the most devastating battle ever fought on British soil. Prince Rupert, licking his wounds, retreated to Chester, but his troops were easily picked off one by one by Sir William Brereton in Cheshire and the Welsh borders, by Sir John Meldrum in the Liverpool area and by Sir Thomas Myddleton in Montgomery.

Even so, old Sir George was cautious. From his temporary base in Shropshire, he suggested (5 July 1644) to Denbigh that Oswestry should be provisioned and fortified and that Denbigh's troops should move nearer to Chester, because surviving fragments of Prince Rupert's army *"will molest us in these counties if not prevented."* Back at Dunham, Booth heard disquieting news and sent an urgent ("Speed, speed, speed!") message to the Nantwich Committee. According to his news, Prince Rupert was in the Preston area with a formidable force of not less than 6,000 foot and horse. Even more seriously, Cromwell had abandoned the pursuit and returned to York, *"so the enemy hath more scope and liberty to advance as he pleaseth."* All the Parliament commanders in Cheshire should therefore *"stand well upon our ward, and rally our forces for the public safety."*

Booth's fear was in fact unnecessary. After all his setbacks and defeats, Rupert arrived at Chester but stayed only long enough to make Byron governor and then abandoned the city and returned southwards.

## The Siege of Chester

Chester remained the only large Royalist base in Cheshire and its strategic importance was as great as ever, with its closeness to possible reinforcements from Ireland. It would have to be taken before a Parliament victory could be guaranteed. However its defences were good: it was receiving supplies through two roads open into Wales where the Royalists were still strong and Brereton's Cheshire forces were quite incapable of storming it or of starving it out.

The Committee of Both Kingdoms (CBK) appreciated both the city's importance and Brereton's relative weakness and frequently requested assistance from neighbouring counties. Brereton needed to be careful about his command structure. At least half of the Deputy Lieutenants were much more moderate in their views than he was and he could not afford to antagonise them. He was on bad terms with the Booth family. Old

Sir George remained courteous, but John and young George Booth were more openly hostile. Nor could Brereton exercise autocratic command, quite beyond the communications systems of the time. He had to bear in mind that although he was commander in one respect, he remained just one of a number of county Deputy Lieutenants and had no more administrative power than any of them. He therefore established a committee of the Deputy Lieutenants, based in Nantwich, conveniently near the siege lines of Chester, and he relied to a large extent on Sir George Booth to organise the northern part of the county.

Chester's defenders were equally determined. They relied mainly on fortified earthworks and did not burn the outlying suburbs, although it would have made the city easier to defend. The ancient walls were not strengthened and could not long withstand the determined battering of cannon, although Byron took steps to line with earth the houses that stood immediately inside the walls.

The siege of Chester began in November 1644, but for much of the eighteen months it lasted, it was not a close siege in the commonly understood term. In fact there were at least four exits from the city of which two were towards Wales. Both sides enjoyed varying degrees of success during the time. At first Brereton's most forward base was at Tarvin and when he attempted to establish outposts in villages nearer the city itself, Byron was quick to counter-attack, so for long periods neither side could establish any clear advantage. Moreover, the Royalists were trying to assemble large forces to relieve Chester, particularly from Staffordshire and Shropshire. Sir George Booth realised that the threat was grave and personally wrote to Sir Thomas Fairfax asking for help. He answered in general terms that he would do what he could, and the Nantwich Committee replied that *"a thousand or two of horse and dragoons, with what possible speed there may be"* would be a great help.

The besieging forces launched a major attack against the Northgate entrance at 6.00am on 27 January 1645. The defenders were ready and put up a stout resistance. A Royalist defender cheerfully described the success of the defence: *"The rebels came with scaling ladders to scale the wall, but they had so hot a breakfast as divers went with bullets for concoction, which hindered their drinking afterwards."*

Sir William Brereton's account of the struggle was much less dramatic: *"Before daybreak we prepared and attempted to storm the outworks of Chester, but we failed to enter: nevertheless we escaped without damage."* He omitted to mention the muskets, swords and pieces of armour the attackers left behind.

The Committee of Both Kingdoms was understandably anxious to give Brereton all possible help and in March 1645 they ordered reinforcements from as far as Lincolnshire and Nottingham, and four cavalry regiments and 2,000 infantry from Scotland. Looking over their shoulders, they also wrote to old Sir George Booth with instructions to secure Warrington against any possible surprise assault.

What they did not say was that there was some reason to suspect the loyalty to them of Sir George's son John, left in Warrington as its governor. Brereton certainly had his doubts, prompted probably by his dislike of the family. As an afterthought to a letter regretting that the Scottish reinforcements were not coming his way, he warned the CBK that he doubted John Booth's loyalty to Parliament, although he does not appear to have had strong grounds for his suspicions.

Certainly John did nothing to dispel the distrust that Brereton felt. Only a few days after Brereton wrote to the CBK, the sequestrators of Bucklow complained to him that in accordance with orders from Parliament they were levying £50 from the estates of delinquents when John Booth not only obstructed them by force but returned the cattle to their owners and imprisoned Richard Starkey, one of the sequestrators.

The background to the affair was that certain townships in Cheshire near Warrington had been ordered by Parliament to aid Warrington when the Royalists were in great strength. Then the situation had changed and Brereton had persuaded Parliament that support for the town should revert to Lancashire. Booth was determined that his personal power and prestige should not be lessened, and he persuaded Parliament that the disagreement should be settled by the Deputy Lieutenants of the two counties. Relying on this ordinance, he now not only ignored the order to support Cheshire but made matters worse by an arrogant and insulting letter to Mr Thomas Warburton, the head of the sequestrators: *"I had hoped... that I might have found the common respect of a gentleman from you.... But I find your proceedings offer violence to mine and your neighbours.... take notice that I am a Deputy Lieutenant of your county and that the former order for the maintenance of this garrison is still on foot and that I will not loose the sequestrators... until the business be settled by the Deputy Lieutenants of both counties according to the order of Parliament."*

Old Sir George was never afraid of showing his independence of thought from Brereton and due consideration for the ordinary men who constituted the troops. Requested by the county committee to raise as many as possible armed and provisioned men to help block the Welsh side of Chester, he answered from Dunham that he had arranged for enlisted companies to be called *"...but for raising the country people I forbear, in regard they are making their seednes, as also they have so often been called together and to so little purpose that they grow sensible that the country is burthened and opportunities neglected..."* His friend William Marbury made the same point. He turned up at the rendezvous but only four others arrived. He sensibly suggested that each township should provide an agreed number of men for temporary emergencies, to return home when the need ended. He, Sir George and Roger Wilbraham would form a sub-committee.

Meanwhile serious discontent was growing among the regular troops. Colonel Duckenfield told Sir George that his regiment was too long unpaid, was sick and discontented, and he asked for pay, good billets and food *"the store whereof of the country is much exhausted."* Sir George was in full agreement and asked Brereton to *"take some orders to give the soldiers content, for there is a general murmur in the country."* Brereton replied that Chester was near to surrender and meanwhile Booth should take steps to raise as much money as possible from previous assessments.

Within a few days the situation reached boiling point when a detachment of cavalry from Yorkshire, based at Wybunbury, almost mutinied. Their presence at Nantwich was particularly important, being the only Parliamentary cavalry there, but they were receiving no regular pay and they considered that the proposal to guard the Welsh approaches was too dangerous, being in the most remote position.  One of their corporals threatened that if they saw Brereton, they would *"cut him small and fresh to the pot"* and the county committee told Brereton that they could not send any more men to Shropshire and no money could come from Wybunbury *"while these robbers are suffered to infest them."*

The Deputy Lieutenants of Cheshire and Lancashire were to meet Sir George Booth at Dunham to discuss the problems. The county was being bled dry and needed substantial funds from London.

Brereton tried to get funds from anywhere.  For at least three years the villages of Cheshire had been complaining about being overcharged and it was becoming impossible to squeeze them any more.  He had himself been financially ruined by the war. *"The enemy hath been possessed of the most part of my estate.  Plundered and taken away my Goods and Large Stockes of Sheeps, Cattle and Horses at Chester, Weston and Handforth, my house at Chester pulled down, Weston House defaced and rendered uninhabitable, and Handforth House quite stripped and left naked of all portable goods.... As also my charge and expense hath been great and extraordinarie and much more than if I had beene onely a private Colonel. As also my debts and engagements are much increased....."*

When the Royalists threatened to relieve Chester at the end of 1645, Brereton was reduced to begging from his friends.  He asked for money, food and ammunition from Mr Crewe, admitting that he had already failed in getting enough from Parliament.  He acknowledged that he had sought financial help unsuccessfully from neighbouring counties and in desperation had sent much of his force to Wales to try and provoke a pitched battle.  The remaining troops were hard pressed. *"The enemy is full of fury and courage, and delight in and practise nothing more than ruin and destruction, as shooting fiery arrows to fire and consume what remains of the suburbs, which they have this day attempted, and which was by an extraordinary providence preserved by the sudden turning of the wind."*

Colonel John Booth in Warrington continued to be wilfully obstructive. The Hundred of Bucklow adjoined the Warrington lands and was raising fewer men than expected.  Sir George authorised a warrant for them to assemble, but one of John Booth's officers, a Captain Alcocke, intercepted them with his mounted troop and sent them back to their homes.  Booth was standing on the strict letter of the law that some of the men had been enlisted from townships under his control and that assessments had also been charged on those townships. *"And if any go about by force to compel either"*, he wrote, *"I shall use my utmost endeavour to make it appear to them that they are in a wrong way.... And in the meantime I hope your town is both able and willing to defend itself...."*

Brereton complained bitterly about John's obstructiveness but realised that he was helpless, and left it to Sir George to sort out.  Old Sir George was furious with both John Booth and the officious Captain Alcocke, and it is likely that strong words passed between father and son.  The Nantwich Committee told John that his failure to cooperate was causing a grave shortage of men and money, either of which could cause the siege of Chester to fail and that John had no right to disobey Parliament or the CBK.  John tried to conciliate the Cheshire Committee by offering three or four hundred men within a week, to be deployed where they would be of most use. *"...and in case I find the country backward in affording their assistance, or refractory in yielding obedience.... I shall not only be very strict in bringing them to condign punishment, but herein I shall crave your aid and best assistance."*

He also agreed to pay the taxes levied and assessed for Ireland, provided they were no more than they should be. He ended: *"You shall find us forwardly willing to apply our best assistance, and my self ready to manifest to you that I am my country's and your true friend and servant."*

The Committee replied caustically and with tongues firmly in their cheeks, that without mutual help and cooperation, their cause would fail, as Colonel Booth well knew. Moreover, everything was done under Parliamentary ordinance *"and for you to cross it, which would be a cross to the design both the Parliament and the Committee of Both Kingdoms have so much taken into their thoughts, will prove we are to cross yourself, whose estimation.... shall we be ever tender to preserve."*

Nevertheless, while great events were unfolding, Sir George still had to find time to deal with local problems. In April 1645 four Deputy Lieutenants including Brereton wrote to him complaining about the antics of Mr Bate, the minister in Mobberley, and Thomas Partington, an Elder in an independent chapel at Duckenfield. Bate used his pulpit to criticise *"particular men that neither wish nor do him harm."* More seriously, Booth had given him orders that any money collected on fast days was to be given to the poor of the parish. However several respected churchwardens and overseers of the poor in Mobberley said that Bate refused to do so, claiming that the paupers were not sufficiently religious. Moreover, whoever had persuaded a magistrate to order collections to be thus dealt with *"were base fellows and drunkards and whoremasters."*

Partington had allegedly managed to lay his hands on money collected in Mobberley for the Warrington garrison and used it to buy corn etc for his own use. Also he had publicly insulted Colonel John Booth, who *"could only staunch his drunken throat with plundering and stealing....."*, an accusation that Sir George refuted indignantly. Old Sir George asked his fellow Cheshire magistrates to make the appropriate charges against Bate. As for Partington, his offences were committed in Lancashire, where Sir George was an inactive Deputy Lieutenant, so Booth wrote to Lord Stanley with a request to deal with him *"as pertains to justice."*

Brereton was summoned to London early in May 1645, leaving the Nantwich Committee with no nominated leader. They suggested Sir John Meldrum, a professional soldier with connections with *"a young gentleman of great expectations"* holding Tarvin. (Young George Booth fits the description). The petition to London is moderate in its request to be able to compound with delinquents, it asks as a matter of urgency for *"a supply of our defect in Parl., having neither knights nor burgess to appear for us there"*. It has all the stately style of his grandfather and was signed by both of them in addition to several of their supporters among the Deputy Lieutenants.

A joint committee of Lords and Commons considered the question of command and came up with the inadequate compromise of another committee to direct all Sir William Brereton's forces for 40 days. Lt Colonel Jones and Major Lothian, both professional soldiers, would command the cavalry and the infantry respectively on a day-to-day basis, but overall strategic command would be in the hands of Sir George Booth, his grandson, Sir William Brereton if present, Henry Brooke, Robert Duckenfield, John Leigh, and the Governor of Nantwich, with a quorum of three.

This did nothing to resolve the problem of pay and supplies. Young George Booth had resigned his command, probably because of his dislike of Brereton and his old regiment was verging on mutiny. The Nantwich Committee told Brereton that *"....unless care be speedily taken, the regiment will be lost and become unserviceable to this county."* Moreover their intelligence suggested that the Royalists penned up in Chester were preparing to launch a surprise sortie of 100 horse to overwhelm the besiegers. Sir George managed to find £200 to pay some of the arrears of the Yorkshire contingent on condition that they would return to service, but the main problem remained of insufficient resources.

Meanwhile, the Nantwich Committee had been thinking over John Booth's offer to supply up to 400 troops from Lancashire. They had sought advice, but Parliament could not make up its mind either. The offer was very acceptable but Parliament would not give them authority either to accept or refuse. In the circumstances, to accept his kind offer would only cause confusion, so they hoped he would not take it amiss if they refused it for the time being. Sir George Booth did not sign the letter, and presumably he disagreed, thinking that the offer should be accepted immediately, leaving the administrative minutiae to be sorted out later.

However, with the threatening advance through Shropshire of the King and the Princes Rupert and Maurice, with a strong army, John Booth came to the conclusion that it was no longer appropriate to be bothering about legal niceties. Many of Brereton's foot soldiers were at Shrewsbury and Booth offered speedy reinforcements to Brereton, *"Notwithstanding any misconceits that may be held of me and whatever your opinion may be concerning me."* He would risk his life and fortune to help.

Unfortunately events overtook him. No sooner had he sent off his letter than he heard rumours of a Royalist force beginning to threaten Liverpool, and he had to ask in great haste for the return of Colonel Ashton's regiment as soon as possible. It was time, Brereton suggested, for an urgent inter-county meeting to thrash out the different priorities and requirements, but it was too difficult for the Lancashire Committee to summon its Deputy Lieutenants from their widespread estates. There was sickness near Manchester, provisions were in desperately short supply and the county was exhausted.

Eventually John Booth and two other Deputy Lieutenants agreed to meet Brereton at Barlow Moor with two regiments of foot. The Lancashire men had secured Runcorn and the important ford at Hale, leaving only Booth's regiment to guard Liverpool and Warrington and a strategic reserve to wait at Ormskirk until there was firm intelligence of the Royalist advance.

But the CBK was in a rare defeatist mood and ordered Brereton to retreat into Lancashire. He had already partially raised the siege of Chester, without apparently consulting his fellow Deputy Lieutenants and the leaders of the Nantwich Committee were very alarmed. On 24 May 1645 Sir George Booth, young George and five other Deputy Lieutenants wrote an indignant letter to the CBK, setting out the situation as they saw it. They objected strongly to the whole strategy of the retreat, as its only possible result would have been to lose Cheshire and to delay a northward advance of the King's army. Their most up-to-date intelligence suggested that the enemy was either retreating or changing its direction of advance, but they still threatened Chester, its Welsh approaches and the strongholds of Beeston, Flint and Hawarden. The Cheshire forces had already loaned out six regiments to Shropshire and could not possibly hold their positions in Cheshire and fight a rearguard action in Lancashire simultaneously. *"Therefore, we have thought fit humbly to desire that the several forces belonging to this county may by your order be confined to the defence thereof during the potency of our intestine enemies and the invasion by others, to which we are continually liable."*

It is worth noting that the "Cheshire Gentlemen" (as distinct from the Nantwich Committee, or a committee of Deputy Lieutenants) did not consult Brereton before despatching this letter to London. They sent him a copy out of courtesy, but were concerned that he would simply carry out the orders from London without demur.

Financing the Parliament forces in Cheshire was always a problem and it was made worse by a large army of Scots commanded by Lieutenant General Leslie who arrived as the enemy army was retreating southwards. The CBK ordered Brereton to find the money to pay them, at which old Sir George almost despaired. He wrote that he would do his best to obey the Ordinance, but suggested that funds previously supplied for the relief of Ireland would be better used to pay the Scots, at least in the short term. *"....there is no one that knows more of the deplorable condition of this county than yourself, and how scarce money is here and difficult to levy."* Then followed an implied criticism of Brereton. *"I am confident that if you or any other had been attending in the House to have informed Parl. of the state of this county, that Cheshire would have been freed....."*

Brereton agreed haughtily that if he had been in Parliament, he would have done his utmost to get them to agree Booth's plan. However now was not a good time, but *"when I attend there according to the great Ordinance, I shall be ready to serve my country and, after the revolution of a short time, I conceive such a motion may be more seasonable than this at present, when the grand affairs of this Kingdom are in agitation."*

The situation of the Cheshire forces was deteriorating fast. Whatever Brereton may have been trying to do, Sir George realised that matters were desperate. The troops were on the edge of mutiny and many of them could no longer be counted on. He sent an express message ("Speed, speed, speed!") to his friend and colleague Edward Hyde of Norbury. *"I have but a little time allowed me. In short, I am to tell you, that if you be one that would save your country, if you be one, respect the safety and credit of your friends, if you regard the conservation of what may be dear to you, you must not fail tomorrow to meet all your friends at Namptwich. To give you some reasons for this my urgency all our trained bands are in a great discontent, two of them are disbanded, the rest threaten, new commands come from above, I beseech you therefore.... let no business of your own, whatever it can be, hinder you from coming....,"*

But luck was Parliament's side. Intelligence came through that the King's armies were withdrawing and no longer seemed to pose a direct threat to Cheshire. The Cheshire forces had been hanging on distantly to the siege in spite of their problems and with the unexpected disappearance of the Royalist army, Brereton, scarcely able to believe his luck, was able to reinforce the Chester siege and to besiege the castles of Beeston and Hawarden. The King's army meandered aimlessly about until on 14 June they were brought to battle at Naseby near Leicester, where they suffered a catastrophic defeat.

Meanwhile, Brereton had finally gone to London in obedience to the Self-Denying Ordinance, leaving command of the Cheshire forces to the Nantwich Committee. In his absence the Cheshire troops were to be commanded by a quorum of Deputy Lieutenants. This quorum, led by old Sir George, was soon in action, writing to Speaker Lenthall with the perennial request for money in a Remonstrance *"that it may please this honourable House - the wealth of the County being well nigh exhausted and not longer able to subsist - to afford such timely assistance of horse and foot as you.... shall think fit for the reducing of Chester... That some money be afforded this County for payment of the horse and dragoons and procuring of ammunition which the County stands in great need of."*

On 19 September they launched an open assault on Chester itself, abandoning normal siege tactics. At 3.00am they crossed the wall with storming ladders and achieved considerable success, capturing the Eastgate suburbs, but were driven back before they could advance further into the city. They could now bombard it from close range and caused much damage with mortars. One unfortunate citizen described the events of 10 December 1645: *"This was a terrible night indeed, our houses like so many split vessels crash their supporters and burst themselves in sunder through the very violence of these descending fire brands."*

On 23 September the King managed to cross over the Dee Bridge into Chester from Chirk, where he had taken refuge after Naseby. He still had a formidable body of cavalry including his own Life Guards, but Parliamentary reinforcements commanded by General Poyntz arrived the next day. A skirmish between Poyntz and Langdale brought no result and both sides drew back. The stalemate was broken about 4 pm, when two cannon shot rang out and Colonel John Booth, under the stern eye of his father, led out a force of 1,000 horse and foot to join battle with Sir Marmaduke Langdale's cavalry. Booth was not interested in any pitched battle, in which the outcome would always be doubtful. He was relying on the superiority of numbers given by General Poyntz and even more on his concealed musketeers who were lurking in the wings of his troops to suddenly open a damaging and harassing fire on the Royalist cavalry's flanks.

The Royalists began to fall back in some disarray but got mixed up with reinforcements from Lord Gerard's men and a number of troops from inside the Chester garrison. Major Lothian was watching, observed the confusion and seized his chance with a scratch reserve of Cheshire infantry and Shropshire cavalry. Small in numbers though they were, they fell on Gerard's horse and a general melee ensued. It was finally broken when General Poyntz's cavalry advanced and drove the Royalists against the mud defences of the city. The Battle of Rowton Moor was effectively over and although Charles himself managed to escape capture, his army was now only a shadow of its former strength.

Sir George Booth was elated, assembled a quorum of Deputy Lieutenants and dashed off a quick report to the Speaker of the House of Commons:

*"Honourable Sir,*

*We still keep the suburbs of Chester, and yesterday joining our forces with Major General Poyntz, God gave us a great victory over the King's Army, whereby God hath not only given us, but the Kingdom much cause of joy and thankfulness. We have such earnest business at present upon us, that we our selves cannot have time to represent to you the particulars, but have commanded the Chaplain to our forces, who was an eye witness to all that was done, to give you a full accompt thereof. All that we shall trouble you with at instant, is to renew our humble requests, that you will be pleased to expedite our Remonstrance and procure a speedy Order for moneys with all possible speed conveyed to us; otherwise we shall not be able to keep such forces together as are necessary for this work.*

*And so with tender of our Service, rest*
*Your most humble servants*
*G.Booth*
*Ph. Mainwaring*
*Rog. Wilbraham."*

Sir George followed up this news with another letter four days later. He was much more optimistic about the morale of the Cheshire army than he had been. He also took the opportunity to make an implied criticism of the absent Brereton. *"Since the House called up their members and committed the Militia to the Deputy Lieutenants, though we found the soldiers left in a mutinous condition for want of pay, and the country quite exhausted, yet it hath pleased God so to render our endeavours prosperous that the country and forces are now reduced to a cheerful and obedient condition, ready and capable of any proportionable design...."* He had heard rumours that some anonymous people had petitioned Parliament for Brereton to return and criticised the Deputy Lieutenants who were commanding in Brereton's absence *"...so insinuating an odium and scandal upon us.."* The return of Sir William Brereton was the last thing Sir George Booth wanted, but of course he could not say so openly without causing a serious breach between himself and his son-in-law.

Even at the height of the siege, there was sometimes room for chivalry. After the Battle of Rowton Moor, the Earl of Lichfield was missing. Young George Booth's men came across an unidentified corpse and Booth sent a messenger under truce to ask if Byron could recognise the body. From the description it was clear that it was indeed that of the missing Lichfield. According to Byron, some of Booth's officers wanted to demand a ransom for it, but Booth *"was too much a Gentleman (though engaged in that ungentlemanlike service) to condescend to so base a motion, and with great civility brought the corpse with a guard of foot and forty horse to a place agreed upon betwixt us, where I met it...."*

Sir George and his fellow Deputy Lieutenants wasted no time in tightening the siege, now that they faced little danger from within the city. Just in case the King managed to find more troops and decided to return, Sir George ordered Colonels Duckenfield and John Booth to join General Poyntz and Colonel Jones on the other side of the river, to guard against a surprise attack.

Meanwhile an artillery barrage began against the Eastgate side of the city. Still the defenders refused to surrender in spite of offers of talks over the next few days. Sir George reported accordingly to Parliament on 10 October: *"Upon Monday last we so straitly begirt the town on both sides the river that none can get forth or come in to them.... Yesterday we again attempted the city by storm.... The service was very hot, in which attempt we spent very much ammunition, for which the gentlemen of the county stand engaged... The premises set out our necessity, and plead for a speedy supply of moneys, without which we cannot continue in this posture. The help of the adjacent counties in provision in a due way proportioned will be in danger to sink under the burden...."*

Brereton returned at the end of October and had immediate success in the capture of Beeston Castle, but the besiegers were grumbling at the lack of money. The Deputy Lieutenants reported again to the CBK that the men were *"beginning to murmur for want of pay."* The better-off gentry were themselves paying for ammunition and were owed £1,600. £2,000 had arrived to pay the men, but it was so little to be divided amongst so many that it would cause more discontent than it would relieve. By December nine of the Deputy Lieutenants personally owed £1,000 to one William Sunderland for the supply of ammunition.

Booth gave Brereton more proof of the discontent in a report to him of his largely unsuccessful attempts to raise another company of 200 men for the Chester siege. A condition of their leases was that they could be called on to serve in Cheshire when required. He had made several journeys to Wilmslow, but had met many refusals and *"...when I know the parties, I shall desire some example may be made."* Just as seriously, one of his tenants, John Bandiford, had publicly announced after a church service, that the recruitment was illegal and he would not send out any of his own tenants. Bandiford had then gone to Lancashire and made the same announcement, although the need was urgent, with the news that the Duke of Richmond had 5000 men and was preparing to raise the siege. Booth had already written to the Speaker with a request that some exemplary punishment be given to Blandiford.

Even the news that Brereton had brought £10,000 for the siege did little to raise the gloom of the Deputy Lieutenants, although it did enable them to pay off their debts to Sunderland. But *"although the £10,000 ordered by the Parliament have a great sound in the country and many may think the same to be sufficient for the soldiers' satisfaction for all the arrears due to them"*, contingents from other counties were to have proportional shares and the amount would not be enough to pay off all the arrears, so they urgently wanted arrears to be collected from every Hundred *"...as well for the satisfaction of our own soldiers' arrears as future payments."* They had to pay soldiers from Derbyshire, Shropshire, Montgomeryshire and Staffordshire and it had been costing £1,500 a week for fifteen months. The county was bled dry of funds and all the rents from sequestered lands had been used, so much that they were compelled to extort provisions rather than money and to pay cash for other food. The Deputy Lieutenants were having to pledge their own credit to those suppliers who still had food to sell.

Lancashire, with its coffers emptied by the long siege of Lathom, could not help and indeed was begging Cheshire for help *"...but we have so long fed our men with promises and small performances.... that even by a letter of Colonel Booth's.... without a fortnight's pay, they will not march."*

The Cheshire Committee, however, was almost helpless. The best they could promise was that if any troops could come from Lancashire, they would share whatever was available, food and accommodation, with the Cheshire forces.

These guarantees were welcome on both sides of the border. Colonel 'Young' George Booth was even then in Lancashire, trying to get their help and briefly visiting his uncle John. One of his problems was that it was essential to gather the views of the Deputy Lieutenants, but they lived considerable distances apart and he had not been able to arrange any general meeting. However he had taken with him firm promises, *"I do engage myself in the behalf of Sir William Brereton, the Deputy Lieutenants and commanders of Cheshire that such forces as the Committee for Lancs shall contribute to the strengthening the siege against Chester shall (for the time they be by the persons above-named required to attend the said service) receive such pay as other auxiliaries do."*

Booth's promises were just good enough. Reports had been reaching the commanders of the seriousness of conditions in Chester. *"They within the city are in a distressed condition, some of them having of late fallen dead in the streets for want, and others extremely pinched with hunger...."* It seemed therefore that one last hard push would capture the city, but the worry still existed that the King had ordered its relief, so the attackers had always to look over their shoulders.

George Booth's report that Colonel Shuttleworth's Lancashire regiment was on its way to Tarporley must have been a great relief to Brereton. His second letter contained mixed news - John Booth's regiment was almost mutinous and he could not promise what use they would be, but at least they were on the march to Weaverham. Colonel Ralph Ashton's regiment had *"broken out into such a mutiny that they are tumultuously run towards Lathom, vowing to cut the throats of those in the house,"* and their officers were chasing after them to try to prevent the massacre.

They were in time. Lathom House and its gallant defenders finally surrendered to John Booth on 2 December 1645. The governor was allowed to keep his own personal arms, those of his officers above the rank of Lieutenant could keep their swords but all other officers and men were disarmed. The entire contents of the house were to be given up to John Booth, who notified Brereton and Booth that the Lancashire forces were now available to join the siege of Chester. But problems over their payment again caused delays and they did not join until after Christmas. Even then John Booth was definitely prickly. Brereton had promised him that 200 cavalry of Colonel Shuttleworth's regiment would stand watch every night, but when only 60 turned up, he complained to Brereton in no uncertain terms. *"If I could command the horse here, they should not have neglected their duty on the Welsh side, but ....they were three nights upon duty there altogether, and the Colonel spares other troops...."*

Parliamentary morale was lifted even more just before Christmas when Lord Kilmorey's butler and coachman found their way out of the city and surrendered to Sir George Booth. They were determined never to return to Chester and wanted only to live quietly at Hallam Hall, a Kilmorey property near Daresbury. According to them, Chester would have to surrender by January unless they were relieved, and indeed there were rumours that Charles was hoping to send in his cavalry on the Welsh side, confirming what the Cheshire Committee were afraid of. Even at this critical juncture, Booth was characteristically concerned at the fate of individuals even if they were on the opposing side. Fearing that Hallam Hall, where Kilmorey's children were living, might be sacked by the Parliamentary forces, Booth made a special request to Brereton to *"....cast your thoughts upon them for their relief in some charitable way."*

New Year came and went, and still Lord Byron was contemptuous of the besieging force. *"Keep your foolishly senseless paper to yourselves"* he answered to yet another surrender demand from Brereton, *"and know there are none in the city such knaves or fools to be deluded thereby."* Brereton could only report to the CBK that the defenders of Chester remained obstinate and were not *"inclinable to embrace any overtures."*

The siege continued, despite the difficulties of both Lancashire and Cheshire in supplying their troops. The contingents of Lancashire horse were very welcome and the Cheshire Committee were careful to thank Lancashire appropriately *"...for your horse they have had as much respect as others and as good accommodation as this poor country can afford.... since their coming into the county none of our horse have received any pay."* By then, however, (9 January 1646) Brereton and the Booths were convinced that their greatest need was for more foot-soldiers and they accordingly appealed to Lancashire for infantry to go with the cavalry already sent.

£5,000 arrived from Parliament on 13 January and the Cheshire Committee thanked the Speaker of the Commons for it, at the same time appealing for more money as soon as possible, because their army *"grows every day more impatient of their hard duty and want of pay."* Their sick-list was growing day by day and desertions were becoming more common. The Cheshire forces were camped in the suburbs of Chester and they feared that their own poor conditions would encourage the defenders to hold out longer *"to the ruin of this county and the damage of the whole kingdom."*

The siege had only days to run. Brereton offered talks on three occasions and finally Lord Byron answered with a list of no less than 36 propositions. But Brereton told the Mayor of Chester: *"Do not deceive yourselves in expectation that I will treat when you please.... The further misery that is like to befall the city be on your own heads."* The situation was desperate. There was little prospect of relief by a Royalist army and the commanders of the city felt that they had no option but to surrender on the best terms they could get. Chester finally fell to the Parliamentary forces on 3 February.

The terms of surrender were not ungenerous. Brereton agreed that Lord Byron could retain his personal arms and have ten men to attend him. The noblemen and gentry could march out with their arms and horses, with specified numbers of attendants according to their ranks, and all the surrendered officers could also keep their swords. No plundering of any kind would be tolerated, the city would remain intact and Brereton undertook to care for any sick and injured left behind.

The King's armies began to fold and the last of his forces surrendered at Stow in March. Chirk Castle was abandoned, Ruthin Castle was captured by Colonel Mytton's troops after a short siege and Bridgenorth followed a fortnight later.

## Post War

The end of the Civil War meant that Booth's active soldiering was over, but his administrative work increased, largely because Sir William Brereton effectively abandoned his Cheshire responsibilities and spent almost all the period 1646-1652 in London. It gave much more power locally to old Sir George and his fellow moderates.

However the fact that the first Civil War had ended did not mean that the county could immediately return to pre-war normality. Cheshire was exhausted. Chester itself was badly damaged - many of the houses in the suburbs, the grain and fulling mills, the old Eastgate and Watergate streets were at least partly destroyed. And just as serious, Cheshire was still beset with the ancient problem of unpaid soldiers in states of mutiny. The soldiers expected to get their arrears from the proceeds of Royalist compositions and confiscated estates of unrepent delinquents - but nothing happened.

The township of Tyldesley, for example, conscious of its financial plight, tried to get away without any taxation, relying on a two year old document allegedly signed by *"several of the Deputy Lieutenants of the county"* which claimed that *"the demayne lands of Shakerley should be freed from all taxes and lays by the inhabitants thereof accordingly as they have formerly been accustomed...."* Their optimistic attempt failed, and the Deputy Lieutenants of 1645, including John Booth, duly ordered that *"the Constables of Tildsley in Shakerley shall henceforth levie all such lays and taxes...."*

The Deputy Lieutenants did not wholly trust Brereton to get money from Parliament and Colonel George Booth, Roger Wilbraham and Jonathan Bruen went to London themselves in order to bypass him. Later their colleagues brought them up to date on the latest situation back at home in August 1646. *"We still stand much engaged to you for your care and pains in the business of the County and we have every week new occasion to write to you concerning it. We have had several mutinies which are not yet punished nor absolutely appeased, the soldiers take great dislike at the Excise, the City and the County almost generally dislike it.... Little will be made of it to prevent present evil, we have told the soldiers that they are to be paid forth out of it, and if that take not there is no way to satisfy them .....we do assure you, if the Parliament resolve not upon some speedy way to send monies for the disbanding of them, this County is in a sadder condition in its above particular...."*

The general population was also in a rebellious mood and there was a danger of rioting. *"We extremely fear, if the soldiers join not in the tumult, yet all or most of them will stand apart and will not assist their officers, and what greater evil may come thereof more than the damage in the Excise in this City, which hath cost much blood, we know not but leave to your more serious consideration....."*

Sir William Brereton, Colonel George Booth and all the Deputy Lieutenants were obliged, in order to avoid full-scale mutiny, to give their signed promises to *ingage themselves for £18,000 at the least... about the business of Chester."* Whatever sympathy they may have felt for the soldiers they had commanded was outweighed by considerations of personal safety, because there was grave danger that their own estates would be plundered by uncontrollable mutineers. Brereton's town house in Chester, St

Mary's Nunner, had been thoroughly looted - it was an unguarded target as Brereton himself had been driven out of the town at the very start of the war.

Even this was not enough for the Nantwich garrison. In July 1646 the Sequestration Committee of the town was at work with several of the Deputy Lieutenants when 500 soldiers, without any officers to control them, openly mutinied and imprisoned them in harsh conditions. Even the Mayor of Chester, William Davies and the Governor, Thomas Croxton, were roughly treated, but Sir George Booth was luckily out of town. The others were thrown *"into the common prison amongst prisoners, Cavaliers and horse-stealers, neither suffering any to relieve us with meat, drink or any necessaries, but what the parsons or some women did privately convey to us, where we (being ancient men) did lie upon the boards.... for the space of 54 hours."*

Sir George Booth and other Deputy Lieutenants tried to intercede but were also threatened. Thomas Croxton, the town's governor, was attacked and injured,and the gentlemen had to escape hurriedly from Nantwich. The mutineers did not give in or release their captives until they were promised that they would not be prosecuted. The discovery of a chest containing £500 and the knowledge that according to one report, troops were being sent against them from Staffordshire, may have helped to make up their minds.

Although an alarmed Parliament promised large amounts of money to pay arrears, not all the troops received enough and the Chester garrison mutinied the following year. One group set off from Chester to Nantwich, where they seized some of the Deputy Lieutenants at a meeting and drove them back to Chester *"like rogues and thieves in base and disgraceful manner and to bring us openly through all the streets (there being no street free from the infection of the plague, it being spread through the whole city) and at their wills and pleasures to remove us sometimes throwing us all being in number fifteen persons into a little room, part of the common gaol, where there was neither bread nor provision of meat or drink nor any accommodation for nature, but publicly like beasts among ourselves, our friends denied to come to us, and being in this sad condition and durance, we were threatened by some of them shouting to hang us, and others to cut our throats or destroy us and cast us into infected houses.... Mr Speaker, to redeem our persons and save our lives (nothing satisfying them but present money) we have been enforced to take upon us the payment of all their four months pay, both of horse and of foot, which together with another months pay which will be due before they can be disbanded with safety to the country will amount to £5000....."*

The captives included Thomas Stanley, Philip Mainwaring, John Legh, Thomas Croxton, John Wettenhall, Richard Leicester, William Davies and James Gartside with two Commissioners of Excise, two Sequestrators, the Committee Clerk of the Deputy Lieutenants and the Governor of Chester. They were crammed into a room near the common prison, without food or drink. They were very worried that they were being deliberately exposed to the plague which was affecting at least 30 houses in the Northgate area.

Old Sir George was luckily not captured, and on the same day that the Committee Clerk wrote the appeal of the prisoners to the Speaker of the House of Commons, above, he and Robert Duckenfield also wrote. They hoped that the House already knew of the soldiers' arrears of pay and complained that the Deputy Lieutenants were actually at a meeting to discuss the problem when the mutineers broke in and kidnapped them. The mutineers *"still are attempting the imprisonment of the rest of the gentlemen of the county if there be not present payment made to them of £4000, for unto so much amounteth their arrears and present demands.... Sir, we know not how far this evil may proceed, nor how deeply the poor county may suffer. And therefore (we) concerned it our duties (who are yet at liberty) to present this short account to your consideration, with our humble desire that the House may be speedily acquainted therewith...."*

Once again, the unfortunate gentry were forced to borrow extensively in order to meet the demands of the mutineers before the prisoners could be released, and this did not happen until at least the end of August 1647.

Cheshire was not alone in being plunged into chaos after the war. Sir Ralph Assheton complained bitterly how difficult it was for anything to be transported safely. He grumbled to his steward, *"You had best be very chary how you return any money, for it seems they will take your money easily enough in the country."* One of his letters was illegally stopped on the road and he suffered so many losses from plundering that he was in two minds to sell his horses *"rather than to have them purloined from me."*

Sir George became involved in the work of the Committee for Compounding. Edward Leigh of Baguley, one of the less active Cheshire Royalists, was fined £300 because he had collected some debts owing to the King and was willing to compound, but the actual ownership of his estates was in doubt. The Committee requested Booth to collect all the papers held by the County Committee and look after them until the matter could be sorted out, because it acknowledged that it had no jurisdiction in disputed land titles.

Sir George had a slight clash with the Committee in 1649, when they ordered the sequestration of the estate of Humphrey Forest of Over Tabley. Four years earlier Booth had ordered it to be discharged, but eventually when the paperwork was sorted out, it was discovered to be still sequestered. Forest appealed on the grounds that he had other debts and many children, and he finally escaped by paying as little as £3-10!

As late as the summer of 1652 Booth found himself a trustee of the estates of Sir William Massey of Puddington who had compounded. (By chance Massey and Booth died at almost the same time late in that year. Massey was heavily in debt and his sequestration was not discharged until 1654.)

Old Sir George had never wavered in his allegiance to the Parliament and had fought long and hard on their behalf. However, the fact that he had done his utmost to placate both sides in an attempt to avert the war and had always been moderate in his beliefs and behaviour was obviously known to the surviving Royalists, and may have been the spur for them to try to recruit his help. In June 1648 he received an anonymous letter from "Your loving friends of the City." They informed him that Parliament was intending to rule through the army and the county militias were being disbanded. They had the promise of counties in the south of England and a body of armed men in Suffolk, which was being reinforced by disbanded soldiers and cavaliers. *"We doubt not but a little will lay Independent flat. Our City stands neuter. We desire you to interrupt publicly or*

*privately, by force or otherwise, the proceedings of Duckinfield and his confederates that*
*we may have a speedier end.  You and Colonel Mainwaring may do much."*

Theirs was a forlorn hope. Booth had never shown the slightest hint of changing sides
and Robert Duckenfield was a friend of his.  He had no great love for a professional
militarism, but equally disliked the arbitrary monarchy that was being overthrown and
would soon end in the death of Charles I on the scaffold.  As for the uprising mentioned
in the letter, it never got off the ground except in Essex, and even there it ended with
the surrender of Colchester and the execution of the garrison commanders, Sir George
Lisle and Sir Charles Lucas.  Booth simply forwarded the letter to Speaker Lenthall with
no comment.

Sir George gave one Adam Martindale his chance as a preacher.  Martindale had
never actually been ordained and could not be a parish priest, despite being a popular
figure - it would have been contrary to the Ordinances of Lords and Commons - and Sir
George did have opposition because of this. When approached by Martindale's
opponents, he at first granted them their desire, but then he received a delegation from
the parishioners of Dunham, who assured him that Martindale was fit.  Thereupon he
referred the matter to the parish monthly meeting, which agreed Martindale's eligibility.
He then arranged a 'preach-off' in front of him, Mr Marbury and Mr John Legh and they
agreed unanimously to accept the long-suffering Martindale.  The Booth family never
regretted their support for this loyal man.

In spite of Sir George's great age at the end of the first Civil War (he was 80) he was
appointed once again to the Commission of the Peace and as a Magistrate.  His grandson
was not included in the list of magistrates.  In January 1649 Henry Hobson and William
Barnes petitioned Sir George.  They claimed that Mainwaring's steward had ordered
them to brew some beer for the 200 people who would attend the Court Leet.  They had
duly done so, despite the fact that they had no licence, and had been fined 20/- each at
Knutsford Sessions, the money to be given to the Poor Fund.  Could their fines please be
remitted?  Sir George Booth showed his strong grasp of justice by refusing their plea.
After all, they could have refused to brew the beer, even if, as they claimed, they had
been ordered to do it, and they would surely have made a nice little profit for themselves.

The case of the late John Mainwaring was very odd.  Samuel Carrington was or had
been Clerk to the Justices.  His wife had deposited some household goods with her sister,
Mainwaring's wife, with a view to avoiding destraint.  Unfortunately, Mainwaring had
died of the plague and his goods had to be sold and the house "cleansed". Thomas
Church and Thomas Barrow, the house clearers, had taken Mrs Carrington's possessions
in addition to Mrs Mainwaring's and refused to give them back to her.  Carrington
therefore on his wife's behalf, petitioned Sir George Booth for an order to Church and
Barrow for the return of a green bed cloth with green and white lace, a Bible and a
geneva print.  Sir George, aged 82, promptly issued the order for the goods to be
delivered personally and for the clearers to give surety for their safe return.

Simon Crouch was a Doctor of Physic and claimed to be a conscientious one.  Plague
broke out in Grappenhall, Thelwall, Latchford and Watton in January 1650, and Crouch
did his best.  He gave medical help and did as much as possible for the recovery of

affected people.  His efforts were apparently successful, because *"all the people in the said townships are now well and at their liberties."*  Unfortunately Crouch had had to abandon his usual paying patients and what with paying money himself to help the starving sick, he was badly out of pocket and was forced to ask for relief for himself.  Sir George was somewhat suspicious and wanted confirmation.  Crouch's claim was to be checked and his accounts verified, and a sub-committee was appointed to do so.  It would be interesting to know if the good doctor's claim was accepted.

Sir George Booth was still active almost until his death.  The printed records show him as being involved in the work of the JPs even at the great age of 85, though the two examples mentioned below would not have pleased him.

In the first, in 1651, Ralph Downes of Etchells had forged the signatures of Booth and Hyde, and had to give surety for appearing at the following Quarter Sessions.  He appeared in front of Thomas Mainwaring at the Nantwich Sessions *"where I caused several wandering rogues to be whipped, they having counterfeited Sir George Booth's paper."*  In the second example, also in 1651, Sir George and his family were strangely the subjects of a petition.  The tenants of the Dunham Massey estates claimed to have had the right *"anciently and time out of mind"* to pasture their flocks on the waste land and commons of the estate, but had been thrown off unceremoniously by John Booth, Sir George's nephew.  Some of the more hot-headed tenants tried to pull down the enclosures that John Booth set up, whereupon Booth had them charged with riotous assembly, against the wishes of his nephew George Booth, grandson of Sir George.  They counter-claimed that *"it was done without any oposicon quarrel or strife, and without any breach of the Peace... and no Ryotous offence by them committed...."*  Furthermore, in asking for their fines to be remitted or moderated, they stated that a Court of Exchequer case pending had been *"forborne"* for several months by the consent of Sir George Booth himself.

In his extreme old age, Sir George Booth became very obstinate and less willing to listen to any point of view other than his own.  This is born out by correspondence with Colonel Robert Duckenfield late in 1651, when Booth was 85 years old.  Duckenfield had learned that one Robert Minshull of Bowdon had failed to pay his tithes to Sir George and Sir George had confiscated two of his horses in lieu.  He thought that Booth's action was perhaps excessive, because *"these times will not allow gentlemen to deal so strictly with the vulgar sort as formerly"*, and suggested giving back the horses quietly without publicity.  Booth replied politely but crustily that he was acting in strict accordance with the law of the land, as Duckenfield should well know, and as long as the State authorised him to collect the due tithes, he was *"so much their servant as to dare to take them and and vindicate them publicly."*  Sir George was conscious of the ancient friendship between their families and reminded Duckenfield that a judge at the last Assizes had stated that delinquents were liable to *"noble"* damages as disturbers of the peace!

In Sir George's last years he was troubled again by the antics and unreliability of his surviving son John.

At the start of the war, John had been exceptionally active on the Parliamentary side - the siege of Manchester, the capture of Preston, the governorship of Warrington and the siege of Lathom House.  As a Deputy Lieutenant of Lancashire, he was in Liverpool in

Sir William Brereton

Marston Moor, an important battle in the Civil War where the Royalists were completely
defeated and thus lost the North of England

March 1644 when Sir Richard Greenvil landed with military supplies for the Royalists from Ireland. Greenvil was an early example of a double agent. In Liverpool he still pretended to support Parliament, but Booth's troops were suspicious. Booth, he recorded, behaved like the gentleman he was *"...And truly, though we had insolencies offered us, yet Colonel Booth, by his Discretion and good Usage of us, kept them from committing those barbarous Injuries I found they were inclined to."*

But as we saw earlier, John Booth's own loyalty began to come under suspicion. In 1645, he was perhaps less energetic than he could have been in raising troops in Warrington, and his father had to step in to mediate. By 1647 or 1648 he was almost certainly playing both sides, because in his petition for help after the Restoration, he described himself as Governor of the town for the King. However he abandoned his governorship very soon afterwards and was arrested in May 1649, suspected of having supplied pistols to royalists. Following investigations by the Committee of Lancashire, he was imprisoned for some time in Liverpool.

The next year he was in trouble again, in spite of serious warnings from the Council of State, and Colonel Birch, the governor of Liverpool, was instructed to ensure that Booth appeared before the Council of State, and failing that to investigate poor old Sir George, by then 84 years old. The Council even ordered Robert Duckenfield, Sir George's old friend, to search Dunham Massey Hall for any illegally held arms, which proves that grave doubts were being entertained about even Sir George's loyalty to the cause. Eventually however, wiser councils prevailed, and they wrote in mild terms to him, informing him (if he needed to be informed) that his son had *"resolved to precipitate himself into further destructive courses... whereof you will hear more particulars ere long."* As for the pistols etc found at Dunham, the Council acknowledged that their purpose was purely defensive and Sir George could keep them.

John was not conciliatory enough however and in October 1650 the Council instructed Sir George to take recognizances of his son and admonish him to be of good behaviour. John was free of arrest and his horses and arms were to be returned to him, but he was warned in definite terms not to do anything prejudicial to the government. Even this could not deter John. One Thomas Coke was arrested and examined for treason. He confessed everything and in doing so implicated John Booth. His story was that he had been contacted by Thomas Doud, an agent for the Duke of Buckingham and that Booth under the alias of Francis Blyth had been helping him the previous autumn (1650). Questioned again, Coke admitted that he had been ordered by Lord Byron and the Duke of Hamilton, who were with Charles II at Breda, to go to Mr John Booth, *"a person that had power and interest in the parts where he lived, and as to one they thought had good affections to serve his Majesty, and should be useful for settling a correspondency with Scotland."*

He had failed to see Booth then, but had caught up with him in London at the Holy Lamb Tavern, thanks to Doud. Here Booth *"did.... express his willingness to do the King service"* whenever Coke could write with firm instructions. Meanwhile, Booth was to help Doud with any help necessary and of course money, but all under the alias of Francis Blyth. When Doud returned from Scotland, he told Coke that he had met Booth at

Warrington, but did not go into details about what if any help Booth had given him.

As the Council of State had reasonably firm evidence against Booth, by 1651 he was in prison in Liverpool again, charged with high treason, and was from here sent to the Tower under close escort. His wife Dorothy was allowed to live there with him, and his sisters were allowed to use the profits of his estates for maintenance, so the confinement was at least gilded to some extent. He was examined by the Council of State and it was not until the end of September that the proposed trial was abandoned and he was bailed in the sum of £2,000. Thereafter, he was much more careful, but was probably involved at least peripherally in the abortive Penruddock Rising of 1655.

As for Sir George, his last appearance in public papers was after the Battle of Worcester in 1651, when the army of Charles II was decisively routed. He was obviously too old at 85 to be personally involved, but he seems to have encouraged his tenants to join the Parliamentary forces and promised them publicly that all those who took part and lived to tell the tale would be granted a free life in their tenancy agreements. The Council of State wrote an official letter of thanks to Sir George. They were *"exceedingly satisfied of his generous resolution"* and said that it was *"a practice which we wish might be exemplary to all."*

Old Sir George died at the end of 1652 aged 86. His latter years had been more full of incident than at any other time during his long life. Stern, but kind and considerate to many less fortunate, he had always accepted his responsibilities as Justice of the Peace, Deputy Lieutenant, Deputy Commander of the Parliament forces in Cheshire and one of the most influential of the gentry of the county, and he had always shown kindness and generosity to those who he believed needed help.

Let Alfred Ingham have the last word, from *Rycraft's Worthies*: *"Free, godly, brave Booth, the flower of Cheshire."*

## Sources

Sir George's land acquisitions, his financial transactions and the building of the first known Dunham Massey Hall are detailed in the Dunham Massey Papers, chiefly EGR Series, held in the John Rylands University of Manchester (JRULM). The purchase of the Warrington estate is taken from Vol 57 of the Chetham Society (Chetham Miscellanies 3.) The salt pans of Dunham are described in Sir William Brereton's Journal, and the story of the Duck Decoy is in his Letter Book in the Cheshire County Record Office. With two exceptions, details of Sir George's career as a magistrate are to be found in the Record Society of Lancashire and Cheshire, (RSLC) vol. 94, 1940. The other two, those of Thomas Haumeire and Cicely Travis are in the archives of the City of Manchester. The volumes of the Cheshire Sheaf give much information on the Civil War in the county, as do Professor Morrill (Cheshire 1630 to 1660, Oxford University Press, 1974) and R.N. Dore, in particular his masterly editing of Sir William Brereton's Letter Books (RSLC, volumes 123 and 128.) The Tanner Papers in the Bodleian Library give the events of the post-war mutiny. Sir George's argument with Colonel Robert Duckenfield are in the Tatten of Wythenshawe MSS in the JRULM, and the Calendars of State Papers reveal the suspicious activities of Sir John Booth.

Sir George Booth 1621-1684,, the Second Baronet and first Lord Delamer.
*Courtesy of the National Trust*

# Chapter Two
## The Second George Booth, First Lord Delamer

Born in 1622, the second George Booth grew up with the rumbles of political discontent sounding more and more loudly in his ears. His father, William Booth, was perhaps twelve years old when Queen Elizabeth died in 1603 after her long reign, and in 1612 Old Sir George passed much of the family estates to him, through *"natural love and affection"*. Assuming that this gift took place when William came of age (his year and date of birth are unknown) it is likely that he was born about 1591. Old Sir George was a healthy 37 year old in 1601 when James VI of Scotland rode south to claim his inheritance by default and become James I of England. Neither could have suspected that the Stuart dynasty was to be the bane of the Booths from the Civil War, made inevitable by the intransigence of Charles I, until the deposition of James II, in which Young George's son Henry played so vital a part.

Young George was three years old when James I died, to be succeeded by his 24 year old son, Charles, and he was 14 when his father William died, leaving him the ward of his grandfather, Old Sir George. When he was fifteen or sixteen years old, the question of marriage appeared, and there were two eligible girls available. The first choice was the daughter of the Bishop of Coventry and Lichfield, but the Egerton family to which George's grandmother, Lady Elizabeth Egerton, belonged, raised the most strenuous objections. Sir George Booth tried to win her round, and when he failed, he asked his friend Sir Richard Brereton to intercede. Lady Egerton was furious. In July 1638 she told Sir George's representatives, James Chantrill and Peter Drinkwater, that the good Bishop's daughter was a bastard and so were all other bishops' children by the law of the land. If George went ahead and married her, *"he should neither have the worth of a groat from her, nor ever have her blessings."*

Brereton pacified her a little by telling her that negotiations had been broken off in favour of the daughter of the Earl of Lincoln, with a dowry of £6000 or £7000. Old Sir George dropped the idea of the Bishop's daughter and took references about Lord Lincoln. The Earl of Kingston described him as *"of a most ancient and renowned family, and held just and religious...."* As for the important matter of dowries, Lincoln could certainly provide better for his daughter than the Bishop, and anyway the Bishop's daughter had other disadvantages - *"The Bishop's daughter had need to have triple portion to the other to make them mean equal matches."*

As for Katherine, the Earl's daughter, she was very desirable, according to John Morton, a distant kinsman of Sir George. His command of English was somewhat tortured, but his meaning was clear: *"And if he gaine her the worlde, can hardly his possession in a woman, she being a fortune in herself (without other fortune) to desire any man living."* He advised that George should demonstrate his earnest intention by making a gift of a gold watch or a diamond ring.

Negotiations proceeded at a dignified pace and as late as the middle of 1639 Lord

Lincoln was writing a jovial letter to young George himself, who was in London learning something of the law. He was quite happy with the way matters were progressing but would appreciate a settlement either with old Sir George or through intermediaries if no meeting was possible. The marriage duly took place, but was sadly doomed to be only short. A daughter, Vere, was born in 1643, but Katherine died soon after. George subsequently married Elizabeth Grey, the daughter of Henry, the first Earl of Stamford.

Young George seems to have been a typical young man of almost any time but especially of his own time and class. As a young man of 17 years of age, he seems to have had quite a serious row with his grandfather and was either sent packing or he left home deeply hurt in January 1640. The dates of the few surviving papers relating to his first proposed marriage coincide neatly with the only surviving letter that mentions his sudden flight to France, so perhaps the disagreement was somehow connected. Another possible cause of the temporary rift is mentioned many years later after his death, by Henry, Young George's son, in an unpublished Elegy. According to this, George apparently had Royalist sympathies as a young man, which would certainly have aroused his grandfather's wrath, but he was soon converted to the side of Parliament.

> "What though some small mistake appears
> To have been committed in thy tender years,
> When the most grave, and wise were led aside,
> By the subtil policies of those
> Who after proved, not their countrey's friends, but foes
> And all their blessings lost they had before enjoy'd.
> Thou soon the guilded hook espy'd,
> Forsook the worse and chose the better side."

Whatever the cause, George reached Calais after a difficult crossing from England, and then thought better of his impetuosity. He did not dare write to old Sir George, but wrote a letter of remorse to the family steward, William Rowcroft, confident that his grandfather would see the letter very quickly: *"I now intend God willing on mundaie to set forwards towards Paris, yet grieved to be chased from my owne home and to have my dear affection rebound to me againe with unkindness, & though I am verilie perswaded I shall never see you all againe, yet I pray you take care to preserve my grandfather in an opinion, that I always have been and ever will be a most dutiful though wilful grandchild, but least you should thinke that I should talke foolishly, I desire to let you know that I have soe narrowlie escaped my life alreadie, as I may justlie maintaine what I have said before, many perplexities have I suffered both at home & abroad, the Lord be my comforter, I have noe more to say, but onlie praying God to blesse you....."*

On his return he was no less quick-tempered, but had the Civil War in which to work off his aggressive tendencies. He was arrogant and boastful, like his Uncle John, but although he was resentful of Sir William Brereton's influence and authority, he could be kept in check by old Sir George. However, when he was away from his grandfather, he could not restrain a careless tongue. In February 1645 he was in London with other Cheshire gentry to check Brereton's accounts and at the same time trying to get some pay for his soldiers. A Mr Goldsmith, who may have been acquainted with Brereton, asked him for his opinion of the latter. Was Sir William Brereton godly and honest, he asked. Booth's answer was curt, contemptuous and tactless, particularly to a gentleman whose allegiance he did not know: *"As any was in Hell,"* he said.

While in London, he was visiting the Earl of Essex and boasted of his deeds to an anonymous man who duly reported the conversation to Brereton. He claimed he had recruited and maintained two regiments with some of his tenants. (A statement of doubtful accuracy anyway. Only one is now known.) He then complained loudly of Brereton's treatment of him, in not only refusing any assistance, but also of assessing some of Booth's tenants to pay Brereton's soldiers and sacking some of Booth's able officers to put in some of his own, who by implication were not as efficient. Brereton resented these criticisms and may have retaliated by threatening to break up Booth's regiment, which was recruited mainly from the Nantwich area. Booth resigned his commission and the Nantwich Committee, headed by old Sir George, protested. The regiment seems to have survived though.

After leaving London, George was passing through Leicester and noticed that the town was poorly defended. He drew the problem to the attention of his brother-in-law, Thomas, Lord Grey of Groby, the heir to the Earl of Stamford, mainly because the town potentially controlled roads to the north western counties and if it fell under Royalist control there were obvious dangers to Staffordshire and Cheshire:

*"My Lord:*

*Being arrived at this place, which, by reason of your public and private interest in it, lays claim to your utmost endeavours for the preservation of it, I shall make bold to present your Lordship with the weak condition it is in, most obvious to the observing eye. By all men's account, there are not above 200 soldiers in the town, and those as peremptory against discipline as their governors are ignorant of it.... 500 resolute well managed soldiers at any time might one day make themselves masters of this town, which if lost will take away all commerce from all the North-west of England; and I can assure you it is God's providence alone in keeping it from the enemy's knowledge... The grand masters, most sensible of danger, and careful of their own security, have all of them houses in a place of this town called the Newarke, where they are fortifying themselves as strong as may be; which will prove, as I fear, of most dangerous consequence; for, I perceive the townsmen much discontented, conceiving themselves deserted by the Committee to the enemy's mercy...."*

Booth was also ambitious, and in this he was encouraged by his grandfather. With the exception of Sir William Brereton - which they would have disputed anyway - they were the leaders of the Parliamentary or Presbyterian gentry in Cheshire and wished to consolidate their influence. It was therefore natural that Young George should seek to become a Member of Parliament for the county, even before he was officially old enough. When he was only twenty, he was writing to Francis Legh of Lyme Hall, confident that their true respects to his grandfather enabled him *"to entreate you would for a kinsman's and a gentleman's sake, be pleased not to promise your assistance to any for choyce of a burgess till I shall wait upon you, which shall be tomorrow without fail."*

The House of Commons had been depleted in numbers since the start of the war:

some members had died, others had excluded themselves by virtue of their Royalist sympathies. Cheshire was a county that needed representation in the House of Commons, since Peter Venables, the so-called 'Baron' of Kinderton, was a Royalist. The other Knight of the Shire was Sir William Brereton. And Old Sir George Booth was anxious to promote the candidature of his grandson, but he depended to a large extent on the parliamentary influence of Brereton, his son-in-law, for the issue of writs. Brereton, a hard-line Puritan with no love for the Booths, favoured John Bradshaw for Cheshire and he also wanted to expand his personal influence in Staffordshire. It was even rumoured as early as April 1645 that young George Booth was petitioning Parliament against Brereton's machinations.

Brereton doubted his ability to keep out young Booth, firstly because of the standing of the family in Cheshire, and secondly because Bradshaw was an absentee and did nothing to publicise his cause. As he told John Swinfen of Staffordshire in a cypher letter deciphered by Mr Dore, *"As touching the business of recruiter election in Cheshire, Col. G. Booth hath so far anticipated as it will be mighty hard and hazardous to erect any other, and John Bradshaw's absence and not appearing in this cause doth much discourage."*

The Booths suspected that Brereton was deliberately delaying the issue of the writ and mustered family support. Sir George thought that Brereton might be more susceptible to an appeal from his daughters, Mary, Katherine and Elizabeth, at home at Dunham Massey. The resulting letter from them to Brereton is confused, suggesting that Sir George may have dictated it to ladies who did not really understand its content or purpose: *"....However, some aspersions have been cast on our family and for that purpose we could have wished to see you at Dunham. But in the meantime give us leave to let you know (as friends) that we are confident they will really vindicate themselves in all ways they may be capable of; who still retain the affections of the country such as they have expressed themselves for our nephew for the knight of the shire. And through the apprehension of their love and respect he is resolved to stand. However, there may appear some discouragement through a report that the writs are come down and concealed, in whose hands we know not. But we made no question but your endeavours will be for a free and clear election...."*

Sir George also wrote to Brereton, assuming tactfully that the writs would come to Cheshire and hoping that the election would be fair. He then informed Brereton, as if he did not know, that he, Booth, had been *"solicited to expose my grandson to stand, which being the desires of his and my friends he hath at last consented as being willing to serve the Parliament in any capacity...."* Just in case that formal notification was not enough, Sir George followed it up the next day (9 November 1645) by letting Brereton know that he was sending *"speedy despatches to all my friends requesting their concurrence and assistance.... I desire by a return to these to receive your approbation and assurance of utmost assistance..."* Brereton did reply by return, but denied even having received the parliamentary writ. *"If the writs had come to my hands,"* he went on, *"they should not have been concealed, but it should be my care that the work might be carried on fairly...."* As for the ladies of Dunham, Brereton was far less courteous: *"I have received your letter, and in answer thereto, thought good to let you know that for the reports you heard there was no ground at all. I brought no writ down."*

Whether Brereton did delay the writ will probably never be known. It was not issued until May 1646, but young George Booth was elected with the support of all the moderate opinion in the county.

While Booth was criticising Brereton for this alleged delay, he was also severely critical of Brereton's failure to adequately pay the troops. It appears that Parliament had issued a 'Model' system of payment, but little is known of it. Brereton had ignored it and paid some auxiliary companies of Captain Duckenfield, leaving unpaid other companies on the same duty, and Captains Grantham and Alcocke had complained to Booth. He asked Brereton not to let his personal feelings towards the Booths cause any partiality; if two of Duckenfield's companies had been given two weeks' pay, why had not the others? Moreover it was insupportable and contrary to Parliament's Ordinances for the pay of some formations to be the responsibility of particular towns and men. Personally, he wanted nothing more than *"the safe carrying on of this great work now before us without interruption"*, but he was having to put up with insults, affronts and *"strange rumours ....which are thought (though I hope vainly) to disvalue me in the eyes of my country."* He would not *"be so unchristianlike to be rash in fixing it upon any particular. But to whom their consciences shall touch them, this directs itself."* In a postscript, he informed Brereton that he and his grandfather were asking the Lancashire Committee for reinforcements against any surprise Royalist assault on the Chester leaguer.

Brereton clearly understood that this was a scarcely veiled attack on himself and he answered angrily that he had paid the men of Alcocke and Grantham before receiving Booth's letter. There was therefore no partiality and Booth should not have claimed there was. As for the other accusations, *"my conscience impeacheth me not of anything therein hinted, but affirms that my designs are (notwithstanding any misconstructions and misapplications of actions, which I wish all would endeavour to shun) to serve my country and the state really, not to bring into undervalue the reputation of any but to preserve it to posterity."* Bad tempered correspondence such as this was further proof of the dislike that the two men felt for each other.

The last Parliament of Charles I had met in 1640, called by royal warrant. With the turmoil of the Civil War, there was of course no chance of dissolving it and calling a general election, and the King had agreed that the Parliament could be prolonged until it wished to dissolve itself. It was therefore a perfectly legal Parliament in spite of its age, and there was no reason why it could not continue until times were more settled. However the two main impediments to a new government following the defeat of the King's forces were the future of the King and the army.

A powerful body of members of the House of Commons were still in favour of a negotiated settlement with the King, based on his surrender of the nominal control of the Army and his submission to Parliament with regard to reform of the Church of England. This body of members were mainly Presbyterians who remained generally in favour of the principle of the King in Parliament, and who feared the violence and fanaticism of the army. Another group of members of an independent turn of mind favoured wide religious toleration and the freedom for congregations to choose their own ministers. There were therefore hopes of an acceptable settlement embodied in the Treaty of Newport. Sir Ralph Assheton showed optimism in a letter to his steward. *"It may be you may see occasion to return again at spring, by which time at God's blessing, we may see a happy issue of this distemper, for praised be God there is a hopeful beginning of the Treaty."*

Both of these loose groups were opposed by the fanatics in the army, in which there were serious problems. They had been ill-used for years and wanted their own reforms. Their pay was always in arrears, so debt was widespread. Moreover, they were expected to live off the land, being billeted and fed by the people of their localities. But these people were also expected to pay taxes for exactly the same purpose. The army was bitterly opposed to any agreement with the King and in fact wanted control of Parliament itself. The obstacle to both the Presbyterians and the army was the King himself. He was still obstinately refusing to sign away his royal prerogative of head of the Church and the army, so there was no chance of reaching any accommodation with the Presbyterian moderates, and his continued existence meant that there was no legal way in which the army could take control of Parliament, with all the power that it represented.

The army took the first step towards gaining overall control by taking possession of the King himself and moving him from Carisbrooke Castle, where his captivity was relatively comfortable, to Hurst Castle, a small gloomy castle standing on a narrow promontory of shingle running into the Solent. There he was guarded by two hundred foot soldiers and forty cavalry, and his imprisonment was complete, although General Fairfax ordered that he was still to be treated with all civility. The clamour of the high command of the army for justice on the King could proceed.

First, however, Parliament itself had to be tamed, and the anti-militarist faction was in the majority. Therefore they had to be excluded. They had refrained from even discussing the army's Remonstrance, written by Commissary General Henry Ireton, and setting out the army's plans for justice, reform, and the trial of the King. By the end of November, the army were so frustrated that Fairfax and his officers spent a day at Windsor, drawing up plans for a march on London, the forcible dissolution of Parliament and the formation of a provisional government.

Not all the generals agreed with the formation of a full military government, and eventually it was decided to proceed with the least possible appearance of irregularity. After all, the Parliament was legally constituted, and to overcome it by force would be a clear breach of the law. What was proposed as a compromise was to purge the Commons of those who were known to oppose military rule, leaving those fellow-travellers who would certainly agree to the army's demands - a drastic step, but even so less drastic than the alternative of forcible dissolution. The events that followed early in December were described by George Booth in the fullest account of Pride's Purge that has survived.

A long debate took place in the House of Commons on Friday and Saturday, 1 and 2 December, discussing the King's answers to the propositions of the Treaty. They were generally unsatisfactory, but the fact that the King showed signs of willingness to compromise at all was hopeful. The debate continued on Monday with a deliberately vague motion *"That the answers of the King to the Propositions of both Houses are a ground for the House* (of Commons) *to proceed upon for the settlement of the peace of the Kingdom."*

This motion was finally carried on the Tuesday by a substantial majority. However the malcontent fanatics were determined to force their own way and Ludlow, Harrison and Ireton, with one or two others, decided to press ahead with a purge of the opposition.

Army regiments took over posts from the trained bands on the evening of 5 December and during the night General Ireton stationed guards at every entrance to Parliament House, with clear instructions to prevent anyone from entering who was not known to be favourable to the Army. Booth was of course on the list and was therefore stopped at the door by Colonel Thomas Pride, whose regiment was on guard in the Palace Yard, Westminster Hall, and the stairs and the lobby outside the Commons Chamber. Pride was charged with physically preventing opponents of the army from entering the House. Despite allegedly humble origins (he may have been a foundling in St Bride's parish), he had gentlemanly manners and, hat in hand, questioned each member with some courtesy. He checked the names of the members against a list, and any who was known to be anti-militarist was forbidden to enter. He was assisted by Lord Grey of Groby, a consistent supporter of the army, and a member since 1640.

Nearly two weeks later, Booth addressed a letter to the electors of Cheshire who *"were pleased to appoint one of your servants in Parliament, which favour of yours having been ever in myne eye hath commanded from me what ever my skill or ability could enable me unto, this I hope I may modestly and safely say, your business I have intended, without designing any private advantage of my owne by place of honour or profit....*

*...the 7th* (actually 6th) *of this instant December, coming as at other times, to do you the best service I could, I was at the step which leads to the outward door of the House of Commons stopp'd by a guard supposed to be of the army, who asked me whether I was a Parliament man, my answer, I was one; then they demanded my name, I told it them; upon that a long paper was brought out by an officer (as I supposed him) which when they had perused, they told me I must withdraw, alleging no reason at all for it. Knowing it to be both imprudent and vain to contest with such force I did withdraw into Westminster Hall, where I met with divers Gentlemen who had received the same usage, with them I joined in a letter to the Speaker of the House of Commons, telling him what interruptions we had in the way of our duties, and desiring him to acquaint the house with it, which I may hope he did."*

Some of the excluded members objected more fiercely than others. Booth's group chose a constitutional approach, perhaps because they did not quite appreciate what was happening or the reasons for it. Others, including William Prynne, made such a fuss that they ended up being detained. Not surprisingly, Prynne had to be forcibly restrained and was dragged away shouting that it was *"a high breach of the privileges of Parliament, and an affront to the House."* Pride told him that his commission was the power of the sword, and proved it by locking about forty of the malcontents up in a cold wet basement chamber for the rest of the day and the next night.

Booth's letter continued his explanation of the events: *"...though thus far I had proceeded, yet could not think my self to have but very incompletely discharged my duty, the principle part, as I conceive, being undone, that was acquainting you with it who employed me, whose servant I am; having faithfully presented you with the whole matter*

*I leave it to you. This consideration... will in your thoughts acquit me from any share of blame... force debarring me from being there where your commands do place me... At what time when it shall please the gracious disposer of all things so to order affairs, that I may with your honour and freedom (for yours it is), I say when thus I may be permitted to do you service, I am ready; till that time and always... I have and hope ever shall have an affectionate heart to the real good of my dear Countrymen the inhabitants of Cheshire.."*

Denied any role in Parliamentary affairs and with the cessation of fighting in Cheshire after the surrender of Chester, George Booth retired to Dunham and spent the next few years expanding the estates. Later events proved that his feelings towards the rule of Parliament were somewhat ambivalent to say the least, but it seems that he totally ignored Charles II's ill-timed and ruinous attempt to regain his throne in 1651, although the Scottish armies must have passed very close to his lands.

His expenses during the Civil War cannot have been too ruinous, because in 1650 and 1651 he spent more than £3000 buying land in Thornton le Moors, Pownall Fee, Bowdon, Dunham Massey and Altrincham. Then in 1652 Old Sir George Booth finally died at the age of 86 and young George inherited the estates, grown enormously since his grandfather had begun his great series of purchases over 60 years before. At the age of 30 he was the proud possessor of several thousand acres, married to a rich and aristocratic heiress, with two sons from her and a young daughter from his first marriage. Almost his first act as Squire of Dunham was to add a new South wing to Dunham Massey Hall, enclosing the courtyard so that the ground plan of the main building became substantially what it is now, in spite of the considerable changes and rebuilding of the next century.

Young Sir George Booth was widely known locally and nationally to be a deep thinking considerate man of moderate opinions. His grandfather had been one of the most respected leaders in Cheshire for six decades and he had inherited a great deal of that respect. Parliament had never heard anything to indicate anything but his reasoned loyalty for the regime. He was, or appeared to be, anti-Royalist and a supporter of Parliamentary government, and he had been notably active in local and national politics. Altogether, he was a man that the Council of State felt they could trust. However General Monck, the Army Commander in Scotland was not quite so sure. He suggested quietly to Richard Cromwell that he ought to gain the confidence of the provincial gentry, among whom he specifically named Pierrepont of Nottinghamshire, Hobart of Norfolk, and significantly Booth of Cheshire.

Not that Sir John Thurloe, Secretary of State, took anything on trust. He encouraged a network of internal spies and informers, and one of these, Captain Griffiths, reported to him: *"...although some of these, such as Sir Thomas Middleton, Sir George Booth etc, in some things possibly were unsatisfied, yet against the cavaliers' interest you may as safely trust them as ever, and it will not be convenient to sleight persons of eminency and interest in the country, being assured of their fidelity."* But Griffiths was wrong, and because of this, Thurloe misjudged his man. He did not understand that belief in a free Parliament did not necessarily mean a belief in the pathetic remnants of the Parliament that (just) existed in 1659. In any case, the Rump Parliament removed Thurloe from his post and replaced him by a Council of State although his intelligence network remained in place. Booth had been opposed to Charles I, but that did not imply support for Oliver Cromwell, even less for Richard Cromwell; he had personally raised a troop of horse at the start of the Civil War but that did not mean that he approved of military rule. More importantly, eleven years before, Old Sir George Booth had quietly passed to the Speaker an anonymous approach from the exiled Royalists, and it was widely known that the young Booth had been strongly influenced by his grandfather. For all these reasons, the Council of State had no reason whatever to doubt the loyalty of Young Sir George.

What they did not know, even with their excellent intelligence system, was that the Royalist exiles on the Continent were just as confident in Young George Booth's loyalty, and with better reason as it turned out. Moreover they were starting to feel that the time was ripe for another attempt to restore the monarchy. The death of Oliver Cromwell, the incompetence and weakness of his son Richard, the Army's dominance over the scorned Rump Parliament, and the widespread concern about likely religious and political anarchy, made them confident the country wanted a King again. They were quite right, but just a few months premature. Charles II had been in contact with Booth several times since the execution of Charles I. As "Mr Adams" he had written to Booth five years before, saying how pleased he was at Booth's return to Parliament and hoping that through his uncle, Colonel John Booth, he would have a care for the writer's affairs.

Thurloe suspected Booth of being involved in Penruddock's plot of 1655 to restore the monarchy. The conspirators had held their first meeting at the house of a Mr Allen, a London merchant, in the September. Booth was not at that meeting, but according to Thurloe's informants had attended subsequent meetings. The Royalists had carefully noted Booth's angry denunciation of the Major Generals as *"Cromwell's hangmen"* and his expulsion from Parliament in Pride's Purge. They were already looking on him as one of the most reliable of their supporters left in England. Sir John Mordaunt, tasked by the King with organising the proposed uprising, told Charles that Booth was *"a Presbyterian in opinion, yet so moral a man, if ever any of that principle were to be thoroughly depended on, I think your Majesty may safely on him and his promises, which are considerable and hearty."*

He told Hyde that he had a *"fair opinion"* of Booth, and gave him details of his career: MP for Cheshire in 1645, excluded in 1648, chosen again in 1654-56, and again excluded in 1656. And with other proven dependable local commanders such as Lord Willoughby and Edmund Waller (though originally a committed Parliamentarian) recruited by Mordaunt, Charles believed that his venture, though risky, stood a far better chance of success than anything previously attempted. He was encouraged by a letter from Mordaunt, also signed by the other commanders that he had recruited, that although no one actually wanted war, there would be little chance of long term peace until he was restored to his throne.

Mordaunt himself was an incurable optimist. The previous year he had been captured and put on trial for High Treason for involvement in a Royalist conspiracy that stood no chance of success. A critical element was to capture the Tower of London by setting fire to a nearby house. When the guards rushed out to help put out the flames, the conspirators would dash in to the Tower and seize it! The vote of the judges was evenly split, and only the vote of the President saved Mordaunt from being found guilty, with the certainty of ending up decorating various gates of the City of London. Failure again would undoubtedly seal his fate, but he remained hopeful and brave.

The basic plan was well-conceived and had the advantage of simplicity. It was quite obvious even to the most blindly optimistic that no single uprising was likely to be successful. The difficulties of communication within England made it impossible to assemble a single large force without alerting the authorities at an early stage. An attack on London, the seat of power, would be bound to fail unless the opposition could be somehow fragmented. At the same time Charles could not return to England until it was reasonably safe for him to do so.

The alternative was a more or less simultaneous series of local uprisings, each involving only a small group of counties. The Army of the Council of State would therefore not only be unprepared but also facing several apparently unconnected revolts in the provinces. and would be split up. They would have to hold on to London and the Home Counties at all costs, and by the time they had secured their base, the various Royalist forces would have had time to join up and consolidate. Before long they would have become stronger than the opposition, and their numerical strength would, it was hoped, make up for their relative lack of training, experience, and expertise. Then, after the Council's forces had been defeated, they would be able to march on London with reasonable confidence.

As for the details, there were going to be two main revolts, in the East and the West, coupled with the seizure of the strategic towns of Bristol, Shrewsbury, Warwick, Worcester and Lynn, and some diversionary risings. Sir George Booth was appointed to command in the north west, but only as a diversion, so that the Council of State would be even less sure where and when the main effort would come. Mordaunt had arranged with the other royalists that Townshend would command in Norfolk, Sir John Boys, Lord Willoughby of Parham and Mordaunt himself in Kent, Surrey and Sussex, while Sir John Grenville and Sir Chichester Wrey would look after Devon and Cornwall.

On the whole the plan was sound, and if it had had the essential element of secrecy, it would have stood a fair chance of success. Oddly enough, in that event, the Booth uprising would have been no more than an historical footnote in the story of the Royalist triumph. But security was exactly what the Royalists could not count on. Even Francesco Giavarina, the Venetian resident in London, was aware of the basics of the plans. He knew that the Royalists were hand in glove with the numerous and wealthy Presbyterians, and that the Council of State was very worried. Their main concern was that if they stripped London of its troops, they might find themselves facing a revolt in the capital itself without the means to combat it. Also they could not have known the real weakness of Booth's forces. Giavarina himself greatly overestimated their strength, putting it at 10,000 men under arms.

The only way of keeping the enterprise under wraps was to decide on a date but to delay revealing it, or any other of the details, until the last possible moment, and even then only to the handful of trusted regional commanders. It would have been fatal to confide the secrets to the foot soldiers, who in any case were mostly still to be recruited.

In fact there had been whispers about an attempt as early as March 1658, and Booth, Waller, Townsend and Willoughby received their commissions from the King in May 1659. This was certainly much too soon. The Council of State's best spy and double agent, Sir Richard Willis, was a trusted member of the Sealed Knot, the Royalist 'underground' in England, and had ample time to discover the main elements of the plot and report them.

The Sealed Knot was very pessimistic from the beginning, because they suspected with good reason that their organisation was hopelessly compromised. Moreover, they were not themselves united. A few considered that James, Duke of York, would be better than his brother; there was disagreement over the question of the desirability of foreign aid. Hyde for instance thought that it would be unwise to owe a debt to European princes and that Charles should rely on his own efforts. All parties were very worried about the logistics of the operation. The organisation was good, they admitted, but they were concerned about the shortage of arms and ammunition and the sheer difficulty of transporting what forces the King had on the Continent back to England.

The rising was arranged for Monday 1 August. Mordaunt insisted on the date in spite of the misgivings of the Sealed Knot, who wanted a postponement, if not a downright cancellation. In fact, Mordaunt was anxious about the slow progress as early as July 1659. Mordaunt and Booth were in London together until late May of 1659, when Booth returned to Dunham Massey after an abortive attempt to make off with the Great Seal of the Rump Parliament - he was aiming to demonstrate his faith in a free Parliament, but he was thwarted by the Army guards.

He wrote to Mordaunt emphasising his determination to carry on with his mission, and regretting that he had not been able to find a trustworthy agent to act for him in London while he was in Cheshire: *"For my constancy you need not doubt," he emphasised, "nor your friend* (the King) *you was with so lately. I hope the bargaine on your part will be performed, that I do not both loose and be laughed at. And for your friend you lately visited, whether there is anything more concerning me, then the civility, ex post facto, yet I am still the same..."*

Back in Cheshire, his first priority was to acquire arms and ammunition without arousing suspicion, and he needed ready cash. To obtain it, he was forced to mortgage Thornton le Moors, an outlying manor of his estates and he mortgaged it to Walter Plumer and his sister Elizabeth of Mitcham in Surrey for £3000. He was already in debt to the tune of £3000 for a mortgage he had taken out the previous year, and his indebtedness was to last him the rest of his life.

While Booth was trying to buy the supplies he was going to need, he and Mordaunt both knew that any change in the arrangements would cause chaos. What they did not know however was that Sir Richard Willis knew a great many of the plans and had passed on the intelligence to the Council. By July 1659 they had a good idea of the Royalist plans and were taking precautions, though it seems that they did not know all the names of the conspirators, or the date of the plot. Regiments could be brought from Scotland as reinforcements and other regiments could be quickly transferred from

London to secure the Midlands.  Precautionary arrests were made, horses and arms seized, and gunsmiths searched.  Sir Ralph Verney heard that *"The times are strangely ticklish",* and that Cheshire and Lancashire were certainly in revolt.

Not that the traffic in intelligence was all one way.  The Royalists had their spies in England, their main problem being to receive the information they supplied without it being intercepted en route because the posts and the ports were being carefully watched. They knew this anyway, through the information of James Herbert, who also told them that *"Every man was betraying his own brother."*  After the beginning of the uprising, one Major Henshaw reported rumours that Booth had an army of 6,000 men, including cashiered soldiers and officers who had previously favoured the Parliamentary cause. With encouraging reports like these, even the cautious Sir Edward Hyde was optimistic enough to think that Booth would easily be able to secure Chester, which would give him a secure base for his operations.

Predictably the result was catastrophe.  Booth had good support in the north west, with members of influential families such as Brereton, Cholmondeley, Stanley and Grosvenor in Cheshire, the Earl of Derby in Lancashire and Sir Thomas Middleton of Chirk in North Wales.  He tried to get help from Piers Legh of Lyme, who was Colonel of a regiment of Horse, immensely valuable as he had almost no cavalry of his own. With his uncle John, he wrote to state that Legh was authorised to enlist more men, *"The people having taken up arms in defence of themselves and the known laws of the land."*

He could rely on his own tenantry of course, but he was handicapped by the lack of a secure base in the area.  The City of Chester was more or less Royalist in sympathies, but Colonel Thomas Croxton with 300 men was firmly in control of the Castle, and although they were not well supplied, Booth could not afford the manpower, the material or more importantly the time for a lengthy siege. Whatever he and his forces did, had to be done with great speed, and no other town in the County could be considered as a worthwhile base or if the worst came to the worst, a refuge.

Booth remained optimistic until almost the last moment.  Then, on 31st July, a letter reached him from the Sealed Knot.  It told him that his enterprise was doomed to abject failure beyond all hope, and from that moment, his mood changed.  Until then he had been outwardly cheerful and confident, but the letter made him deeply depressed. Everything he had been agitating for seemed to be lost, and even if, in spite of all, he went ahead with the plan, his own life and estates were certain to be forfeit.  But he was a man of honour and proud of his position and authority in Cheshire.  He was responsible for the Royalist plot in the county, others depended on him, and his sense of duty would not allow him to abandon them.  As Mordaunt said in a letter to Hyde: *"...certain persons of quality assuring him of their ruin in case he desisted, he frankly determined on the attempt and from that time carried himself very worthily in it,"*

No one else did, however.  The Council of State was too well-informed thanks to Willis, who had also, in his capacity of double agent, sown much dissension within the senior ranks of the Sealed Knot and thus persuaded other Royalist leaders that to carry on with the plan would be fatal.  As a result, only handfuls of Cavaliers actually turned up at the various meeting places in the South and Midlands on 1st August, and the troops of cavalry sent out to oppose them dispersed them without trouble. Tunbridge, Redhill, Salisbury Plain, Gloucester, Hereford, Bristol and Chichester were all named rendezvous; they were all occupied by Government forces and prisoners taken. Sir John Mordaunt himself loyally arrived at his Surrey rendezvous and was horrified to find not only that no other Cavaliers had turned up, but also that a well armed troop of cavalry was waiting in case they did. Luckily for him, he saw them just in time and managed to slip away quietly before they saw him.

Meanwhile the Council of State had largely ignored the North West. Perhaps they were not aware just how successful Booth had been in his preparations, or more likely they considered that the region was sufficiently remote as to be not worth bothering about at least in the short term. It was essential for them to keep firm control of London and the neighbouring counties, and their known supporters with the army could (and did) take care of the Midlands, so any risings in more distant parts could be mopped up more or less at leisure. In any case, they had received several scraps of information that there would be such a rising and Colonel Croxton was prepared to hold Chester Castle against all comers. Lieutenant General Edmund Ludlow also leapt into action when one of his officers gave him brief details of the rising. He was actually en route to Ireland at the time, and as soon as he reached Dublin he despatched 100 of his soldiers to reinforce the small garrisons in the Welsh towns of Denbigh, Beaumaris, Carnarvon and Holyhead, in case the rising had any considerable support in those areas.

While Booth was reading the depressing letter from the Sealed Knot, church bells were already ringing and drums were beating to mark the start of the uprising, demonstrating that there was widespread support for it. It was almost too late to stop. Carts carrying the arms he had bought were seen on the road to Dunham Massey. The Reverend Henry Newcome in the Collegiate Church in Manchester had been told that a Quaker rebellion had been discovered, and the people had to be ready to suppress it. He did not for one moment believe this transparently false cover story, however. *"I did know that they were very insolent, and troublesome, yet was unsatisfied that the thing was true, that they were up in arms."* But although he was certain of the real reason behind the preparations, he did nothing personally to help or hinder the enterprise, merely let his curate unsuspectingly make the announcement about the Quakers.

The Reverend Adam Martindale was even better informed, and realised that Booth's men were inadequate for such a vital task. *"Raw, undisciplined men,"* he called them, *"...not well formed into an armie, nor sufficiently furnished with armes and ammunition."*

Booth himself went to Manchester on the evening of 31st July, a day of torrential rain, and recruited perhaps 500 men. On the same day, after sermon, the drums were heard to beat in Warrington, and about 500 more horse and foot, fully armed, joined the Booth colours. The next day he rode to an agreed rendezvous in Warrington, where he met his subordinate commanders and the 500 recruits. On Tuesday 2nd August he called a muster on Rowton Heath near Chester, an unhappy memory for the Royalist cause, but with the promise from John Booth that the city gates would be open to him. *"Which day they accordingly met, being above three thousand Horse and Foot, well mounted and arm'd, with drums beating, Colours flying, and Trumpets sounding."*

After this brave show and some basic practice manoeuvres, Booth called the whole army together and issued a solemn Declaration, a plain statement of exactly why he had taken up arms for the King. But he carefully made no mention of the King himself or indeed of the monarchy in general. He was not and never had been a convinced supporter of the monarchy, but he could not admit that to his men at this juncture. His main ambition was simply the return of a free Parliament, not beholden to the Army for its existence, and not subject to arbitrary dissolution:

*"The Declaration of the Lords, Gentlemen, freeholders, and Yeomen, of this once happy Kingdom of England.*

*Since it hath pleased Almighty God to suffer the spirit of division to continue in this distracted Nation and to leave us without any settled foundation of Religion, liberty or property; the Legislative power usurped and contemned at pleasure; the Army, raised at first for our defence, Abused and misled into unwarrantable Actions, by the Cunning and ambition of some of their superior Officers; no face of Government appearing, either in any single person or Body of men in Council lawfully Constituted, to whom the Grievances of the People may with any Probability of success be properly addressed,*

*We being Conscious of our Duty and sensible of our own and Nation's ruin if these distractions continue, or resolve into a more fixed oppression, by some corrupt settlement inconsistent with Laws, Peace, & interests of the Nation, have taken up arms in defence of ourselves & all others who will partake with us in the vindication & maintenance of the freedom of Parliament, against all violence whatsoever of the known Laws, Liberty, and Property of the Good people of this Nation, who at present groan under Illegal, Arbitrary, & insupportable taxes and payments unknown to our Ancestors.*

*This being our Duty to God and Man, and our only design, we cannot despair of the blessing of him that giveth victory, nor of the cheerful concurrence of all good men, nor of the undeceived part of the Army; whose arrears, increase, a further pay, & Advancement to higher commands we shall by all means procure, suffering no imposition or force on any man's conscience. To this we doubt not but all true Englishmen will say Amen."*

This appeal was probably widely, but secretly circulated around the county. George Booth also circulated *"A Letter from Sir George Booth to a Friend showing the reasons for his present engagement"* which largely repeats the contents of his Declaration and is pitched at the nobility and gentry to gain their support. The last time that a House of Commons had been legally (in Booth's opinion) elected was 1640, and only 40 of them were left. The Government were *"the meanest and fanatick spirits of the Nation"* who wanted everyone to *"be warmed into the same zeale"*, and Englishmen no longer had any *"settled foundation of religion, liberty or property."* Really the Army was in control, busily practising themselves what they criticised in others, usurping power and tyrannising the nation. They had usurped legislative power and the common people had nowhere in which their grievances could be redressed.

*"What is this but to necessitate men to complain... Let the Nation freely choose their representatives"*, called Booth. *"But we are faithfull and peacefull in the land, and if they in authority.... will agree of a means to admit the old members of both Houses, or to call a new free Parliament... he only is truly a Traitor that reserves not his judgement and*

*obedience into their determinations."*

Booth's third manifesto, *"An Express from the Knights and Gentlemen now engaged with Sir George Booth",* was aimed clearly at the citizens of London and all other freemen of England. All Englishmen, he said, had the same birthright with *"a common and equal bond of freedom and unity.... general, equal and impartial to all, without respect of persons, rank, quality, or degree."* But their rights had been stolen from them, and they were left with arbitrary imprisonment and taxation, all contrary to the Magna Carta and the Petition of Right. These undemocratic powers were exercised by only a few ambitious high-ranking men with no respect for God or conscience. Religion, said Booth, should be a matter of individual freedom and universal toleration, and he appealed to the *"gathered separate churches"* to join with him and his Presbyterians to protect the laws and liberties of the people. Many reforms would be put in place - annual elections of all officers, succession of Parliaments, trial by jury, abolition of all new taxes, and the protection of the rights of the poor. Finally Booth returned to his favourite hobby horse, the free Parliament, which would have final authority.

He was dismayed to hear that Warrington had openly declared for the King, and commented that it would be their ruin. His initial successes had been extraordinary, far greater than he could have expected. He was supported by the Earls of Manchester, Derby and Stafford, Lord Willoughby of Parham and Sir William Waller. Essentially he could count on a large part of the counties of Cheshire, Lancashire and Staffordshire. In Cheshire there had been no opposition more than passive resistance, because those gentry who did not join him prudently disappeared from view. Even so, the overt support he had received was quite considerable. Wrexham was the bailiwick of Sir Thomas Middleton, and men gathered to his standard there; Denbigh and Flintshire were strongly Royalist, and men came to join him in sizeable numbers.

However there were serious desertions from the cause. His forecast that it would be ruinous to declare openly for the King was only too accurate. Many of his troops shared his desire for a free Parliament but also remained Puritan in sympathy and seeing no need for the return of a King, deserted Booth's army as being altogether too dangerous. Thomas Rugg, a barber in London, said that he was *"extreamly beloved of his country and tenents"* and many of them *"did attend him with horse and armes."* However very few others remained faithful to him. When battle lines were drawn, a newsletter estimated probably pessimistically that he had no more than 1,300 men left.

Booth's local successes were not backed up anywhere outside the North West. As early as 5th August, Bulstrode Whitlocke reported to the Council of State that *"the enemy"* commanded by Sir George Booth was confined to Cheshire and Lancashire. Even then he was exaggerating slightly, as only the southern part of Lancashire was involved, other than Cheshire of course. Nevertheless the Council of State were startled by the suddenness of the rising and took it very seriously, with many emergency measures. Two Members of Parliament, Messrs Brookes and Dunch were fined £100 each merely on suspicion of leaning towards Booth!

Outside Parliament, there was even panic among people who had only rumour to go on. Dr William Denton in London advised Sir Ralph Verney to hide his horses in a wood and even to pull off the shoes from his best mare so that she could pass as a colt and be less likely to be commandeered. *"We have all a mind to be out of the towne, but yett hopes, feares, & jealousies doe soe distract us, as that we can resolve of nothing. I wish my papers & other things were with you, for we doe not thinke ourselves at all secure here.... but the open face of things at this presente appeares thus, viz. noe considerable force, if any at all, up anywhere but with Sir George Booth, who with others are now proclaimed traitors."* Significantly, however, Denton mentioned that the city was calling for a free Parliament, which of course was precisely what Booth was wanting.

The two most significant actions were that Major General Lambert was ordered north with 16 troops of horse and heavy dragoons to crush the rebels, and warships were sent to prevent any supply ships from entering the port of Chester. Major General Fleetwood was being particularly subtle. He encouraged Lambert to accept command, which put him in an awkward position. Obviously there was a risk in leaving London to seek battle with forces of unknown strength, and he was rather unwilling to leave Fleetwood, his rival, holding the reins of power in London. In fact, Lambert was never in any danger from Booth's army. The estimates of its strength varied widely from 1,000 to 7,000, and even 12,000 according to the wildly optimistic Royalist Thomas Ross in his report to Colonel Hollis. The true figure will never be known, but a maximum of 3-4,000 is likely.

Colonel Thomas Birch learned of the rising from a Quaker gentleman who stopped him on the road. Greatly alarmed, he wrote to the Speaker of the Commons and informed him *"obscurely of great preparation of arms, and that Sir George Booth and some other gentlemen of Lancashire and Cheshire, who live next door bordering upon the confines of both counties, were endeavouring an insurrection.... Upon the Friday I went to Manchester, where I was much more confirmed in the truth of it; and that night I heard of some cart-loads of arms carried forwards Manchester to Sir George Booth's house in Cheshire; whereupon forthwith I sent my man to our county troop and another troop of the army, that were about twenty miles off, to give them notice and the better to avoid a surprise, that they would keep moving and quarter together for their safety."*

Birch also warned Colonel Bradshaw and Colonel Croxton, the Governor of Chester Castle, the Sheriff of Lancaster, and various other gentlemen whom he could trust. He heard that Booth had been joined by Colonels Ashton, Holland, Ireland and others, and asked the Governor of Chester to notify the Council of State urgently in case they did not already know. His own problem was that *"where I was at home, surrounded with them all about me, it was not possible to send to you (Parliament) either by letter or messenger... Sir, I stayed at home the longer, and to the greater hazard than discretion allowed me, that so I might give you the more certainty of their proceedings.... they tell much of the expectation they (have) of other forces out of Wales and neighbour counties, but I hear of no stirring elsewhere. I hope you will pardon this sudden distracted relation, having scarce time to write it...."*

On 7th August, Booth went back to Manchester on another recruiting drive, but by then he must have known that his cause was hopeless. He told the Reverend Henry Newcome that he had been basely deserted, and that although he had received promises from five hundred of the country's leading gentry, they had all been prevented or had failed in their intent.  Newcome understood Booth's position and advised caution.  He suggested that some attempt should be made to bring about mediation between Booth and Lambert, but Booth's rising was too far advanced for this.

Booth was the only Royalist commander who had had any success at all.  All the other risings had barely started before being ignominiously quashed by the army, and without large-scale help, he stood no chance.  It was then that he lost all sense of purpose and direction.  His experience of military strategy was negligible, and over the next few days, it showed.  In essence he had only two options open to him.  He could either gather all his forces around him and try to beat Lambert in a single decisive battle, or he could storm Chester Castle in the hope of capturing it quickly so that he would have a secure base and sit out a siege until the King arrived.

In fact he did neither, and just wandered helplessly and aimlessly around mid Cheshire.  His only decisive action seems to have been to send his uncle, Sir John Booth, to Chester to try to arrange for the gates to be opened for him.  According to Thomas Ross in his report mentioned above, he was furious at the collapse of all his promised support and *"rageth most horribly, and vows the discovery of all those that promised to join with him and most unworthily failed.  If he do so, I think few will blame, but rather pity him to have to do with unworthy men."*

Nor were George's troops very reliable, as was shown by the experience of Henry Bradshaw of Marple, a nephew of the President of the Council of State, whose house was ransacked by Booth's forces.  He complained to Booth as friend and neighbour:

*"The undeserved respect which my late father and his family have formerly had from your late renowned grandfather, and that which I have hitherto experienced from your honor, hath laid such an obligation upon me and mine as will never by me be forgotten, and I am confident had you been acquainted with any design of any under your command against me, I should not have had my unfinished house so rifled, and my estate so carried away, my poor wife, children and family, so affrighted as they were upon Friday night last by persons calling themselves soldiers sent by Col. Holland, as their captain alleged.  Sir, I had not, nor have in the least measure advised, acted, or consented, up to any thing against you or any in your army, or that hath relation to you, neither was nor am privie to any plot, contrivement, or raising of men, either directly or indirectly against you, or the cause you have in mind."*

Two days later he wrote again, warning Booth that a Parliamentary army was heading his way.  *"I... intreat you that you would seriously consider of the cause thereof, of your public intentions and actions, and the consequence thereof, and in time desist....."*

The Council of State proclaimed Booth a rebel and traitor, and ordered the proclamation to be read in all market towns, but no hard news reached London until 12th August.  A small detachment of State troops under Major Creed had had a brief skirmish with some of the rebels and found them easy meat.  As Lambert contemptuously reported to Whitlocke, they were *"rather inclined to fly than to fight, their foot being mostly forced into the service and unarmed.  A few days will try their temper."*

While Lambert was advancing and Booth was vacillating, what of Booth's other commanders?  He had committed one of the cardinal sins of warfare by splitting his forces exactly when he needed to concentrate them. Moreover, while he with the bulk of his army and the aged Sir Thomas Middleton was wandering vaguely round Cheshire, he left his principal subordinates in Chester watching but not really besieging the castle and not having any firm idea what was happening or what his plans were. Even Booth's Uncle John was baffled. He and his colleagues wrote despairingly to Booth, hoping that the letter would eventually find him. It is obvious that their theoretical military expertise was much greater than Booth's:

*"We.... are much amazed to think of your drawing off so far as Northwich, leaving us here. What the real cause may be we cannot imagine but in the meantime it still disheartens your friends and hath occasioned already many tears in this city, and we have so far considered the business that we cannot imagine your return before you have engaged, neither can there any intelligence pass betwixt you and us, nor can you think other than that the enemie will immediately clap betwixt you and us and so obstruct all passages.... We could wish we had been made known to your intentions sooner, but this sudden result and motion relisheth not well and looks with a very bad face to all...."*

Surely no senior officers ever wrote a more gloomy, pessimistic and it must be said, more accurate resume of the situation and forecast of its outcome.

All this time, Lambert's army was steadily approaching, but with troubles of his own. The weather was foul, with heavy rain and strong winds, and many of the troops were reluctant to march at all. According to Giavarina *"the infantry stopped several times on the road, protesting that they would not advance unless they were paid what was due, as they did not receive a penny before they started. They were induced to proceed with fair words and promises after the mutiny had lasted some hours."* Many of them wanted a free Parliament just as Booth did, and their reliability was distinctly doubtful. Lambert even had to order his cavalry to enforce his orders, and some men were wounded before the others *"resumed their march, but grumbling and very dissatisfied, especially as the march is long and toilsome and they are harassed by terrible winds, very unusual for the season, and by rain which has fallen almost incessantly since they started."*

In spite of his confidence he was taking no unnecessary risks. Booth had to be defeated come what may, and he left as little as possible to chance. He stopped briefly to pick up two more infantry regiments and a massive force of cavalry, and detached a small force to pick off the town of Stafford, which had risen in support of Booth but where there was only a weak Royalist garrison. Then he proceeded to Nantwich, where even more reinforcements joined, but their intelligence was not good enough to tell them exactly where Booth's army was.

Lambert and his forces were actually on the march to Chester on 18th August when, as night was falling, they almost bumped into Booth's army heading towards Northwich. A small group of Parliamentary horse were riding to Warrington from Wigan, when they encountered Booth's scouts and challenged them. They replied with a counter challenge, to which they answered *"For the Commonwealth."* Booth's men fired a quick volley without causing any damage and then retreated hastily. It was too late to give battle that night, and Booth and his men got safely to Northwich while Lambert and his army stopped overnight at Weaverham. Even Booth probably did not clearly know why he had decided that Northwich was a good town to garrison.

The next day, 19th August, marked the very last battle of the English Civil War, although 'battle' is too grandiose a word to describe the events at Winnington Bridge. Booth had a good eye for country, whatever his shortcomings as a military commander, and with his detailed local knowledge he picked out excellent defensive positions. The opposing forces made contact briefly at Hartford Green early in the morning, but the Royalists fell back northwards in good order to the River Weaver. There at Winnington they held *"a fair stone bridge"* as Lambert described it. They could hope to hold it *"in regard the river was unfordable, the bridge narrow, flanked with a strong ditch on the far end and a high hill up which no horse could pass otherwise along the side in a narrow path."* With a steep slope and good cover at their backs, an experienced commander, with well-trained troops, might have achieved a great deal. Unfortunately, not only were their opponents hard battle trained veterans, but they themselves were raw unblooded novices.

Without any waste of time, Lambert cleared the defenders off the bridge with two or three carefully aimed volleys, and ordered his horsemen to cross it as quickly as possible in small groups. Badly aimed defensive fire from Booth's men had no effect, and the horsemen charged up the slope without hesitation. Being in small highly mobile groups they presented no sort of target to the Royalists, suffered no casualties, and efficiently cleared Booth's cavalry from the crest of the slope. Lambert's infantry followed close behind and charged uphill against Booth's foot soldiers, who broke and ran without offering any worthwhile resistance. That was virtually the end of the 'battle'. It was a rout, neither more nor less. Lambert's troops suffered one casualty, Booth's perhaps 30. In fact there was so little resistance from the Royalists that Ludlow commented that Lambert's troops were *"more ready to save than destroy them."*

A few isolated groups of Booth's forces stopped and in desperation offered token resistance, but without effect. One of his officers, Captain Morgan, bravely tried to cover the retreat but was killed. By midday all semblance of cohesion and control had disappeared. The Royalist officers had ordered 'every man for himself', and were trying to reach some safety themselves. Lambert's dragoons reached Northwich to find two companies of foot soldiers and two troops of horse, who fled northwards, hotly pursued, until they were almost at Manchester. As for Booth, he went south to Chester, and got there just ahead of Major Creed and his men. When they reached the walls of the city, Booth sent out messengers under a flag of truce to discuss surrender terms. They were allowed to pass through the Army lines to Lambert, still 15 miles away. Booth still had his pride left, and he told Lambert that he wanted only a free Parliament and was prepared to open discussions on those terms. Lambert knew Booth's reasons already, of course, and his reply was contemptuous. Booth's forces, and the city itself, had until 10am the following day to surrender unconditionally. If they did so, the city would not be sacked and plundered.

There can have been very little discussion among the Royalists. Their fine plans had been defeated almost without a struggle, they were tired, and their morale must have been at rock bottom. Their only thought was survival, and even that looked unlikely for their leaders. Only surrender on Lambert's terms offered even the slightest hope. Sir Thomas Middleton and Lord Kilmorey left Chester hurriedly, some remaining troops of horse mutinied and tore up their colours, and the gates of the city were formally opened for Lambert to ride in, take possession of the city, and relieve Colonel Croxton's hungry garrison in the castle.

As for Sir George Booth, he had slipped away earlier at the Northgate, realising that only by hiding could he really hope to save his life and estates. He was reported to be heading towards Chirk, where Sir Thomas Middleton had gone to hold the castle, but he had no clear idea where he would go in the long term or what he could do. Perhaps there was some vague idea in his mind of slipping away to the Continent to join the King and his other exiles. Mayor Waring of Shrewsbury had sent messengers to bring him the latest situation, and when they returned from Lambert, he sent an express to London with the news that Lambert was splitting his forces to Chester and Warrington, but the remnants of Booth's army had been told to *"shift for themselves."*

One of Lambert's officers, Richard Ashfield, also sent the Committee of State some even more reassuring news:

*"Since our coming we have taken many prisoners, some of quality. Col. Holland hath voluntarily submitted himself, so hath Peter Brook of Cheshire, several other gentlemen of this county. I daily expect either by their coming in freely, or gathered up by the horse that are quartered at several places, the country likewise begins to take them and bring them in; so that in a short time I shall be able to give you as good account of all the considerable persons that have been in this late rebellion..... here is no convenience of prisons, which puts us to a great strait how to secure them, but I think there is no great fear of their making any escape, they knowing not whither to go; for any party of them, small or great, together I fear of none. God, I hope hath scattered them, that he might establish righteousness in these nations."*

Mayor Jones of Chester was more concerned with establishing his own innocence, fearing *"lest we should be looked upon as engaged in the design..... the truth is and will so appear that we were altogether ignorant of the design in the proclamation mentioned, were strangers and knew not of their approach till upon us, we were altogether without defence to oppose them, our walls in a great part down, had no force within, and the least resistance would have made us prey to them. When they were got in they acted the military part as to the carrying on their designs... and appointed a Governor of the City without our consent, we were strangers to their councils and resolutions...."*

Mayor Jones had created two companies of militia *"to provide some kind of force for our defence against that violence which we were in danger from"* but refused to use them against Lambert's army, *"resolved rather to open the gates to the Parliament forces and submit to mercy than oppose, which caused the other forces to leave the city, and we know not other means but God that we were preserved from hurt by them when they left us, and that the city was open to the Parliament forces when they came but by the benefit of those two companies so raised by us......"*

All Booth's efforts had come to nothing. His army and his hopes had been routed.

What followed a few days later had elements of slapstick farce: the doltish innkeeper, the man clumsily dressed as a woman, even the happy ending (though that could not have been foreseen then.) But it was desperately serious for Booth. The scene was the Red Lion inn in Newport Pagnell. Two gentlemen arrived on horseback about 7pm and asked for a room for themselves and some friends, including a lady, Mistress Dorothy, who were following on behind. The innkeeper showed them several rooms, but the gentlemen said they were all unsatisfactory until he showed them the poorest room in the house. Entry to it was through another room which made it inconvenient to say the least, and the innkeeper was rather puzzled when the gentlemen accepted it immediately. He then heard the clatter of horses' hooves and found another man and a lady riding pillion behind him arriving. Naturally he offered to help her down from her horse, but she leapt down from it with agility, ignored him completely, strode off into the inn and commandeered the upstairs room.

The innkeeper was getting very curious indeed, but he began to prepare supper - two joints of meat - for his guests. The woman stayed in her room. While the meal was cooking, the gentlemen called for a barber to shave them - there was nothing unusual about that. They admired the barber's razor and enquired if they could buy it. The barber refused, because it would break his set of razors. However he had a spare at home, and they could have it if they wanted it, for half a crown. The men accepted the offer at once, although the price was very high.

Supper being ready, the maid servants offered to help the lady to get ready, but through her friends she refused, which itself was very strange. One of the men told the innkeeper that Mistress Dorothy would not come down but would eat in her room. Then he asked for a bowl of hot water, and went upstairs again with his expensively bought razor. At last it dawned on the innkeeper, who seems to have been rather slow on the uptake, that there was something very strange about Mistress Dorothy. He slipped out to consult a relative, the local apothecary, and the two then went to find the village constables. Suspicious people had booked in and one of them might be a man in disguise. What should they do?

The constables agreed that there was something very wrong about the affair, and assembled a strong posse of ten armed men. They prudently set a guard at the back of the inn and demanded admittance to Mistress Dorothy's room. At that 'she' and the other men tried to leave hastily via the backstairs, only to find the constables' men waiting. They saw that the game was up and offered no resistance. The apothecary took control of the situation. Producing a pistol, he went up to "Mistress Dorothy" and pointed it at her. At first 'she' claimed to be simply a gentlewoman travelling from Derbyshire to London, but the apothecary pressed her again.

"*I ask for quarter,*" she said.

"*Are you a woman or a man?*" asked the apothecary.

"*If you will spare my life, I will tell you.*"

"*Speak the truth and I will.*"

"*I am a man,*" replied Mistress Dorothy, to no one's surprise.

"*As you are a gentleman, tell me the truth.*"

"*I am that unfortunate gentleman, Sir George Booth,*" he said reluctantly.

Within two or three days Booth had been taken to London under close escort, wearing a new suit, hat and shoes bought for him in the village. The news of his defeat and capture spread like wildfire.

For the pamphleteers and ballad-mongers, it was a gift from Heaven. Some were carefully thought out and intelligently written, such as a refutation of Booth's "*Letter of 2nd August 1659, Shewing the Reasons of his Present Engagement.*" Booth and his supporters claimed to be "*considerable members of our Countrey*" and as such had "*more sober and contagious thought in time of extremity than other men have.*" The reply was that Booth ought to be more thankful to God than people who had less, and that he was obliged by God to think twice before starting a war, with all the harm it would cause. Did owning a great estate give him the right to act thus? "*Have personal discontents, and revenge, upon presumed wrongs by denying your access to sit in Parliament, put you in Armes? Shall the root of your revenge be watered with the blood of your Country?*" asked the pamphleteer sardonically. Booth complained of heavy taxes and the raising of a militia. The scornful answer was that he himself had previously been a tax raiser when necessary, and that to start a war would only increase them again. "*What is this but to quench fire with oil, and to put it out with gunpowder?*" Booth wanted a free Parliament. What, asked his anonymous critic, did he mean? Would it not be packed with "*idle, and profane superstitious, ignorant and scandalous suppressed Ministers? ....the most profane, cursing, swearing, drinking, blaspheming Royall Reformadoes, and their cursed crew of Papists, Atheists and bloody men....?*" If Booth really wanted the restitution of the old members of both Houses of Parliament, he must mean either some or all. If the former, it would not be free, and if the latter, it would not be representative of the feelings of the whole nation. "*Let the Nation freely choose their representatives*", called Booth. The army were committing acts of usurpation and tyranny, and were men not right to complain?  English freemen had ancient rights of liberty, which were being eroded, infringed and denied by the unelected military. Booth's critic countered this by asking rhetorically what was Booth's own authority to *"take up Armes, raise partyes, levy a warre, kill and slay those that oppose you?"*

And so Booth's quoted claims and the counter claims continued: Booth: *"A mean and schismaticall party must depresse the Nobility, and understanding Commons."* Opponent: *"So must a Tyrannical, Popish, Prelaticall, profane and wicked party."*  As for Booth, he had well deserved his reputation of *"a Gentleman of honour, prudence and piety"*, but he was truly a traitor, having changed sides.

*"Sir"*, he concluded, *"we pray for you, though you war against us: your liberties, for your sakes, are as dear unto us, as our own, for our own sakes.  That the cause of God and his truth.... may be preserved from violence, and blood, and blood-guiltinesse, is my most sollicitous, and habituall desire, and for which I shall      CRI IN HOPE."*

It was very unsubtle, but as a piece of state propaganda, it was probably effective.

Just as biting and sarcastic was an invented conversation between Sir George Booth and the imaginary Sir John Presbyter at their meeting near Chester.  Given Booth's religious beliefs, one would expect total agreement in their conversation, but it did not quite happen.  Their conversation was, unsurprisingly, largely religious in content, as distinct from the "Answers to a Letter".  It was again tongue in cheek.  Sir John, for instance, wants to chase out all the Sectaries (small religious sects) in England. Sir George offers to secure them for him, but does not know who they are.  Sir John answers that they are *"those which cry down Magistracy and Ministry"*, Anabaptists, Independents, Quakers, Ranters, ten groups altogether.  Booth is grateful for the information, *"as they fall into my hands, I may take care to have them dispatched out of the way."*  The joke is that Presbyterians were themselves of course a minority religious group, belonging neither to the old established church nor to the ultra fanatical Puritans.

However, says Sir George, his army is dwindling, because the King was proclaimed too soon.  His enemies are all around and are too strong.  Sir John tries to encourage him and promises to curse the enemy by bell, book and candle.

Booth and Presbyter meet again in the Tower of London and Booth bitterly blames Sir John for his failure.  Sir John replies that he never intended Booth to take up arms: *"You were too heady, and you did want discretion"*  Booth should have gone to Lambert as soon as he realised that his chance had gone, and surrendered his army, claiming that he had unearthed a malignant plot....headed by *"some desperate cavalier."*  *"But is this not Dissimulation and Equivocation?  How shall I know what to believe when I hear you preach?"*  *"If you would know what I mean when I preach, you must look upon my actions, and not my words....."*

It is a vicious attack on the Presbyterians and blames Sir George Booth for having been tricked by them, even though he was one of them.  The message is very clear, that they are not to be trusted, even among themselves.  Too late Booth realises that they are *"a pack of very knaves, hypocrites, and base dissemblers... I am ashamed that ever I owned you.  I did abhorre to think of such perfidious impudent Cheats as you.  Let me see you no more.  Amen."*

If Booth ever read this, he must have smarted, because it was an attack on his own religious beliefs. Personally he was moderate in his views and the pamphlet made him look a fool at having been deceived by the fanatics. What made it even worse was that none of it was really true. The Presbyterians were not involved religiously with the uprising; Booth's motives were entirely political.

This doggerel verse is pitched at a much lower level:.

*"From Anabaptists and quivering Quakers,*
*From those that rule us like bow-legged bakers,*
*From those that undo us yet are good law-makers,*
*Good Lord deliver us!*
*From Sir George Booth and his Cheshire lies,*
*From being taken in disguise,*
*From those that send us that devil, Excise,*
*Good Lord, deliver us!"*

A

# DIALOGUE

BETWIXT

## Sir George Booth,

AND

## Sir John Presbyter,

At their meeting near

# CHESTER,

UPON

The Rendezvousing of the Army:
Wherein, most of the Machinations depending upon
that Affair, are discovered.

LONDON,
*Printed for* William Wild, 1659.

Some years later, however, the *Mysteria Revelata* printed some much more complimentary and slightly better verse from the Royalist perspective.

> *"I'm sure the instructions that Wilks did bring*
> *With's fellow treaters show'd us no such thing*
> *Nor did Monck, though solicited, comply*
> *With loyal Booth, but on the contrary*
> *Assisted Lambert, till he flew so high*
> *The people, yea, the Presbyterians all*
> *With one consent inclined to stand or fall*
> *By what th'ensuing Parliament should act*
> *Which they unanimously hope in fact*
> *Would soon restore the King, the only way*
> *To a just settlement, which every day*
> *They saw perverted, and new projects found*
> *To lay the nation level with the ground*
> *Which they could not endure, but all about*
> *The spirit raised by Booth afresh breaks out."*

The Council of State was delighted that the rebellion had been put down with such ridiculous ease and so cheaply. Even Lambert's emergency war chest of £14,000 was hardly touched, and Booth was locked up safely in the Tower of London, without access to pen and paper. His prospects could hardly have looked bleaker. His goods and estates were likely to be confiscated by order of the Council's puppet Parliament, as were those of Randolph Egerton, Robert Werdon, old Sir Thomas Middleton and *"any others who have supported Charles Stuart since 7th May last."* Booth's papers were to be seized and kept, and those who had helped him were to be held securely. Even one of his servants, John Tippin, was to be confined in the Tower to await trial on a charge of high treason. Peter Harrison, the Rector of Cheadle, got away quite lightly. Accused in October of aiding and abetting Booth, he was given the choice of a £4 fine or having his house looted. Not surprisingly, he opted for the fine!

The Council had only to interrogate Booth to find the last few missing bits of information, and Sir Henry Vane and Sir Arthur Haselrig took on the job. Meanwhile, it was necessary to reward the people who had helped in Booth's downfall. The inn keeper of Newport Pagnell was given £40, and each of the servants £10. The men who had escorted him to London shared £60, and even a man who had swum across the River Dee to tell Lambert that Chester Castle was open received £10.

The Council of State openly gloated. Colonel John Bamfield said *"such a fine settlement here as this is likely to remain a Commonwealth."* Lord Lockhart, the Ambassador to France, was sent the news on 25th August, and M. de Bordeaux, the French Ambassador in England, informed Cardinal Mazarin that the mere appearance of Lambert's army had routed Booth's forces. As for Booth, it was total disgrace, but in Bordeaux' opinion, he could have avoided it by shutting himself up in Chester, accepting the siege and refusing to give battle. However it would have taken a much more

# THE
## Lord Lambert's
# LETTER

To the Right Honorable

The *Speaker* of the PARLIAMENT,

Concerning the Victory which it hath pleased
God to give the Forces of this Commonwealth over the Rebels under

Sir *George Booth* in *Cheshire.*

*Read in Parliament, Monday Aug. 22.*

To which is added

A LIST of the Officers which are
Prisoners, with the number of Soldiers and Colours
taken ; according to the Relation made by
Captain *Brown,* who was present
in the Fight.

London, Printed by *Tho. Newcomb* over against *Bainards*
Castle in *Thames-street,* 1659.

My Lord:

73

I must begg yᵉ pardon if I renew my suite in the behalfe of Maior Harrison, a person I do engage shall be as observuant & seruiceable as yᵉ lᵖ can desire; at my request yᵘ were pleased to promise him employment assoone it should fall: He being at this time with me in this iourney, my doubt is he may suffer by his absence; that yᵉ Excellencies many Businesses may make him out of yᵉ memory, & so he may come short of the fauour yᵘ intend him; I haue desired Colonell Knight to ~~remember~~ minde yᵉ lp. Let me obtaine

Rochester: May . 11-

excuse for this trouble from him that is:

yᵉ lord:

yᵉ Excellencies most faithfull & humble seruant:

G:Booth:

Sir George Booth to General Lambert. *Courtesy of The British Library* experienced campaigner than Booth to appreciate the grand strategy of abandoning the offensive and accepting the defensive while waiting for relief.

By 3rd September Sir Thomas Middleton had accepted the inevitable and surrendered Chirk Castle. Lambert was ordered to demolish it and make it untenable. Middleton was treated with surprising leniency, perhaps because of his age, and instead of joining Booth in the Tower was allowed two months liberty to attend to his affairs, after which he could apply to Parliament for mercy.

The Royalists in exile were deeply despondent, the more so because at first they had very little hard news. A rumour circulated that Booth had been put to death without trial. Sir Edward Hyde thought it was all Booth's fault anyway, because he had reportedly refused to admit Catholics. Hyde also received a note from an agent in England that *"Booth's glorious pretext of a free Parliament and the subject's liberty, is all ended under a woman's petticoat, which makes many conclude him to be rather a fool, knave, or coward"*. Even Hyde's geographical information showed a lamentable ignorance. One report he received told him that Booth had been defeated in a pass near Northwich!

Sir Edward Nicholas, the King's Secretary of State, reported that there was no hope at all of more risings in the foreseeable future. There was no one left in arms against *"the rebellious government."* He did not even know where the King was, and just hoped against hope that he had been warned in time to prevent him leaving.

Mordaunt wavered between optimism and pessimism. In one letter, he claimed that there was still a chance. According to him, Norfolk, the west country and parts of the North were willing to try again. But in another report he wrote that the Parliament would either be purged or broken up, with the risk of civil war again. If it happened, he thought that the Presbyterians would side with Parliament for a republic *"being dissatisfied with the treachery of the cavaliers in Sir George Booth's business."* If they prevailed, the prisoners would be set free; if not, and Lambert was successful, they would be put to death. There was only a hint of real optimism. An anonymous report to Hyde in December spoke of many Cavaliers who were true to the King, and *"as for Cheshire, the same persons engaged with Sir George Booth are in the present business and most of them still have their arms."*

Sir George's wife Elizabeth was naturally scared for her husband. She had stayed quietly in the background during the rising, but now that George was in prison and his life was in grave danger, she was determined to do everything she could for him, although she was only just recovering from the birth of another son, brother to William and Henry. Starting at the top, she wrote to John Bradshaw, who had presided over the court that had tried and executed Charles I. His advice was simply that she and Booth should admit everything they knew about the plot openly and fully. This however would have made Booth's trial and execution even more certain.

As it was, he would cooperate to a certain extent with his interrogators. He was no fool and realised that they already knew most, so it would do him no further harm to appear helpful. Moreover he could admit his real motives, which did not necessarily include the return of the monarchy. He had never called for its restoration, he told Vane and Haselrig, in fact he had positively refused to proclaim the King.

As for the active part of the rising, some of his alleged supporters had made approaches to Lambert against his advice and then fled. He had been over confident at first, even refusing to admit some Presbyterians who wanted to join him. And just as important, there were some high ranking gentry he thought he could count on - with their tenants of course - who kept their heads so low they were invisible. He felt, in short, as if he had been abandoned by God.

But there was one thing Booth would not divulge, the names of his co-conspirators. Some were known of course, and Booth admitted to his dealings with Mordaunt who had disappeared abroad again out of the Council's reach. Booth was an honourable man, a gentleman by rank and birth. He was doomed, he thought, but he would not condemn others to death, even if by so doing he might just save his own life. So when Vane and Haselrig asked him to name those gentlemen who had supported him and were not taken, he proudly asked for understanding. Yes of course he could name them, but would not willingly do so. It would wound his honour, and that to him was as important as life.

Lady Elizabeth Booth did her best to give her husband some sort of alibi. The Council had collected all their papers, hoping to find something even more incriminating, and she promptly wrote to Haselrig. She confirmed that she had co-operated fully with the searchers, and among the documents they had taken was one that was still sealed. Some visible bits were in some kind of cypher. John Mordaunt's wife had given it to her in London, she claimed, but some friends had arrived before she could speak to Elizabeth about it. *"...which paper as it is now delivered to the bearer I received, but never showed the same to my husband or acquainted him with it."* Even Booth admitted that she had the letter, which he thought came from the King, but he claimed to know nothing of its contents. A thin defence indeed, but perhaps better than nothing.

To everyone's surprise, nothing much happened. Lambert took more than 700 prisoners, but released most of them, detaining only senior officers and those who admitted having served in the Royalist armies in the Civil War. Booth himself was examined several times, but true to his resolve gave very little away. He remained in the Tower of London, but no steps were taken to put him on trial. By the middle of September he was being permitted visitors, and his aunts Katherine and Frances, with his first father-in-law, Lord Lincoln, were allowed to speak to him on private affairs, in the presence of the Lieutenant of the Tower.

The Committees for Compounding and Sequestration were rather more busy dealing with other conspirators. As early as August the estates of Booth, Middleton, Randolph Egerton and Robert Werdon were ordered to be confiscated, and anyone who concealed their property was to be fined double the value of the concealment.

John Ratcliffe of Chester was particularly hard put to it to explain his own involvement. Why had the Sheriff opened the gates on 2 August? Why were bonfires lit in the streets when the news broke of a rising in Derby? (not true) Why were there shouts of *"God save the King"*? Ratcliffe nervously explained that the times were very dangerous for him and the city; there were soldiers inside and outside the walls, which were too weak to withstand an assault. As for the defenders of the city, they were all untrained volunteers. He personally had never acted against the interests of Parliament.

The Committee surprisingly believed him, but with reservations. As they explained to the Committee for Cheshire, accused people would always cause as much trouble as they could, because *"their great aim is a delay, in expectation of further changes."* This statement is curious. The implication is that they were already aware of a groundswell of public opinion in favour of a restoration of the monarchy, although a further six months were to elapse before it actually took place.

Only just over fifty men were named as Booth's helpers, and not all were sentenced. John Werden for example had died in 1647! However Robert was described as *"a most violent enemy"* who had *".....administered general astonishment and terror to the whole county."* There was not enough evidence against Lord Chesterfield and only one man would speak against Thomas Fanshawe of Ware. Sir Thomas Leventhorpe of Hertfordshire had only one accuser, as did John Harris of Devon, named by his own footman. George Philpott was a known Catholic and had left home just before Booth's rising and stayed away for several weeks. Very suspicious thought the Committee, but not hard evidence.

Others were sentenced to sequestration, but closer examination of their affairs showed that their estates had already been seized years before! Finally, only Booth, Werdon, Middleton and Egerton would have been sequestered, but even they were going to retain their personal estates, since the Committee feared *"with good reason.... that the moneys would have been seized by the soldiers."*

It is time to examine why Sir George Booth deserted the Parliamentary cause and took up arms apparently for the King. An examination of his political philosophy shows that he never actually abandoned the principles he had held certainly during the first Civil War. For him, the authority of Parliament was of fundamental importance. It was the fount of all the ancient rights and liberties of the people, but its power and influence had waned drastically, and it was no longer free. Without its authority and protection, Englishmen had no guaranteed rights of property or religion, nor had they any redress of grievance if their rights were infringed.

But how had this state of affairs come about? Charles I had believed in the divine right of Kingship and the people had not enjoyed the freedoms that they might have done in an ideal world. Nevertheless, the case can easily be made that they never really had such freedoms, and in any event the country had been remarkably stable under Oliver Cromwell's Protectorate. However, although Cromwell's death caused hardly a ripple of excitement on the surface (*"the same or a greater calm in the kingdom than had been before"*, as Edward Hyde, Earl of Clarendon, gloomily wrote) the effects were far-reaching.

Richard Cromwell had none of the charisma of his father, and had amassed large debts. As a second Protector, he was useless, and a number of senior Army officers, including John Lambert, John Desborough and Charles Fleetwood, felt that in them was the real power in the country. Nevertheless, when Protector Richard Cromwell faded into Tumbledown Dick and political obscurity, he was succeeded not by the army but by the Council of State, which we have already seen investigating Sir George Booth and his uprising. But although the Council of State had the nominal power, the country was in effect governed by the eleven Major Generals of the Army, each of whom had command in one area of the country. This meant that the Council could operate only at the whim and pleasure of the generals.

It was this arrogant usurpation of power by the Army that Booth detested. If an army was necessary, it had to be an executive arm of the state, subordinate to the government. The government in turn should be a Parliament freely elected by the people, not subject to improper influence, and with a duty to uphold ancient rights, freedoms and privileges enshrined in common law and precedent. These liberties, Booth maintained, should include importantly freedom of individual conscience to worship how one wished, provided of course that it did not threaten the state. such a parliament should in his view consist of surviving members of both houses of parliament, i.e. the so-called Long Parliament of Charles I, or be newly elected.

It is clear that Booth's politics were always very moderate, and were heavily influenced by the views of his late grandfather. Perhaps he had been a firebrand in his younger days when he had personally recruited four regiments of foot to fight against the Royalists, but he had calmed down, and essentially his philosophy had not changed. The changes there had been were in the machinery of government and the abandonment of its old ideals. The rising Booth led was an attempt to restore the status quo with a properly constituted government. He had remained true to his original principles. The Booth leopard had not changed its spots.

The King managed to get a letter of thanks through to him in December, which interestingly foreshadows his later declaration of Breda, allowing tender consciences. The Declaration itself was still four months in the future, so even as early as December Charles must have felt that he still had some grounds for optimism. His letter ran:

*"Your handsome and considerable engagement gave me not only full satisfaction for your earlier actions, but a tender sense of your particular misfortune, and if it shall please God to bless me, neither you nor yours shall ever have cause to repent it.*

*So signall a testimony as you have lately given of your inclinations to me, makes me very willing to encourage the generous returnes of misled persons and to assure them they can no sooner acknowledge their error, than I shall have a value and esteem for them. Your good friend my Lord Mordaunt hath given me a particular account of all your proceedings by which I clearly finde you intended my restoration, and my kingdomes tranquillity, and this induces me to give you the assurance of my being your very affectionate friend, Charles R."*

It is significant that in this letter, dated 16 December, Charles gives advance notice of the Declaration of Breda, still four months in the future, so even then he must have felt that he still had grounds for optimism.

Booth was examined several times and divulged nothing important, but there was no shortage of evidence to put him on trial. The mystery was that there was no move to do so. By January 1660 Booth began to hope for survival after all and petitioned the Committee of Safety for his freedom. He was, he claimed, weak because of fever, bad food and unwholesome air. His family were in want of subsistence, so he asked for the sale of his estates to be suspended and for them to be restored to him on any reasonable terms.

While he was stuck in the Tower, he probably knew nothing of the activities of General George Monck, one of the eleven Major-Generals, and commander of the Army in Scotland. There were curiously close parallels between the political careers and philosophies of Booth and Monck. Both men had fought in the Civil War; neither had played any part in the trial and execution of the King; both had been loyal to Oliver Cromwell, and had no respect at all for Richard; neither had been suspected of being a secret Royalist; both realised at about the same time that the Protectorate had collapsed; and both concluded that to prevent the chaos of another civil war, the 'old order' - the King in Parliament - had to be restored. One, the amateur, failed. The other, the professional, succeeded.

The exiled King had known for some time that Monck was at least not hostile to the idea of monarchy, and that he had done nothing personally that could not be overlooked. Moreover, popular feelings had been slowly changing. The Protectorate experiment had clearly failed, and the more fanatical Puritans had won no friends. There was a general desire for calm and stability and it seemed that only the King could provide it. There was a feeling in the air that it was time for him to return and a few people began to realise it. In January 1660, Lord Ormonde told Henry Jermyn that *"the general disposition of the people ...seems to promise great advantages to the King; four parts of five of the whole people, besides the nobility and the gentry, being devoted to him."*

Perhaps it was this indefinable sense that change would not long be delayed that saved Booth's life. Nothing could have been easier than for the Council of State to arrange a quick trial. It would have been over in a day, the death sentence inevitable, and carried out in a few days at most - just long enough to build the scaffold. But it did not happen. In fact the Rump Parliament was not bloodthirsty and none of Booth's participants were executed.

On New Year's Day 1660 General Monck and his soldiers began their famous march from Scotland to London. Monck had realised that firm action was needed to get rid of the scorned, useless Rump Parliament and the hated, unelected Council of State. There was a real danger of an uncontrolled slide into anarchy and another civil war. Also, his soldiers were long unpaid! There was considerable discontent in the army ranks. Monck had even been asked to sign a petition circulating from other army regions, but had refused. *"It hath been alwaies against my way to sign any petitions at all..."*

In spite of the danger to the Council of State from General Monck, Booth was still in greater danger. On 10 January the House voted to confiscate all the estates of his supporters. Meanwhile however, Percy Church told Secretary Nicholas that *"Monck is courted by all persons and parts of the Kingdom... All is at a stand till the arrival of Monck, which is expected at Barnet next week... Most of the counties have declared for a free Parliament... nothing else will satisfy the people... who begin now openly to drink the King's health."*

Bonfires were lit in London to celebrate his arrival and Samuel Pepys saw them, as he saw most things: *"In King Street, seven or eight; and all along burning or roasting, or drinking for rumps... indeed it was past imagination, both the greatness and the suddenness of it."* The London apprentices caught the excitement and two or three of them were killed demonstrating for the return of a free Parliament. Major General Fleetwood thought it was all managed by the Cavaliers and Booth's supporters, wanting to be avenged for the death of Charles I.

Monck had two objectives, to restore the sovereignty of Parliament and to get pay for his deprived men, but he specifically did not include in his demands the restoration of the monarchy. One of his first acts when he reached London was to force the Rump to readmit to its ranks those members expelled in Pride's Purge. Even so, the Council of State remained obstinately deaf and blind to developments, and as late as 7 February extended the powers of the Commissioners of Sequestration to cover all delinquents in the Booth affair.

Nevertheless, the re-admission of the expelled members was the catalyst for the release from the Tower of Sir George Booth. For at least two months he had been an embarrassment to the authorities. Now their power had virtually ceased to exist. Monck had become the de facto ruler of London, and the newly enlarged Rump Parliament had the overwhelming support of the people. Clearly if there had ever been a suitable time to try and execute Booth, that time was past, and the readmittance to the Commons of the excluded members was enough reason for him to be released.

This indeed was one of the first things they insisted upon, as Pepys remarked, but Booth was instructed to give security on bail of £5000 that he would appear before the excluded members when summoned. This condition, however, was exactly the same as that which would probably have been exacted earlier by his captors.

Booth indignantly refused to agree to any conditions. He had already attempted to do just what the members were now trying to do and any conditions imposed would be illogical and injurious to his honour. If he were to be released, it would be absolute. Seeing him adamant, the members agreed to drop the condition and so Booth was set free on 22 February 1660, after six months uncomfortable imprisonment, to resume his place in society and care for his estates.

He was very soon active again, and Edmund Verney saw him and Sir Thomas Middleton and hoped they would both do well. So did Samuel Pepys, seeing him in Westminster Hall on 2 March. At about the same time the Rump ordered the release of all those concerned in the uprising and quashed the taints of traitor and rebel that had described them.

The future was still very uncertain, and rumours about a future head of state abounded. *"Great is the talk of a single person,"* wrote Samuel Pepys, *"and that it would now be Charles (II), George (Monck), or Richard (Cromwell) again."*

However the Rump Parliament wanted a free election, and dissolved itself. At the same time, the King wrote privately to Monck, diplomatically acknowledging his current power and influence, and stating that he trusted Monck entirely. Monck's reply was typically cautious. He would not commit anything to paper, nor did he openly suggest that it was time for Charles to return. Instead his secret oral message simply advised Charles that as Spain and England were still officially at war, it would be unwise for him to remain in Brussels, which was nominally at least under Catholic sovereignty. Charles took the hint and removed to the neutral town of Breda.

It was from Breda that Charles wrote formally to the Speaker of the House of Commons on 4 April, and issued his famous Declaration of Breda. Perhaps this document above all was most influential in allowing his return, because it was so moderate in tone. Only the actual regicides would suffer his full furious revenge for the death of his father, and all others would have a full and free pardon if they appealed for his grace and favour within forty days. Moreover, religion, like elections, was promised to be free. Charles recognised that different religious opinions had produced discord, and wished wholeheartedly to calm things down. He therefore declared *"a liberty to tender consciences"*. No man was to be *"disquieted or called in question"* on account of his region, provided that it did not threaten the peace of the country *"....we desiring and ordaining that henceforward all notes of discord, separation and difference of parties be utterly abolished among all our subjects, whom we invite and conjure to a perfect union among themselves, under our protection, for the resettlement of our just rights and theirs in a free Parliament, by which, upon the word of a king, we will be advised."*

Charles also recognised that many estates had changed hands legally during the Commonwealth. What would happen if their previous owners demanded restitution? His declaration suggested that Parliament would be the best place to decide such contentious matters. These bold statements of intent were precisely what Sir George Booth had been campaigning for. The restoration of the monarchy it seemed was necessary to bring about the reforms, both religious and political, that he had desired for many years and had risked his life and fortune for.

The King's letter and his Declaration of Breda were read out in the Commons on 1 May, and on the same day they passed an official resolution desiring the King to return to his native land as its reigning monarch. Sir George Booth's efforts on behalf of the King were recognised by his being in the official delegation from the Houses of Lords and Commons to go to the Hague with a navy escort to fetch the king home again after his exile of 15 years. When they arrived in the King's presence, Booth was honoured by being the first to kiss hands with His Majesty.

On the day they left, Booth found time to drop a quick line to General Monck, reminding him politely of a promise he had made to find a place for one Maior (sic) Harrison, perhaps the same Reverend Harrison, Rector of Cheadle, who had paid £4 rather than be plundered. Harrison was accompanying Booth and Booth feared that he might suffer by his absence, *"that yr Excellencies many businesses may make him out of yr memory, & so he may come short of the favour you intend him."*

That day, Samuel Pepys was overwhelmed with work, but had time to delight in the aristocratic company he was keeping, and the pleasure of hearing the 30 gun salute from Dover Castle as the fleet sailed majestically past. Charles' official welcome in England after 12 years exile was marked by huge pomp and ceremony. He reviewed many of the great nobles and gentry of the country, each with his own troop of horse. The Duke of Buckingham, the Earls of Cleveland, Oxford and Warwick, and Lord Mordaunt, newly ennobled, were just a few of the peers, and Sir George Booth was in the company of his old friends Sir Horatio Townsend and Sir Humphrey Townsend among many others. *"....the brave horses, rich sadled, evry man with a feather in his cape, foot men in rich*

The fortunes of the Booths was intimately involved with those of the Stuart dynasty.

Sir George Booth, the First Lord Delamer, was present at Charles II's arrival at Dover (above), he visited London with his friend Reverend Newcome in 1666 to see the aftermath of the Great Fire (left), and like the good Presbyterian he was, soon became disenchanted with Charles, his court and his many mistresses
(below: Charles and Nell Gwynn).

*liveryes and the great atendance that waighted* (on) *his Majesty..."*

The arrival of Charles II marked the beginning of a deluge of requests and petitions from hosts of people who claimed that they had supported him, tried to help him and in many cases suffered for him during his absence. They had apparently good reason to hope for reward or at least recompense, as he was *"very graciously intending such ...as shall really find to have corresponded with the Lord General* (Monck) *or Sir George Booth in order to His Maties restoration shall reap the fruit of his grace and goodness towards them."* Most applicants were doomed to disappointment, however.

There were over 140 requests for Church preferment alone. Over forty petitions referred to hardships suffered during or after Booth's uprising, and asked for recompense or preferment. Some applicants were obviously no-hopers, such as John Stone, who claimed merely that he had served under Charles I and *"armed a man under Sir George Booth"* and William Bruce who alleged that Charles I had promised him a viscountcy

Others had stronger cases. The Reverend Joshua Stopford had done excellent service as chaplain to Booth's army and by preaching to them. He wanted to be Prebendary of Normanton and provided a certificate of recommendation from Booth. Others, such as John Cross, John Dowthwaite and the Reverend Samuel Cryer had been engaged in the 1659 uprising and petitioned for minor posts as rewards.

Others had harrowing stories to relate and lost no time in doing so. Mary Groves petitioned on behalf of her husband, who had lost an estate of £600 per annum and £2000 after the Battle of Worcester; Malcolm Smith had been 32 weeks in the notorious Gatehouse Prison in Westminster and was starving; Sir Gervase Lucas was *"ruined by eighteen months in prison"*; John Aylett had been 20 weeks a prisoner *"on Sir George Booth's business"*; and the late William Gery, according to his daughter Anne Dartiguenave, *"was himself plundered to his shirt and imprisoned"* for following Booth, and Anne herself *"was left to inherit nothing but sadness."*

Samuel Terrick related how he had been wounded in the Battle of Winnington Bridge, his estates had been confiscated, his house plundered and himself imprisoned. George Duke had lived on *"pump water and pottage"* in prison for five months, until his release in April 1647 *"half dead and naked."* Even then he had stayed loyal to the Royalist cause, sent secret reports on Cromwell's Council, and raised 500 men for Booth. It is pleasant to see from the State Papers that he was granted his petition as Secretary to the intended Council for Trade, with ample opportunity to restore his lost finances!

Not everyone was as successful. Henry Millett was the owner and commander of a small ship, *The Judith*, which had been carrying weapons to the Booth insurrection. On 1 September 1659 he was captured and imprisoned and his ship confiscated. Could he have his ship back please? He would even pay £16 for the cost of feeding his crew. He was out of luck. By June 1660 when he petitioned, his ship was long disposed of.

Many were quite modest in their requests. John Greeneway had *"suffered much under Sir George Booth"*, but merely wanted to remain as Postmaster in Crewkerne, as did William Carter in St Asaph. Major John Harlinge wanted only a position of £40 a year as consolation for being captured and imprisoned for 67 weeks after the Battle of Worcester. Lt Col Thomas Egerton, who had served the Royalist cause from the beginning of the Civil War right through until 1659 and had personally saved the Royalist Standard from capture at Dorchester, just wanted his old place in the Privy Chamber. Captain Joseph Smyth claimed to be entitled to a pension of £5, but it had been docked under a false claim that he had served under Cromwell, whereas he had left the army rather than fight against the King. Moreover, he had been put in prison for desertion and lost £26. His testimony was superb; 9 'gentlemen' and 27 other officers certified that Smyth had assisted the King's cause by helping men who had served under Sir George Booth. His pension was restored and he was given £5 in hand.

And Sir John Booth, Sir George's uncle, recounted his personal losses: £2000 and his horses when he was Governor of Warrington; £6374 (precisely!) when he was put into the Tower; £1800 in *"Lord Wilmot's business"*; £3750 in plate and jewels stolen by his *"fanatick wife"* when he supported his nephew in 1659; and miscellaneous debts of £2300. He petitioned for part restitution, or a baronetcy, or the lease of the Manor of Berkhamstead, but the State Papers are silent about his success.

Many requests were not intended to be considered by the King, but were much more appropriate to be dealt with at local level, such as petitions for promised pay. John Ingham of Millington served under Captain Davis, but the township refused to pay him without an order from the Cheshire Justices. William Whiteley of Northenden was responsible for arranging four soldiers for Booth's army, under the command of Colonel Legh of Adlington, each of them to be paid £3 10s. They were given arms and £1 15s on account, but Whiteley could not afford to pay them the remainder. The soldiers were suing him and he asked that the arrears be paid by the people of Northenden.

Adlington and Thomas Legh cropped up again in January 1661. Adlington had a quota of soldiers to provide for and promised £3 to Robert Adshead and Thomas Burges, who agreed to enlist themselves for the village. At the end of their service they were discharged and asked for their money *"yett the said Inhabitants have hitherto denied and refused to make paym't thereof and still doe refuse to doe the same, against all right equitie and good conscience and to the great loss and hindrance of your petitioners."*

A final example is the case of Thomas Mason of Dutton who was captured and taken to Chester after the battle. He was told he was *"an impudent rogue"* for claiming that he had been sent by Lady Kilmorey to join Booth, but even Sir George Booth said that Mason joined up quite voluntarily. When Mason was put on trial, the JP, Mr Gerrard, jokingly said he would be hanged without mercy. When Mason smiled, Gerrard fined him 4s on the spot! Gerrard's sense of humour seems rather grim. When he ordered the constable of Stretton to arrest escapers from the Battle of Winnington, they were to be shot on sight, and any house they sheltered in was to be burnt forthwith.

For at least a decade the petitions kept coming in. In 1665 Robert Calcott killed Henry Banastre in a fight. Although it was in self defence, he was sentenced to death, but the Countess of Derby enlisted the help of 17 Cheshire Justices on the grounds that Calcott had been active in the Booth affair and had only just avoided being hanged then. He was reprieved. Three years later, Ben Coling asked for a Waiter's place in the Custom's House, having been *"often in prison on Sir George Booth's business."* And in 1670 it was reported that Charles White of Derbyshire had been *"long kept in loathsome restraint and his whole estate seized and embezzled, for associating with Sir George Booth to promote the Restoration."*

Some people took the opportunity to settle old scores and reported on the activities of known Parliamentarians. William Downes had been a Cromwellian Roundhead trooper and had searched stables in Hereford with the object of concealing horses from people likely to support Booth. A Dorset Vicar, one John Wesley, had been *"diabolically railing in the pulpit against the later king.... rejoicing at Sir George Booth's defeat."* William Stevens of Chippenham had always taken the Parliament side. After the Battle of Worcester, he had rejoiced that *"the rogues are routed."* Moreover he had stolen mail to Bristol and given it to Cromwellian soldiers *"to the great prejudice of Bristol people."*

And in Cheshire the gentry torpedoed any hopes that Thomas Stanley of Alderley may have had, by certifying that he was disloyal to the crown, that he had indicted supporters of Booth for High Treason, and that he was unworthy of a baronetcy.

The King was bombarded with so many requests that most had no real hope of success. His finances could not have stood the strain, even before his string of mistresses began their careers of extraordinary rapacity. Only those who had powerful influence could realistically hope for even quite minor grants. Booth himself gave certificates of proof of service to Richard Arscott who had served under him and mortgaged his estates to do so, and to James Stevens, who had been imprisoned.

Some who had given conspicuous service were, however, justly rewarded. At one end of the scale, Sir Edward Hyde became the mighty Earl of Clarendon, and at the other end, the Penderel brothers received pensions from which their descendants benefit to this day. As for Sir George Booth, on 20 April 1661, he was granted the style and title of Lord Delamer of Dunham Massey, with *"two bores (sic) sable, armed and bristled"* as the supporters of his coat of arms. His wife Elizabeth had the right to retain the rights and privileges of an earl's daughter, her father being Henry, 1st Earl of Stamford.

Even more substantial for Delamer was the cash grant of £10,000 from the King. Charles originally offered £20,000, but Delamer was either too altruistic or suspected the true state of the royal finances and only agreed to accept half the sum.

Booth quickly faded out from public life. The petitions for relief mentioned his name for years, but he seems to have spent the rest of his life quietly at Court or Dunham. He asked for and received a full royal pardon for any possible misdeeds during the 1659 uprising, just in case... *"of which Wee will ever retaine a very particular sense, as more especially in justification of him, for what hee did and acted in Order to our happy Restauration.... to declare that the same was done, acted and commanded by him in vertue of Our said Commission."* (empowering him to raise Cheshire and the Northwest.) The Reverend Henry Newcome saw him once a month at Dunham and in the first years at least of Charles' reign, he was enjoying life. He played bowls: *"In bowling greene with Lord Delamer till five, & it raininge ye gentry were driven off ye greene."*

The death of his eldest son William aged only 13 in February 1662 affected him deeply. For some weeks his grief was uncontrollable. Henry Newcome, who knew him well, commented that his condition was very sad. A man in his position should know himself thoroughly, his sins, temper, grace and assurances, but as it was he was *"sorely afflicted with melancholy and little better than distraction."* As late as August, Newcome and Martindale spent hours with him trying to offer consolation. Even when he was recovering, he could be very moody and Newcome learned that it was wise to speak to Delamer's family in private *"lest he should have taken hold of them to his further disturbance, because of his distemper."*

In 1662, he was *"pretty cheerful"* and *"very fair and noble and pious."* Newcome spent several days at Dunham in the summer of 1664 and wrote that *"There were great store of gentlemen and gallants, and nightly entertainments."* Newcome's Puritan soul did not really approve of these jollifications, for he believed that rich and poor could both enjoy contented lives according to their stations. As for Lord Delamer, *"he is bound hugely to be thankful for all these things, and he also that can do without them."*

Delamer remained a firm believer in government by Parliament. Unfortunately Charles grew increasingly disgusted with his Parliaments for not acceding to the royal will. When he first came to the throne he spoke lovingly of his Parliament, and declared that neither King nor Parliament could function properly without the other. However this cosy relationship did not last, because Charles was nervous about the possibility of a new revolution, while Parliaments were equally worried about the return of absolutism.

The King dissolved the Cavalier Parliament in December 1678, paving the way the following February for the first General Election to be held in 18 years. The King was no easier with the new Commons, especially in the difficulty over the succession to the throne. Charles was in robust health, but Queen Catherine had not produced an heir, and the country as a whole was against the King's brother, James, Duke of York. Parliament went so far as to prepare a Bill of Exclusion, which would have effectively removed James from the line of succession, and not surprisingly aroused the King's fury.

He dared not antagonise the Commons too far and suggested to James that he should leave England temporarily until the fuss died down. At the same time he showed the iron hand in the velvet glove to the new Commons by announcing that he would accept any law that might preserve their religion provided that there was no interference with the descent of the crown in the direct line. This did not satisfy the Commons and the Exclusion Bill received its second reading in May 1679, whereupon Charles used another of his weapons, that of prorogation. The Commons duly went on enforced holiday, supposedly until August, but in July the King dissolved Parliament altogether, fearing that if the Exclusion Bill passed, Monmouth's supporters would put him forward .

So another General Election was held. But Charles was beset by difficulties - more revelations about an alleged Popish plot; the impeachment of the Earl of Danby, his Lord Treasurer, the open hostility of the Earl of Shaftesbury, the problems over his brother James and his son, Monmouth - and the King decided not to meet his new Parliament at all. He went further by announcing that Parliament would not actually meet until January 1680, and then, in the middle of his secret negotiations with France, which he thought might even obviate the need for it, he indicated that Parliament would not meet until November 1680. This was too much for the House of Lords. On 6 December sixteen senior peers, led by the Earl of Huntingdon, submitted an address to the King. They included the Earls of Shaftesbury and Stamford, Lord Saye and Seal, Lord Grey of Warke and Lord Delamer, who unanimously petitioned for Parliament to sit. Delamer had a particular interest, as his son Henry had been elected Member for the county.

*"Sir,     We... do humbly beg that your Majesty would consider the great danger your royal person is in, as also the Protestant religion, and the government of these your nations. We humbly pray that in a time wherein all these are so highly concerned, you Majesty will effectually use your great councils, the Parliament. Sir, out of the deepest sense of duty and loyalty to your Majesty, we offer it as our humble advice and earnest petition, that the Parliament may sit at the time appointed, and that your Majesty would be graciously pleased to give public notice and assurance thereof, that the minds of your Majesty's subjects may be settled and their fears removed."*

There can be no more sincere proof of Delamer's devotion to the principle of a constitution of the King in Parliament than this petition.

The question of money crops up frequently in the family papers, and it seems as if Delamer never quite recovered from having to mortgage his estates in 1659. Also, his financial plans for his daughters were far too ambitious for a man of no more than comfortably moderate means, indicating that he had no great understanding of money matters. His difficulties began in November 1660, when he consolidated the two existing £3000 mortgages, but it cost him £454-10-0 to do so. In 1671 he transferred large parts of his estates to trustees to raise a marriage portion for his eldest daughter Vere, by Lady Katherine, his first wife. Then in 1680 he decided to arrange financial security for Elizabeth and Diana, his daughters by Elizabeth. Again he over-reached himself. Elizabeth was engaged to the Earl of Conway and Delamer arranged a portion of £5000 for her and £5000 for her sister, who was to marry Sir Ralph Delaval of Seaton Delaval.

Adam Martindale, chaplain to the family was privately opposed to the arrangements and in particular to what Delamer was willing to concede. He thought that they were unreasonable and unaffordable, and importantly they made no mention of any refund in the unfortunate event of Elizabeth's early death or her inability to have children.

Delamer was clearly bent on climbing the social ladder, at least vicariously through Elizabeth, and Conway was after all a Secretary of State and the Deputy Lord Lieutenant of Ireland, second to the Marquis of Ormonde, and an important man in his own right. Other people recognised Delamer's ambitions, not to mention his lack of judgement, and a cynical and anonymous report said of Conway that his *"celebrated virtue and honour renders Lord Delamer more ambitious of his alliance than the other, though great, charms of honour, family and fortune."*

Even if the praise of Conway was sincere, his main concern was to establish that he was not about to marry into a family with any suspicion of taint. Obviously he knew that Delamer was a peer of first creation, that his reputation rested on his unsuccessful deeds of twenty years before, and that he was of a family of relatively minor provincial gentry. But he had also heard scurrilous rumours. Was Delamer perhaps losing his reason? If so, it would be disastrous for the marriage. Cautiously, he commissioned confidential reports, which, if Delamer had got wind of, would have made him break off instantly.

As it was, the reports were complimentary, even flattering. Hamilton Mawson claimed 25 or 30 years acquaintance with the family. It was *"more ancient than most in the country where he lives, and as to the reflections on his lordship and his family, I stand amazed at their impudency.... Such reports... must certainly be mere malice... there not being a person of more honour than the lady's father."* Another report, by one John Tattersall, dismissed any possible imputation on Delamer's sanity. *"As for the lord being mad, there was never such a thing spoke of."*

Elizabeth Booth herself was very well spoken of. She was *"a proper, comely lady and fine-skinned. The only thing in her person is her nose being a little too high and sometimes red"* according to C. Magenis. Tattersall also agreed that she was *"comely and virtuous."* Adam Martindale, who was in the best position to judge, said she was religious and virtuous, and far too good for Conway, whom he disliked and distrusted. Elizabeth herself was very pleased at the prospect of marriage to Conway, and was more than a little in love with him. She replied to a letter from him: *"Your lines bringing me fresh evidence of the place I hold in your memory give me freedom of returning your thanks, with this addition, that your thoughts are not more often here than mine with you."*

She became pregnant very soon after the wedding and told her mother the good news as soon as she was sure. Lady Delamer was naturally delighted and wrote to Conway congratulating him. His new wife, she said, *"will make you as happy in the relation God has made her to you now as she has ever been to me and her father."* Sadly, this was not to be. Early in July 1680, Elizabeth, Countess of Conway, died after giving birth to a dead baby. Martindale was very scornful about Conway, who *"was proling at Court in a gainfull office for money"* when she died. He would not even attend her funeral on the grounds that his grief was too great. In fact *"this excessively mournful Lord",* as Martindale described him, was not exactly inconsolable, and found comfort in the arms of *"a young airie lady"* and re-married in five weeks. He even proved that Martindale's suspicions were right by refusing to refund Elizabeth's portion to Delamer. He kept half of it and agreed only that the other £5000 would go towards Diana's portion.

Perhaps Delamer's depression dates from this time. Apart from his unmarried daughter Vere by his first wife, Catherine Fiennes, Elizabeth had given him no fewer than twelve children, from 1648 onwards. But three girls, Anne, Jane and Sophia had died in infancy, his eldest son William was 13 when he died in 1662, and his third son Charles had died in France in 1675, not long after Delamer had hosted a glittering party at Dunham with Lord Denbigh, the Crewes, the Cholmondeleys, various Breretons and Mainwarings, and the Bishop of Chester to lend tone to the proceedings.

Before and after his elevation to the peerage, Booth did much to help his friends. Reverend Henry Newcome, had been a minister in Manchester for some years, but had no official stipend and depended uncertainly on a proportion of the tithes. He was considered suitable for a Fellowship of the Collegiate Church, which was headed by a Warden, Mr Richard Heyricke. The College had been founded by Charles I. By the time of Charles II's restoration there were three vacancies in the four places. The King began by granting the three vacant Fellowships to five men! This was clearly an impossible situation, so he cancelled two. It was feared that the King might easily select one of the two incomers, and over four hundred citizens of Manchester signed a petition to the King in favour of Newcome. He had been *"for these several years past as one of our ministers, and unanimously and freely chosen to the place; who is a man of a sober and peaceable temper and demeanour, eminently qualified for the work of the ministry. He hath been in his laborious preaching, and by his exemplary pious conversation, a successful instrument of much good unto us; and one who hath signally owned your majesty's cause, running the utmost hazards with us."*

Sir George Booth willingly agreed to present the petition to the King, with his personal recommendation. Charles was reluctant to issue his warrant, but agreed to add his weight to the request. With this somewhat doubtful help, Booth went to Lord Clarendon, the Chancellor, and asked him to halt all proceedings at least for the time being. Things were beginning to look up for Newcome and Booth diplomatically arranged for the Manchester gentry to write a thank you letter to the Chancellor. He sent a progress report back to Newcome. *"...I have spoke both to* (the Chancellor) *and Secretary Morrice; who both promise their endeavours to persuade some of the fellows of Manchester to accept the prebend of York designed for you and to release the fellowship they now have unto your hands. But before I would proceed, I did desire to have an account from you of all the new fellows; what other benefices they have, and which of them you apprehend may be the easiest persuaded to exchange..."*

Newcome doubted that any of the new Fellows would willingly resign: Mr Johnson, being fair-minded and living in London, might just be persuaded. When Booth eventually received the information in February 1661, he again badgered Clarendon and Morrice, but it was too late for Newcome to get his Fellowship. As compensation Newcome was awarded a prebend from the Province of York, which was perhaps more important to him than the Fellowship because it gave him the financial security he needed.

Delamer took his friend Newcome in 1667 to London to see the sights. The city was only starting its slow recovery from the Great Fire of the previous year and Newcome was dismayed at the *"woeful spectacle of that ruinous heap."*

In about 1672 Lord Delamer appointed the Reverend Adam Martindale as his family's chaplain and instantly struck a good rapport with him. Martindale's duties were not arduous. He was only required to attend when Delamer was in residence and Delamer was in the habit of spending the winter in London, so Martindale normally attended only from May until October or November. His pay was based on his attendances, so the maximum of £40 a year was usually only £20 or so, often even less. Martindale never quibbled, although his expenses for clothing etc were considerable, because *"as things were the salary was as much as was ever promised me, and truely paid; yea, and noble for the time I attended, and such as (I question not) many a worthier person would have beene glad of."*

Martindale was quite busy when the family was in residence at Dunham. He was expected to undertake family duty twice a day, and before dinner he would give a prayer, read a chapter from the Bible, and then give a longer prayer before the dinner was served. Then before supper, he had to read another chapter from the Bible, followed by a psalm. One hopes that the meals were not actually congealing on the table while these services took place! On Sundays of course, full services took place in the family chapel, involving long sermons. But in addition to this ecclesiastical work, he was often expected to accompany Delamer on his local journeys around the county, so his chaplaincy work was not exactly a sinecure.

Martindale was unwilling to sign the Act of Uniformity and so was ineligible to be a parish priest or curate. Having time on his hands, he undertook private tuition, although there was considerable opposition to him from such bigots as Sir Peter Leicester of Tabley, who disapproved strongly of self-confessed non-conformists being engaged as tutors in society families. Martindale needed to learn some mathematics himself however, knowing only basic arithmetic and a little about decimals. Lord Delamer had a good knowledge of the subject, and was happy to give Martindale private coaching. So Martindale *"fell close to the studie of decimalls in a more artificial manner, logarithms, algebra and other arts ...in which work I was encouraged and assisted by my noble Lord Delamer, who gave me many excellent books and instruments, lent me his choicest manuscripts, imparted freely any knowledge he had, and (which was as useful as anything else) put me upon answering hard and tedious questions...."*

Lord Delamer's last involvement in contentious politics was from his point of view involuntary and unwelcome. By 1682 he was in his 60th year, feeling his age and generally content to stay in his home county, entertaining and being entertained by his friends. In September of that year, His Grace the Duke of Monmouth came to Cheshire, and by the actions of his son Henry, Delamer was plunged against his will into events that threatened disaster to him and his family. Monmouth was the eldest son of Charles II. He was young, handsome, athletic and charismatic. Charles James Fox later described him as *"in the bloom of youth, with a beautiful figure, and engaging manners, known to be the darling of the Monarch"*. Even at sixteen, he was *"the most skittish, leaping gallant"* that Samuel Pepys had ever seen, *"alway in action, vaulting, leaping, or clambering."*

At first the King could deny him nothing. He was Duke of Monmouth and Buccleuch, Earl of Doncaster, Earl of Dalkeith, Baron Fotheringay, Baron Tynedale, Knight of the Most Noble Order of the Garter, a Master of Arts of Cambridge and Oxford Universities, Captain of His Majesty's Life Guards of Horse, Lord High Chamberlain of Scotland, Commissioner of the Admiralty, Master of the Horse, Chancellor of Cambridge University, Lord Lieutenant of Staffordshire and Captain-General of all troops and land forces to be raised in England and Wales. And moreover he was the darling of the people, and that was to prove his downfall - and nearly also Lord Delamer's.

Monmouth suffered from one insuperable disadvantage. Despite being the King's eldest son, he could never constitutionally inherit the throne because of course he was illegitimate, being the product of Charles' liaison with Lucy Walters during the early years of his exile. In the continued absence of any legitimate heir, and Queen Catherine seemed to be barren, the next king would be Charles' younger brother, James Duke of York, who was deeply unpopular because of his open Catholicism.

Monmouth began to lose favour with his father; he lost the post of Captain-General, petulantly resigned command of the Guards and went into temporary exile on the Continent. He returned without the King's permission to show that he was no traitor and was not privy to the Popish plot. The King was furious and banned him from the Court.

It is likely that the fires of rebellion were beginning to stir in the young Duke, in spite of his protests to the contrary.  His travels in the north west were ostensibly in order to indulge in one of his favourite sports, horse racing, but in all probability his real purpose was to cement his support in Staffordshire and Cheshire, where he knew he was very popular and had many influential friends.  He received a tumultuous welcome wherever he went, and the journey had all the flavour of an official royal progress.

He spent the evening and night of Friday 14 September at Dunham Massey, on the invitation of Henry Booth, Lord Delamer's eldest son. (See chapter 3)  He was treated like the royalty he was.  Henry ordered the servants and tenants to form a double rank guard of honour as he walked from his horse to the hall. Whatever the private feelings of the tenants, they dared not risk incurring their master's displeasure, either at Dunham Massey or at Gawsworth Hall a day or two later, where he had a similar welcome.

Monmouth dined in public in the Great Hall with Henry Booth and over 40 other notables, and the tenants were allowed to file in through one door and out of the other so that they could goggle at the great man. Others clustered at the windows, shouting *"A Monmouth, a Monmouth!"* and were, it was alleged, given pieces of blue ribbon to wear as tokens of their allegiance.

Even more seriously, it was said that a list was made of the names of Monmouth's chief supporters. This was potentially a very grave development. Was young Monmouth thinking seriously of usurping the throne for himself, in defiance of his uncle James? Was it a list of those who could be counted on to take his side in the event of open rebellion?  Clearly, anyone whose name appeared on the alleged list, or who gave him more the usual hospitality called for by gentlemanly good manners, could be considered potentially disloyal, and this could be fatal for the culprit.

Lord Delamer had been put into a highly embarrassing and potentially dangerous position by his son's behaviour.  Monmouth's journey through Staffordshire and Cheshire, accompanied as he was by a 20-strong retinue, was far more than a normal visit, and the welcome he received from Henry Booth was more rapturous and deferential than would have been called for by ordinary politeness.

Delamer might have let the matter pass, but Sir Leoline Jenkins, Secretary of State, was actively trying to discover those who were definitely loyal to the King and those who were likely to be disaffected.  To this end, he had a network of informers, among whom was Delamer's near neighbour, Sir Robert Leicester of Tabley.  Leicester, as a Justice of the Peace, had dutifully reported everything to Jenkins - the welcome, the ribbons, the listing of names - but without the courtesy of letting Delamer know, although he was friend and neighbour.  Delamer heard of Leicester's actions, but was ill with gout at the time, so Elizabeth his wife wrote on his behalf to Lord Conway for his advice.  Conway told Jenkins that Delamer flatly denied giving out ribbons or taking any kind of register, and was *"very hot upon it to justify himself."*

Conway then admitted that he had no personal knowledge of the events.  He wrote to Lady Delamer that he had been otherwise informed about the matter of the ribbons. He then suggested to Jenkins that Delamer should be invited to produce any relevant documents, because it would be impossible to conceal any list of Monmouth supporters. Understandably indignant, Delamer was left with no option but to state his case formally and publicly proclaim his innocence.  His letter bristles with stiff outrage.

*"Dunham Massey, 6 October.*

*Myself being at present much afflicted by gout, particularly in my hands, my wife last week acquainted Lord Conway that I had been affronted by a neighbouring justice pretending authority from you.  All my design by that letter was only to keep the thing in mind till God enabled me to write you the particulars, but I find by a letter from Lord Conway that he and you have had discourse about it, that you own the authority given, having been informed that I had given ribbons to many thousands of young men, and had taken their names in writing.... I pretend to so much learning as to know what the law thinks of those that list men without the King's authority.*

*My loyalty being thus attacked, it will be no strange thing to a person of your great loyalty to hear that I am resolved to the utmost to defend it and to this purpose, when I have strength to crawl to London, you must expect a letter desiring you to supplicate his Majesty to appoint a day that before him in Council my accusers and I may appear that... I may be either publicly condemned or publicly absolved...."*

Unfortunately Jenkins' answers have not survived, but their content is clear from Delamer's letters.  It seems that Jenkins did not read Delamer's first letter carefully enough and accused him of things he had not even written.  Delamer replied indignantly on 18 October, only four days after the date of Jenkins' letter: *"...if you peruse my letter again, you will not find so much as the mention of the words arbitrary and illegal nor any charge against you...  All my design was, and still is, to declare a resolve of justifying my own loyalty.  This, I hope, cannot offend any."*

Jenkins apparently tried to dissuade Delamer, but his truthfulness was in question, in addition to his loyalty, and he returned to the fray: *"...I am not to be affrighted from bringing this affair to a trial.  The first of next month I design to begin my journey towards London, though very unfit for such a voyage and very doubtful how I shall be able to endure it...."*

Jenkins did not even bother to answer, so Delamer went to London in spite of his poor health.  He was determined to have a formal hearing, because Leicester had openly enquired into the events at Dunham Massey and particularly questioned one of Delamer's servants.  With such open investigation, the news would be bound to fly around the county that he, Lord Delamer, was under suspicion for disloyalty and perhaps even for treason, and he would not tolerate such high-handed conduct from his neighbour, a fellow justice: *"With God's goodness and no little difficulty I am come to this town and....  I must entreat you to solicit his Majesty that Sir Robert Leicester of Tabley particularly and whoever else have made any complaint of me to his Majesty may be summoned to make good their complaints before him in Council, that so they or I may have public punishment and shame, where it may prove due."*

This persuaded Jenkins to action and he spoke to the King about the matter. Unfortunately for Delamer, the King gave it only cursory attention before telling Jenkins that Leicester had done nothing to justify being summoned before him, and that if Lord Delamer still considered that Leicester had exceeded his authority as a JP, then he had a remedy at law. Delamer was very affronted at this treatment and replied in hurt tones, very much on his high horse: *"...since I find I am become so despicable and unfortunate that my loyalty, credit and what else can be dear to me is of so very little account with his Majesty, you shall have no more trouble for this affair from me."*

So, not being allowed to get justice or to clear his name by proving his innocence, Delamer wanted to close the episode, unsatisfactory though this course was to him. However Jenkins and Leicester were still suspicious. There was no doubt at all of the political allegiance of Henry Booth; his home was at Mere, close to Dunham Massey and to Tabley; his father had once famously changed sides. Was he doing so again? Did he protest his innocence too much? And was rebellion again being plotted in Cheshire? Jenkins and Leicester looked only at the obvious facts, and paid no attention to Delamer's public record of always supporting the principle of the King in Parliament. As far as they could see, Delamer was a grave potential danger and needed deeper investigation.

One way of finding out was to search the houses of the Booth's tenants. If arms were to be found, it would be almost conclusive proof that rebellion was being planned and that the Booths were deeply implicated. Moreover, even the absence of any arms would not in itself prove that there was no plot, merely either that they had not yet been acquired, or that they had been safely hidden. But to make a search at that time would probably be premature, as Leicester realised. Yes, he could search and disarm as necessary, but it would surely give the game away. In any case, a previous search of Henry Booth's house had revealed nothing except three cases of pistols, suspicious perhaps, but nothing unusual for a gentleman.

Leicester could not with certainty rely on the personal loyalty of the searchers, his own tenants. The word would fly around the county faster than any search, and any remaining arms would be securely hidden away, as they probably had been already. The alleged plotters would be free to continue their dastardly plans, safe from any official interference, and the danger they posed would be even greater. The only effective intelligence would be to question blacksmiths if they had been commissioned to forge quantities of weaponry. Jenkins saw the point and decided not to take any further action just then, but it is safe to assume that the matter remained in his mind.

Delamer's financial problems plagued him until he died. He spent only about half the year at Dunham, sometimes even less, leaving for London in October or November, and not returning until about May. His expenses were always heavy, especially in London, where he would be expected to live and entertain in a manner befitting his station. Even in Cheshire he enjoyed a busy social life, made more hectic and tiring by the problems of travelling on roads that were hot and dusty in summer and deep in mud during the winter. In the spring and early summer of 1681, when he was getting elderly, he found himself at least once a week dining in company with Sir Willoughby Aston at Dunham and at Aston's house, or with his old friends the Mainwarings. He was often to be found at Mere with his son Henry (who was usually racing). Others in his circle were the Earl and Countess of Derby and Lord Brandon, the son of the Earl of Macclesfield and a close friend of Henry. The death of poor Elizabeth so soon after her marriage to the Earl of Conway obviously broke this social scene for a while, but by July 1681 the dinner parties were starting again.

Martindale was in a good position to understand Delamer's finances, and he explained the situation as follows: *"...having parted with so great a share of their estate to their eldest sonne, and being still to bring up five sonnes more in a costly way of education, and otherwise to provide for them, and three daughters, which must have great portions, and my Lord's attending the Parliament, or pursuing other business every winter at London, was so exceedingly costly, what could be saved fairely must not be expended. It would have been some hundreds of pounds advantage if they had staid at home all the yeare; and I doubt not my Lady would have beene well content...."*

1671 had been a particularly expensive year. It began in May, when the marriage of his eldest surviving son Henry caused him to protect his own wife's position if he should die unexpectedly. He therefore arranged a settlement for her which would provide a steady income for her during her lifetime, and simultaneously, he put property in to the hands of trustees to raise a portion of no less than £6000 for Vere, his eldest daughter - who remained unmarried until her death in 1717.

There was also Henry to consider. His marriage in 1671 to Mary, the daughter of Sir James Langham, had already taken place without benefit of prior legal arrangements about portions, but a gentlemen's agreement existed between Langham and Delamer. By this, Langham was paying £10,000 as Mary's portion, with another £10,000 in the event of his death, but Delamer for his part had to organise an annuity of £400 for her by placing more property in trust.

In 1680, four years before his death, he was forced to arrange portions for Diana and Elizabeth, and by then large parts of his estates were mortgaged. Staley (Stalybridge), Matley, Tintwistle and Saddleworth were followed by Carrington, Ashton on Mersey, Partington and Sinderland, and Thornton le Moors followed in September. Even the core property of Dunham Massey Park and Hall were not immune. They were transferred to trustees in 1680 as part of the settlement to provide the jointure for Henry's wife, Mary, security for Lady Delamer in her widowhood, and annuities of £50 each for Henry's younger brothers George, Robert, Neville and Cecil.

Lord Delamer now in his early 60s was very gouty, full of melancholy and devoting most of his time to study. The pain in his hands and feet was ascribed to gout, but this was a catch-all diagnosis common in the medicine of the time and could well have been any form of arthritis. The melancholy is not surprising bearing in mind the debts on the estates, coupled with the fact that he had never been allowed to clear his name. A late period portrait of him hangs in the National Gallery of South Australia. Delamer is shown to the waist, looking pensively to his right. His hair or wig is past shoulder-length, and he wears a neatly trimmed moustache. His eyes are clear, but his expression is of great sadness, reflecting the melancholy of his latter years. His depression was made no easier to bear by the problem of Henry's future.

Charles II was of course still alive, but the question of his successor loomed large and Delamer was in no doubt which way Henry would jump when the King died. He would certainly not favour the Duke of York and treason was a dreadful possibility. Delamer himself had never wavered in his belief that the English constitution should be the King in Parliament. He had fought for it in the Civil War, had risked his life and fortune for it prematurely in 1659, and had petitioned for it only four years before.

He died in August 1684 at the age of 62. Adam Martindale had two good reasons to regret his passing, *"the unspeakable loss of my deare and faithfull friend my noble lord Delamer, together with all hopes of employment at Dunham"*, from which it appears that Henry did not share his father's friendship with Martindale. Martindale was not alone in his sorrow. Sir John Arden in Stockport wrote a private letter to his friend Sir John Crewe of Utkinton in extravagant praise of Delamer: *"....the tragedy of my good Ld Delamer's death; a virtuous prudent gentleman and my assured good friend.... I never did nor can love any Lord soe well as I loved him..."*

Henry Booth shared the grief at his father's death, although he did not arrange for a memorial to be erected in Bowdon Church. Perhaps he could not afford it, but in any event it was left to William Andrews, the family steward. This monumental inscription was unfortunately not replaced after the restoration of the Church in the last century, but the wording has survived.

> *"Under this monument are interred the remains of George, Lord Delamer, Baron of the ancient and noble house of Dunham Massey, who was distinguished by his piety, fidelity, and affection to God, King and Country, and who in the sixty-second year of his age exchanged an earthly coronet for a celestial crown, and died on the 10th day of August, in the year of our Salvation 1684. William Andrews, deploring the death of his most honourable Lord (in whose service he had continued for upwards of thirty years, faithfully emulating and partaking in the loyalty which his master showed to his King), this monument to his ever-blessed and happy memory has been erected, consecrated, and preserved, and a hope added that when his life at the same time with his official duty to that noble family came to an end, at the entrance to this tomb his ashes might rest, until the day when they might rise, together with those of his master, into the new and eternal life.*
>
> *Died 25th July 1685."*

Lord Delamer left the residue of his estate to his wife after deductions of £5 to each surviving child, but this was not enough. She insisted on staying at Dunham, which meant that Henry had to continue to live at Mere, and in January 1685 he arranged an annuity of £630 for life for her. Sir John Arden wrote of her, in the letter to Sir John Crewe quoted above, that she was not well. *"She may probably please the heir: and not displease neighbors if she haste after hym."*

Richard Legh called on to pay his respects to Lady Delamer and offer his condolences and was very surprised at what he found: *"As I passed by Dunham I sent in a compliment to the fair Lady there, who takes her loss very patiently, but whether like a good Christian or noe, I know' not. She hath long waited for this, and the last time I saw her I thought it was like a Raven that sate cawing over a sicke horse; how she will manage her joy a little, time will show; some say she will disparke both Dunham and Bollen unless her Son come well off and will give more than they are worth."*

Henry Booth acknowledged his father's death in a poem. It survives in a small manuscript in his hand preserved at Dunham Massey Hall:

An Elegy on The Right Honorable George Lord Delamer
who deceased August 8th 1684 Carmen Pindaricum

> Were I inspired with Cowley's happy Muse
> I then might better dare to choose
> Thee for my subject and attempt to raise
> Altars unto thy praise
> And memory
> Which sure will last
> Till time be past
> And swallow'd up in vast Eternity.
> He could have done what man could do, but yet
> Too little to express deserts so great as thine,
> Which bright and clear, ev'n as the Sun did shine.

Sources

The Tatton of Wythenshawe MSS give the negotiations for young George Booth's marriage and the mysterious Calais letter. I have taken his letter to Thomas, Lord Grey from Jeff Richard's biography of Grey, and the background to Booth's election as a Recruiter MP from the Brereton Letter Books. The latter also include several mentions of him during the Civil War, as do the various volumes of the Cheshire Sheaf. Booth's expulsion from Parliament in Pride's Purge is in the Clarke Papers (Camden Society 1894, reprinted 1994). The Thurloe State Papers and the Calendar of State Papers give the contrasting opinions of his loyalty, and John Mordaunt's Letter Book (Camden Society, 1945) is the most useful source for the arrangements for and beginning of the 1659 revolt. The revolt itself and its aftermath are dealt with in the Bath MSS of the Historic Manuscripts Commission (HMC), the Calendar of State Papers Domestic (CSPD), the Lancashire and Cheshire Antiquarian Society Volume 4, the Calendar of the Committee for Compounding and R.N. Dore's *The Cheshire Rising of 1659* and *The Civil Wars in Cheshire*. The petitions to Charles II for relief are all in CSPD. The latter, with Martindale's pungent comments describe the marriage negotiations for Booth's daughter with Lord Conway. Booth's protestations of innocence about the visit of the Duke of Monmouth are also in CSPD.

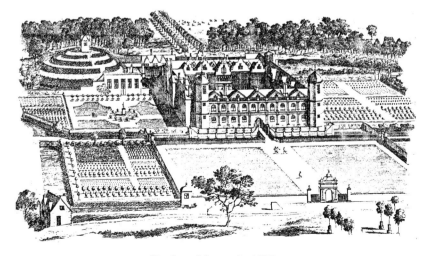

Dunham Massey in 1697

Henry Booth, Second Lord Delamer and First Earl of Warrington

# Chapter Three
# Henry Booth,
# Second Lord Delamer and First Earl of Warrington

Henry Booth's life was short but tumultuous. Born in 1651 when the last hope of the Royalists seemed to have vanished for ever, he survived the reign of Charles II, becoming more and more opposed to the King's increasing tolerance of Catholics, and was largely responsible for the sacking of James II, whom he hated. He inherited the impulsiveness and impetuosity his father had shown a young man and he carried them to the point of fanaticism. While his father, and in particular his great grandfather, always had a touch of tolerance and moderation, for Henry there was no middle ground. There were only black and white, and when he hated he did so with a terrifying fury. He loathed the loose morals and debauchery of the Court, the corruption of the judiciary and Catholicism in all its forms, particularly the extremism of the Jesuits.

Did he really know anything about the Rye House plot? Did he carry his overt liking for the young Duke of Monmouth to the point of rebellion? Did he really plot the death of a king not once but twice? We do not know. We do know that he became too familiar with the Tower of London, that he was in the gravest danger of his life on a charge of high treason, and that he was probably very lucky that his peers found him innocent.

The second of the twelve children of 'Young' Sir George, the first Lord Delamer, Henry Booth became heir to the estates when he was eleven on the death of his elder brother William. This was in 1662. After the strains and stresses of the Civil War and the failed uprising of 1659, his father had more or less withdrawn from public life. It is likely anyway that his stern Presbyterian upbringing clashed with the open immorality of the Charles II's court. It was by no means compulsory for a lord to be part of London life, and Lord Delamer was usually content to relax on his estates, but he did spend significant time in London until he became too infirm..

As a young man, Henry did the same, and could have expected to do so for the rest of his life. He would inherit a rich estate, even though it was less rich than it had been before the Civil War, and there would be no need to become embroiled in the intrigues of life at Court. Even attendance at the sessions of the House of Lords would not be compulsory. He could if he wished, remain at Dunham Massey, care for his estates and play his part among his local friends and colleagues as a country gentleman. But instead he came near to sacrificing his life for the extremist causes he believed in.

As a young man, his greatest passions were hunting and racing and in that he was typical of his time and class. Both he and his parents spent much time with the other Cheshire gentry, including Sir Thomas Mainwaring and Sir Willoughby Aston. He hunted a buck with Mainwaring in 1674. In September 1675 the Booth family were to have dined at Peover but were tragically prevented by the death of Charles, Henry's younger brother.

About 1671 he married Mary Langham, and set up his own independent residence at

Mere Hall, about two miles away from Dunham, where he often hosted his parents and friends. Racing was a great pleasure for him and he seems to have excelled at it. In May 1681 he won a plate and a saddle at Newton Races, and the next month he competed with seven other riders, including the Mainwarings, Sir Thomas Grosvenor and Peter Shakerley. Three weeks later at Knutsford, against stiff competition, he won the plate. Two years later, he won £50 in a race against the Earl of Derby.

The gentry of Cheshire had a wide and detailed social round. They spent much of their time progressing around the county and being entertained as guests in each others' houses. Lord and Lady Delamer, Sir Willoughby and Lady Aston, Sir Thomas Mainwaring, Jack Mainwaring, Lord Delamer's younger brother Nathaniel, Sir Robert Brooke, the Earl and Countess of Derby, the Earl of Macclesfield and his son Lord Brandon, the Shakerleys, the Warburtons, even the mighty Grosvenors, all formed a tightly knit social group who were constantly to be found hosting each other. The enmities and warfare of the Civil War were long since put behind them depite that many of them had been on opposing sides during that bitter conflict. Life was pleasant and easy-going, and there was no obvious reason why it should not continue.

Henry had some civic duties. He was elected to the House of Commons as one of the two County members in 1678, but in December of 1679 the King announced that he would not need a parliament until November 1680. In fact it was recalled in the October, but did not last long; in January 1681 the king dissolved it and announced that a new Parliament would be elected to meet in March in Oxford. Henry was again elected, and wrote to his brother-in-law the Earl of Conway to tell him the good news.

*"I suppose you may have heard that Sir Robert Cotton and I are again elected for this county. We have been put to a great charge by a faint opposition, as you will understand when Mr Andrewes waits upon you. The Papists all voted for Sir Robert Leicester and Sir Philip Egerton. One man was giving his vote for these two and, because two Papists came to vote for them, he gave his to me and Sir Robert Cotton. It is computed that I had polled 1,500, Sir Robert Cotton about 1,200, Sir R. Leicester 340 and Sir P. Egerton 280. I believe they might have about 300 more to poll. We, I am confident, had at least 3,000 more. They are much ashamed of their undertaking. I wait on my sister as I go to Oxford."*

The political situation at that period was already tense and getting more so. Charles II's honeymoon with his people was over and undercurrents of discontent were growing. Queen Catherine showed no signs of giving him a legitimate heir, an ironical situation given the large numbers of illegitimate children he had fathered, and his eldest son the Duke of Monmouth, a bastard who could not inherit the throne, had a wide popular following. He had seen which way the wind was blowing and abandoned any allegiance to Catholicism. His uncle, Charles' brother James, the Duke of York, was the legitimate heir, but James was openly Catholic and as stubborn and unbending as his father.

While he was a Member of Parliament, Henry made one bitter enemy, and the repercussions would come to haunt him years later. The Chief Justice of Chester was Sir George Jeffreys, who was at the same time Recorder of London. How he could hold two such important posts at the same time was beyond Henry's understanding, particularly as he seemed to be quite incompetent in his Chester office - lazy, unpredictable, arbitrary, and often drunk. Henry was determined to uphold the honour of his city in Parliament and in 1680 he made a speech in which he violently attacked the corruption of judges in general and that of Jeffreys in particular. He believed that the government of England was the best in the world, but it had one great defect: *"Whatever benefit we have by the Laws.... depend on the Will and Pleasure of those who are to see to the execution of the Laws: For Laws that are not put into execution are vain and empty things... So it is out of doubt that they who are entrusted with the execution of the Laws, it is an indispensable duty incumbent on them that they take care not only that the Laws be duly put in execution, but also that they pursue their proper end and design, in short, that neither the innocent be condemned, nor the guilty acquitted."*

Henry's speech was carefully prepared. He had studied the work of Sir Edward Coke, Solicitor-General, Attorney-General, Chief Justice of the Common Pleas, Lord Chief Justice and champion of the common law of England in the reigns of Elizabeth and James I, a man whose forthright views brought him into conflict with both those monarchs. Henry quoted Coke's exposition on Magna Carta, that justice should not be delayed or denied. Even the King's Great Seal was powerless to disturb or delay Common Law. Henry said, *"... let any Man deny if he can, whether our Judges have not transgressed in all these? Has not Justice been Sold, and perverted?"*

He then showed his true feelings about Catholics. Only the year before, the House of Commons, rightly distrustful of the Duke of York, had attempted to exclude him from the King's Privy Council by debarring Catholics from office, a measure which would certainly have had Henry's unqualified support. In the event, the Queen's servants were exempted, but the King told both Houses that *"he was ready to join with them in all the ways and means that might establish a firm security for the Protestant religion."* This was the time of the Popish Plot and the Queen's Physician, Sir George Wakeman, had been acquitted of involvement by the Lord Chief Justice, William Scroggs, and there was wide suspicion that Scroggs had been got at. Henry certainly thought so:

*"Witness the acquittal of Sir George Wakeman.... Has not Justice been denied; Witness the abrupt dismissing of the Grand Jury when an Indictment was to have been given in to prove the Duke of Y–, a Papist, and to prevent that great service to the Nation; the Jury was dismissed, notwithstanding they had several other Bills of Indictment in their hands; by which Justice was not only delay'd but deny'd.... So that our Judges have been very Corrupt and Lordly, taking Bribes, and threatening Juries and Evidence: Perverting the Law to the highest degree...."*

Booth emphasised his case by referring to punishments meted out to corrupt judges under Alfred, Edward III, Richard II and Henry IV. He then turned to his main theme and attacked Jeffrey violently by name, accusing him of almost everything that a Judge should not do:

*"The County for which I serve is Cheshire, which is a County Palatine, and we have two Judges peculiarly assign'd us by His Majesty: Our Puisne Judge I have nothing to say against him, for he is a very honest Man for ought I know. But I cannot be silent as to our Chief Judge, and I will name him, because what I have to say will appear more*

*probable. His name is Sir George Jefferies, who I must say behaved himself more like a Jack-Pudding, than with that gravity that beseems a Judge. He was mighty Witty upon the Prisoners at the Bar, he was very full of his Joaks upon people that came to give Evidence; not suffering them to declare what they had to say in their own way and method, but would interrupt them, because they behaved themselves with more gravity than he..... but I do not insist upon this, nor upon the late Hours he kept up and down our City; it's said he was every night drinking till Two a Clock, or beyond that time, and that he went to his Chamber drunk, but this I have only by Common Fame, for I was not in his Company. I bless God I am not a Man of his Principles or Behaviour.....*

*But that which I have to say is the Complaint of every Man, especially of them who had any Law Suits. Our Chief Justice has a very arbitrary Power, in appointing the Assize when he pleases, and this Man has strained it to the highest point; For whereas we were accustomed to have Two Assizes, the first about April or May, the latter about September, it was this year, the middle (as I remember) of August before we had any Assize; and then he dispatched business so well, that he left half the Causes untryed, and to help the matter, has resolved that we shall have no more Assizes this year.*

*These things are just cause of Complaint: It cannot be supposed that People can with ease or delight be in expectation so long as from May to August to have their Causes determined; for the notice he gave was very short and uncertain.*

*And I beg you is it not hard for them that had any Tryals, to fee Councel, be at the charge of bringing Witnesses, and keep them there five or six days, to spend their Time and Money, and neglect their Affairs at home, and when all is done, go back and not have their causes heard. This was the case of most People the last Assize."*

In the light of later events, it was not wise for Henry to make such a vehement and outspoken attack on one of the country's chief Judges, who soon became Lord Chief Justice. Booth, however, was not only brave to make the speech, but factually correct, even though some of his accusations were based only on hearsay. Jeffreys was savage, coarse, bad-tempered, largely ignorant of law, biased and corrupt. He was also cowardly, which was proved in 1688 when he was stripped of office. But in 1680 he was almost at the height of his power and Henry Booth made a dangerous enemy.

At this point, Booth may not have been totally opposed to the rule of Charles II, which was becoming more tolerant of Catholicism; alternatively he may have considered it politically and personally advisable to be at least superficially a supporter. Whatever the thoughts in his mind, his brother-in-law Lord Conway introduced him to the King in January 1682, and he kissed hands as a token of his allegiance, although it seems strange that he had not previously had a formal introduction.

His fidelity to the King lasted a mere six months. By July, he was in some danger in high places. Secretary Jenkins doubted his support for the King enough to consider sacking him summarily from his position as Custos Rotulorum (Custodian of the Rolls) of Cheshire, which involved little or no work, but was an honorary job of considerable importance. Within days, Jenkins was also getting serious and well-founded reports from his agents about Booth's reliability. According to Dr Matthew Fowler, the North West of England was very doubtful if it should come to a choice between Charles and his bastard son the Duke of Monmouth, or in the event of the King's death without a legitimate heir, between Monmouth and the King's brother James, the catholic Duke of York. Dr Matthew Fowler described Staffordshire, Cheshire and Lancashire as *"very rotten"* because of the leading gentry who would certainly favour Monmouth. He was apprehensive about Chester, which he thought was *"rotten at the heart"*, and he hoped devoutly that the castle was in safe hands. Mr Offley of Staffordshire was rumoured to be planning to spend £500 to host Monmouth on his forthcoming visit to the area, and in Cheshire the Earl of Macclesfield and his son Lord Brandon, Sir Robert Cotton, Sir Thomas Mainwaring, and Henry Booth would also escort the Duke.

When Monmouth arrived in Cheshire from Staffordshire early in September 1682, Fowler's information proved to be not only correct but under-estimated. Monmouth came to Nantwich in a coach provided by a Mr Leveson and Sir Robert Cotton met him in his own coach. Also in the procession were the gentry Fowler had already named, together with other members of their families, Roger and John Mainwaring for example. The Earl of Macclesfield provided at least 100 horse, with others arriving later.

Henry Booth was in the welcoming party with his elderly uncle, Nathaniel, and Nathaniel's son George, the Protonotary for Chester. They met the Duke about three miles out of Nantwich, and when they entered the town itself, Monmouth treated the occasion as if he were the King himself. Boys marched proudly in front of him and many of the towns people lined the hedges to get a glimpse of him. He was immediately preceded by Lord Brandon and Henry Booth as his ceremonial honour guard. They *"encouraged the beasts of the people to shout for joy at his coming, which was done in such great volleys that the streets and country round about were deaf with the confused noise, neither the Duke nor any other forbidding the use of such popular applause as wanted nothing but a Vive le Roy to complete a rebellion."*

Thomas Stringer, the innkeeper, had no love for Monmouth, and had to watch from the safety of his room. He described Henry Booth as *"well mounted and armed, finely habited, with rich furniture on his horse, several led horses and servants going before."*

The welcome Monmouth received from the townsfolk was overwhelming. People went down on their knees before him, and he thanked them kindly and courteously. The minister and the churchwardens refused to ring the church bells, but an enterprising supporter grabbed the keys from the sexton and the church bells *"trolled full merrily all the time of his stay"* in welcome for the Duke, and the people thronged the streets *"shouting and throwing up hats before him so employed the multitude that not one word could be heard but, Monmouth"*. A notable absentee was the Mayor of Nantwich, who observed the proceedings unofficially but took care not to be introduced to Monmouth, and only one of his aldermen met the distinguished visitor.

Monmouth's tour was becoming more and more like a royal progress. His popularity was obvious. The concern was being transmitted to lesser dignitaries and when Monmouth reached Chester, the Dean of the Cathedral personally ensured by taking away the keys that the bells would not be rung. In fact Monmouth's reception was slightly less enthusiastic than they had feared; only about 150 people accompanied him, mostly known dissenters and *"such ordinary mean persons as they can procure."*

Sir Geoffrey Shakerley, a reliable loyalist, had just been appointed Governor of Chester Castle. He sent Jenkins a fuller report of the events, listing all the gentry he could recognise and said that Monmouth's unofficial entourage was not less than 200 riders. Not only were many of the leaders of the Cheshire gentry there, but also gentlemen from Staffordshire, Shropshire, Flintshire, and as far away as London. Monmouth had a riotous reception as he entered the gates of Chester. With the exception of the Cathedral and St Peter's, all the church bells were ringing, and *"a great number of rabble and boys shouting before them and throwing up hats, and that night several bonfires were made. The bells, bonfires and rabble, 'tis supposed, were encouraged by the Mayor, at whose house the Duke lodged.... The Mayor having a daughter to be baptized, the Duke was godfather and she named Henrietta.... Let Monmouth reign"*, cried the mob, *"let Monmouth reign."* Usefully, Shakerley ended his report by noting Monmouth's planned movements over the next few days. To Jenkins, it was looking more and more like a deliberate attempt by Monmouth to drum up support for the future.

Sir Geoffrey Shakerley's son Peter gave more details. The Chester mob were well lubricated by free beer provided by Alderman Street, and were encouraged to show their support for the Duke by Lord Brandon waving his hat and Henry Booth by his side. The Duke dined at The Feathers in Bridge Street with Macclesfield, Brandon, Booth, and others of the gentlemen who had accompanied him from Nantwich. The next day, Sunday, he attended the morning and evening services at the Cathedral, where he heard Dr Fogg, a nonconformist, dutifully pray for the health of the King, but omitting the Queen and the Duke of York. After that, Monmouth went to the Mayor's house and consented to act as godfather to his baby Henrietta.

One of the magistrates, Matthew Anderton, was very scared. His house was stoned, St Peter's Church was broken into to ring the bells, and bonfires were lit in the streets. He estimated that there were at least 500 rioters on the streets and the Mayor would do nothing because he supported Monmouth himself. *"Where this will end, God knows,"* Anderton wrote hastily to the Deputy Lieutenants. *"I dare not go home, and I appeal to the Lieutenancy for relief.... I implore your aid for his Majesty's service and the preservation of this city and the peace thereof.... God help the poor cavaliers that must live here. Really there will be no abiding for the King's friends, if bonfires must be permitted on every idle occasion and the rabble encouraged in their unspeakable licentiousness."*

The next day, Monday, Monmouth and his entourage left Chester and travelled to Wallasey for the races on Tuesday. Peter Shakerley was trying to pass himself off as a loyal Monmouth supporter, but Henry Booth realised that he was not to be trusted as such and engaged in *"a frivolous discourse, with intent to sham me off."* Booth, the Mainwarings and others did their best to provoke him, but he kept his temper when at dinner the discussion turned on the Exclusion Bill.

The Duke of Monmouth was a keen horseman and loved racing. In that he was joined by Henry Booth, who rode up to him before the first race and said something that Peter Shakerley could not quite catch. Whatever it was, the Duke approved and embraced Booth very cordially. Monmouth was in an excellent temper. Not only was his tour progressing as well as he could possibly have hoped, but his racing was on form and he won the Twelve-stone Plate with a prize of £60. Henry Booth came third, but won a challenge race at the end of the day. The party then crossed the river to Liverpool, where Monmouth's welcome was less enthusiastic than at other places, although Nathaniel Booth was seen to give money to buy powder for celebration musket volleys.

On Wednesday the party returned to Wallasey and Henry Booth beat Monmouth in the second Twelve-stone Plate, winning a purse of £30. The side-betting was high and could have been even higher when Monmouth offered to bet £1000 on his horse. Perhaps luckily, no-one was willing to accept the bet and Henry Booth rode off to Dunham to make sure that everything was ready for his royal guest's visit the next day. Meanwhile trouble flared again in Chester when the mob spotted one of Monmouth's horses being led through the streets. They took it as an excuse to relight their bonfires, and when a loyal alderman protested, one arsonist hit him and said he cared not a f... for the King or Parliament, God save the Duke of Monmouth!

Henry met Monmouth on Stockton Heath with as many tenants as he could muster and escorted him to Dunham. He had arranged a ceremonial guard of honour of his tenants who formed a double rank, wearing the Duke's favours in their hats and shouting *"A Monmouth, a Monmouth"* to guard him and his company as they passed from the stables to the hall. There the Duke and his entourage of about fifty gentlemen dined in the Great Hall and the *"rabble"* were allowed to file in through one door and out of the other, so that they could have the privilege of gawping at the great man.

One who had an even better chance to see and talk to the Duke was Henry's niece, the eleven year old Katherine, the daughter of George Booth. Her grandmother Lady Delamer encouraged her to sit at Monmouth's feet *"by himself on a couch, and tell him who everybody was and many things he asked me, and when he danced he made me dance with him (tho' I had never learnt) but he told all the company that whoever lived to see me a woman, would see me the first dancer in England...."* Nearly eighty years later she still remembered the event clearly. With such natural charm, it is no wonder that Monmouth captured the hearts of so many people. He had the indefinable quality of personal magnetism and always knew exactly how to speak to people who were overawed by his lofty position.

From Dunham, Monmouth proceeded a short distance to Mere Hall, Henry's own house, where he dined the following day, before continuing to Gawsworth Hall to spend the night and hunt deer. Again Monmouth was cheered by a large crowd on his return from the hunt, but the loudest cheers were reserved for Henry himself. *"A Booth, a Booth,"* they shouted, *"as if they had been again choosing him a member."*

Sir Leoline Jenkins was deeply suspicious of Monmouth, as was the King, who forbade him to appear anywhere in Whitehall or indeed anywhere near the King. Henry Booth's behaviour also made him a marked man. Lord Delamer, his father, was deeply upset by his conduct, particularly as he was put to great trouble to clear himself from the charge of distributing ribbons to and taking the names of those who supported the Duke. His health was not good enough easily to stand the difficult journey to London, and six months later, Sir Willoughby Aston commented that he was very ill and badly swollen after his journey and was virtually confined to his chair.

Henry was now a prime suspect in any plot against the King, whether there was any evidence real or even imaginary. Jenkins received reports that many of the gentry of Cheshire had even held a secret meeting in Delamere Forest, in which they pledged their loyalty to the King, which made him seriously consider the possibility of civil disturbance. That possibility came a step nearer in the spring of 1683 with the discovery of the Rye House Plot. Rye House (a previous owner had been a maltster) lay at a narrow point on the Newmarket road in Hoddesden and the idea was to assassinate both the King and the Duke of York on their way to or from a meeting. Fortunately for the king and his brother, an accidental fire at Newmarket made them leave early and the plot failed.

Chiefly under suspicion were leading Whigs with no love for the Court or for the Duke of York. Lord Grey of Werke escaped, Lord Russell and Algernon Sidney were arrested, tried, condemned and beheaded on fairly flimsy evidence, and the Earl of Essex cut his own throat. Henry Booth was also arrested and flung into the Tower of London for the first but not the last time, on 13 July 1683. The authorities had no evidence against him except that some arms were found in Chester, and they seem to have decided to imprison him only on the general principle that he was a leading and outspoken critic of the government. Whatever his feelings about the King, he was certainly a supporter of the Duke of Monmouth and an opponent of the Duke of York. These were enough to cast suspicion on him. His family were of course very distressed; his wife Mary left for London immediately on hearing of his custody, and Lord and Lady Delamer followed within a day or two. Lord Delamer made a personal appeal to the King himself and was exceptionally eloquent. It was said that *"he hath made ye application to ye King most winning on his Maty of any of our great men...."*

Many of the gentry of Cheshire were deeply disturbed by the news of the plot. Sir Willoughby Aston had to call out the Militia with four days pay, and the Deputy Lieutenants received orders that the Earl of Macclesfield's house at Gawsworth was to be searched and certain other gentlemen were to be disarmed. The Grand Jury at the Chester Assizes claimed that there were *"strong apprehensions of danger from a dissatisfied party in this County who not only showed their disaffection openly by addresses made to Henry Booth esq and Sir Robert Cotton... at the last election of the Knights of the Shire tending to alter the succession of the Crown.... but also by their several meetings and Cabals since which administer greater suspicion by the store of Arms many of them were provided with. And for that the same persons unanimously assembled with schismatics in the public reception of James Duke of Monmouth, who has appeared a prime Confederate in the late Treasonable Conspiracy..."*

Casting their net very wide for safety's sake, the Grand Jury also named many of Cheshire's leading gentry - the Booths, the Mainwarings, the Macclesfields and many others. But naming possible conspirators and proving involvement were very different matters and nothing could be proved against Henry Booth. He was a firebrand, he was hostile to the establishment, he loathed the increasing influence of Catholics in general and the likely succession of the Duke of York, and he was a known supporter of the Duke of Monmouth, but these were not proof. He was confined in the Tower of London from 13 July 1683 until February the following year, and in September he was dismissed as a magistrate.  But he did not share the fate of Lord Russell and Algernon Sidney.

Henry was certain that Lord Russell was innocent and that the trial itself was improper, and some years later he gave his reasons in writing.  The indictment included conspiring the death of the king, intending to levy war and to that end seizing the Guards.  The Guards, however, had not been established by Parliament and did not exist at all when the law on High Treason was formulated during the reign of Edward III.  *"A Needle may sooner be found in a Cart-load of Hay, than any Statute that has established the Guards"*, wrote Booth.  They were not therefore a legal force and to seize them would have been no more than a felony he claimed.  He also adduced other highly legalistic reasons, such as that there was no precedent for any indictment for High Treason under Common Law, so no Court other than Parliament itself had the power to try the offence.

As for the evidence against Russell, it was in Booth's view quite insufficient.  One of the chief witnesses stayed only 15 minutes with Russell and other conspirators.  Furthermore he could not remember clearly if he had actually been at an important planning meeting or had only heard about it.  Another witness began by claiming he had attended two meetings with Russell but when pressed could only recollect one.  And a third said that even if he had been an enemy to Russell and to Monmouth, he would have sworn before God that neither of them intended to kill the King.  The indictment had been brought for the obvious reason that treason was against the peace.  But Russell's trial seemed to be based on the premise that if an act is against the peace, it could be construed as being treasonous, which was clearly false logic.

The Cheshire Grand Jury's verdict was too all-embracing for some.  Sir Willoughby Aston had always been a loyalist and he was outraged at being named among the 28 possible malcontents. Moreover there were strong rumours that pressure had been brought on some jurors to sign the list of names, so Aston seriously contemplated suing for false malicious conspiracy.  He refused in fact to give a bond for future good behaviour, on the grounds that it was tantamount to a guilty plea.  His loyalty can never have been seriously doubted - he had nothing but scorn for *"the old Pack still unhang'd amongst us, still hot upon the scent of Royal blood, would start the same Game up again."*

Early in December 1683 Henry Booth had applied for release under the terms of Habeas Corpus and was brought from the Tower to Westminster with Lord Brandon, Francis Charlton, John Hampden and Major Wildman, all escorted by 60 musketeers.  They were indicted for high misdemeanours and bailed to appear on the first day of the next legal term on sureties of £2000 and £1000 personal bonds.

Henry returned to his family at Mere Hall and plunged himself again into the social round of racing, hunting and dining with his friends.  In February the news came through that the case against him in London had been dismissed; there was no evidence of any kind against him.  This, however, was not enough for the Chief Justice of Cheshire, Booth's old adversary George Jeffreys.  Booth and the others must be bound over to keep the peace and provide security.  Binding over was not a punishment, he claimed, merely a caution.  Private inconvenience was preferable to public mischief and gentlemen should agree to be bound rather than that peace should be hazarded. Booth, through his attorney, Mr Williams, predictably disagreed.  He had been imprisoned merely on suspicion and had been released without charge and without a stain on his character. There was no reason therefore why he should be bound over. Just as predictably Jeffreys disagreed. Booth was free, but he, Jeffreys, had been given no formal indication that all proceedings had been dropped. Booth's situation was therefore technically no different from that of the other gentlemen and he must agree to be bound. Booth had no answer to this and grudgingly agreed.

Henry Booth succeeded as the second Lord Delamer on the death of his father in August 1684, but only six months later he was plunged into the most serious episode to date of an already turbulent life. At noon on 6 February 1685 Charles II died after a stroke and several days of agony at the hands of his doctors. He was succeeded by his younger brother, the Catholic James II, an event which opened the floodgates for what became famous as the Monmouth rebellion. Monmouth was in exile in The Hague when the news reached him a fortnight later, and at first he was grief stricken. The chance of ascending to the throne soon occurred to him, and he was not without agents at home, including one Major Wildman, now at liberty after being involved in the Rye House Plot.

The accession of James II did not bode well for Henry, Lord Delamer. His fanatical hatred of all Catholics, and James II in particular was too well known, and the Rye House plot had not been forgotten. He was thought to pose a danger, and shortly after James' accession he was committed to the Tower for a second time. There was nothing concrete against him and no obvious reason why he should be imprisoned, so he was soon released and took his seat in the House of Lords on 19 May 1685.

His liberty did not last long. At dusk on 11 June 1685 the Duke of Monmouth's small invasion fleet approached the port of Lyme in Dorset on its doomed enterprise. Twenty seven days later Monmouth was captured after the disaster of Sedgemoor. James II began to seek victims. Only a few days after the capture of Monmouth, a King's Proclamation was issued requiring Delamer to present himself before the King and the Privy Council within ten days, and he obediently surrendered himself to it. He was again imprisoned, and this time there appeared to be some solid evidence against him. George Jeffreys at least thought so. He had a cast-iron witness who he hoped would be corroborated by two others, and that would be ample to seal Delamer's fate.

Delamer remained in the Tower for months with no word of any trial. In November, he petitioned the House of Lords on its re-assembly foe release or trial. After what Narcissus Luttrell described as *"some hot speeches"*, they decided that no trial could be ordered because no charges had yet been laid against Delamer. The Lords sent a deputation to the King to ask why Lord Delamer was not in his place. This roused the authorities to action and only two weeks later Delamer, Sir Robert Cotton and Mr John Crewe Offley (Luttrell gives the name as Ostley) were bailed under Habeas Corpus on enormous securities of £10,000 and personal bonds of £20,000 each. The Lords were told officially that directions had been given that Delamer was to be put on trial for High Treason and that at the time of the Monmouth rebellion he had gone to Cheshire with the specific purpose of inciting a rising there.

*"The Tryal of Henry Baron Delamer for High Treason"* took place in Westminster Hall on 14 January 1686 before the Right Honourable George Lord Jeffreys, Lord High

Monmouth begs mercy from his uncle, James II.  He was executed in 1685.

Chancellor of England and constituted Lord High Steward for the occasion.  The Serjeant at Law was Sir Edward Lutwich, Chief Justice of Chester, and 27 members of the House of Lords assembled to hear the case against Henry.  For a peer of the realm to be tried for High Treason was a rare event and created such a sensation that even the King of Denmark, with the Crown Prince and Crown Princess, visiting England, were among the spectators.  The gentry of Cheshire also travelled down to London in force for the trial. Aston, after all, was indicted by the Grand Jury, his brother-in-law John Offley and their mutual friend Sir Robert Cotton had their huge bail sums to protect, rich though they were. In addition, other members of the Aston family, the Mainwarings, the Willoughbys, Lady Biddulph, Lady Cotton supporting her husband, the Earl and Countess of Derby, Colonels Whitley and Worden, were all in London for the occasion.

Jeffreys began by assuring Delamer that he would receive a fair trial and instructed him to hold up his hand to answer to the charge.  Delamer replied haughtily that he was a Peer of the Realm.  Was he to hold his hand up as a mere commoner would?  Jeffreys turned to the jury of peers and said that it was only a formality and signified nothing. Delamer interrupted.  Was the Lord High Steward (Jeffreys) one of his judges.  No, replied Jeffreys, he was one of the judges of court, but in this case not one of the tryers. Henry had had ample time to make his preparations and must have known this important fact, but he wanted his enemy to say it to the peers who were his jury.

The Clerk of the Court then read the indictment against Henry: *"Henry Baron of Delamer, thou standest indicted in the County Palatine of Chester... contriving, practising and with all thy might intending, the Peace and Tranquillity of this Kingdom of England to disquiet, molest and disturb, and War and Rebellion to stir up, move and procure, and the Government... to subvert, change and alter, and our said Lord the King to depose... and to Death and final Destruction to put.  On 14 April 1685 at Mere in Cheshire and divers other days and times conspire to raise money and armed men and*

Judge Jeffreys and the Bloody Assizes after the Monmouth Rebellion

THE

# TRYAL

OF

*41656*

# HENRY

## Baron Delamere

FOR

# HIGH-TREASON,

In WESTMINSTER-HALL,
the 14th Day of *January*, 1685.

Before the Right Honourable *George* Lord *Jeffreys*, Baron
of *Wemm*, Lord High Chancellour of *England*, Con-
ftituted Lord High Steward on that Occafion.

On which Day, after a full Hearing, the Lord *Delamere*
was Acquitted from all Matters laid to his Charge.

*LONDON*,
Printed for *Dorman Newman* at the *Kings Arms*
in the *Poultry*. MDCLXXXVI.

*to seize Chester Castle and City."* On 4 June at Mere *"in further prosecutions of thy unlawful, most wicked and traitorous purposes aforesaid, divers liege people and subjects of our Lord the King did excite, animate and perswade..."*

Delamer, playing for time, asked that the indictment be read again. He wanted to be allowed to speak before pleading, on a matter of law. Jeffreys said that Delamer must plead before he could be allowed to speak. Delamer repeated the request, and Jeffreys, his patience wearing thin, said that if he had any plea, he must make it. Delamer was determined and at length Jeffreys reluctantly compromised by allowing him to read a paper. Delamer stated how he had been summoned to Parliament and duly attended before being arrested and imprisoned in the Tower of London. After four months he had petitioned for release and the House of Lords had asked why he was not present. The trial had then been arranged, but Parliament had been prorogued until 10 February but not dissolved. Delamer argued that by ancient custom he could not be tried during the continuance of the Parliament and in any case he should be tried by the whole House.

The Attorney General advised that nothing in law could supersede the jurisdiction of the present court. Delamer countered by saying that as the point of law had been turned down, he wanted a counsel. Jeffreys ignored this and said that Delamer's plea was based on an error of fact; the indictment had not been put to the full House of Lords and had appeared after the prorogation. There were actually precedents.

Delamer stubbornly asked for counsel again, and Jeffreys agreed that he would hear his counsel's arguments. Delamer said he did not have a counsel and could he have one to argue the point of law? Jeffreys refused, on the grounds that no counsel could be assigned until it was known that there was in fact a point of law to be argued and Delamer's plea was therefore frivolous. Delamer quickly seized on this statement and accused Jeffreys of describing the rights and privileges of peers as frivolous.

*"Pray good my Lord,"* replied Jeffreys, *"do not think that I should say any such thing, that the Privilege of the Peers is frivolous; for you do not hear me say that this is one of their privileges."*

Would the Lord High Steward, in view of his last remarks, consult with the peers to discuss the question of privilege, asked Delamer.

Jeffreys lost patience and showed his teeth. *"Good my Lord, I hope that you that are a Prisoner at the Bar, are not to give the direction, who I should advise with, or how I should demean myself here?"* he growled. Delamer realised that he had probably gone too far and begged Jeffreys' pardon. Jeffreys answered that he would hear no more arguments and would do his duty *"with all tenderness"*, but would hear no more arguments. Delamer protested that he still had not been granted a counsel, to which Jeffreys replied that that was Delamer's problem, his request was overruled and rejected, and he must now plead guilty or not guilty. Giving way, Delamer pleaded Not Guilty and he would be tried by God and his Peers.

Sir Thomas Jenner, a Sergeant at Law and the Recorder of the City of London began to summarise the indictment. On 14 April, Delamer *"did Maliciously and Trayterously Assemble, Consult and Agree with Charles Gerrard esq, and other false Traytors, to raise great Summs of Money, and procure Numbers of Armed Men, to make a Rebellion*

*against the King, and the City and Castle of Chester to seize, with the Magazines there."*
On 27 May he returned from London to Mere *"to accomplish his Treasonable Intentions",* and on 14 June he tried to coerce other traitors to join him.

Monmouth had sent one Jones from Holland back to England with a message that he proposed to begin his rebellion in England rather than Scotland and to let Delamer and others know that he would soon sail over and land in the west. Nevertheless he considered Delamer to be one of his chief supporters. Jones was to give the message to a Captain Matthews, who was responsible for passing it among Monmouth's supporters, but could not find him or Major Wildman. Eventually Jones met Brand and Disney, since executed for treason and gave him the instructions. On the evening of 27 May, Disney met Lord Delamer at a London coffee house and that very same night, Delamer left town with only one servant, travelling by side roads as fast as he could, and going by the name of Brown. It was circumstantial, but he would prove that the purpose of Delamer's hurried and secretive journey was to raise men and money.

The first prosecution witness was Lord Howard of Escrick, to give an account of the conspiracy. Howard declared he *"must always repeat with shame and confusion for my guilt, as I cannot but always reflect upon it with sorrow and horror."* He knew of Lord Shaftesbury's involvement and that 8-10,000 men were ready to rise in London. However other leaders backed down and Shaftesbury felt abandoned. Monmouth tried to reassure him, saying that the insurrection would proceed, but not hastily. When questioned, Howard admitted that he knew nothing of Lord Delamer's alleged involvement, nor of any planned rising in Cheshire.

Lord Grey of Werke took Howard's place, and his evidence was more serious for Delamer. He harked back to Monmouth's triumphal progress through Cheshire, and claimed that even then a rising had been agreed between the Earl of Macclesfield, his son Lord Brandon, the first Lord Delamer, and his son Henry. Captain Matthews' task was to arrange a meeting with Macclesfield, Brandon and Henry in connection with the planned rising in Scotland. Grey had not personally seen Jones's message, but knew that only Macclesfield and Brandon were actually named in it.*

The prosecution then called Nathaniel Wade. He told of discussions between Monmouth and the Marquess of Argyle about a rising in Scotland when Monmouth landed in England. Lord Delamer, he alleged, was a friend in Cheshire, and when Monmouth landed at Lyme in Dorset, his plan was to march towards Gloucester and later join up with the Cheshire forces. Macclesfield, Brandon and Delamer were to be told of the landing and to join forces with him. Jones's mission was to notify Monmouth's friends in England that he would soon arrive. Jones was to contact Major Wildman, who

*Grey had been captured at an inn near Charing Cross and was escorted to the Tower of London in a coach by a Mr Deerham. When they reached the Tower, the sentry turned them away because it was too late. Mr Deerham was told to look after Grey until morning. Grey sent for some friends and together they drank 14 bottles of claret to while away the night. Deerham managed to order a hackney in the morning, but fell asleep on the journey. Grey himself was so drunk he completely forgot why they had returned to the Tower. He knocked on the gate and ordered the sentry to fetch an officer for the prisoner. Only when the sentry had left his post did it occur to Grey, through the fumes of claret, that the prisoner was himself! Just in time he grabbed his opportunity and ran, but was later arrested in seaman's disguise. He turned King's Evidence to try to save his own neck. (State Papers Domestic, 28 June 1683 and Gilbert Burnet *History of my Own Time*) would then be responsible for passing the word to Macclesfield, Brandon and Delamer.

Jeffreys turned to Delamer and invited him to put any questions to Wade. Delamer refused, claiming that he had never seen or heard of Wade in his life.

The Attorney General next called Richard Goodenough, who had been in Holland with Monmouth and confirmed that Jones had been sent with a message to Delamer to be ready for the Duke's landing but meanwhile should take care not to be arrested in London. *"My Lord Delamer,"* he said, *"was one of those Lords that had promised to draw swords on his behalf."* According to Goodenough, Monmouth had told him personally that he hoped Lord Delamer would keep his word to him. Delamer again claimed that he had never seen the witness in his life.

The next witness was Jones himself, who seems to have been thoroughly untrustworthy. He had already told the King everything he knew and was now coming to Court to give witness against Delamer. He had travelled to Holland in April on private business but had heard rumours from Disney that something was afoot. Wanting to know more, he had offered to take any message to the Duke of Monmouth,. The message was very cryptic and was to the effect that Monmouth should stick to the constitution given in a letter on its way - but if the letter miscarried, the advice to Monmouth was that he should stay in Holland or go to Scotland. Monmouth flew into a great rage when Jones delivered the message. It was that villain Wildman's work, he shouted. It was too late to change the plan. He still intended to sail for England. As for Wildman, he should either hang for him or fight for him. A few days later, Jones returned to Monmouth who gave him a sealed letter for Captain Matthews. Matthews was to notify Lords Macclesfield, Brandon and Delamer that Monmouth, would soon leave for England. Jones had actually opened the sealed letter as soon as he was at sea, and it clearly stated that Taunton would be the rendezvous point, and that Lords Macclesfield, Brandon and Delamer were to be told the date and time of the landing. Jones had landed on 27 May and had made contact with Disney, but both Matthews and Wildman were out of town, so he could not deliver his message. Instead, he made off to Lyme in time to meet Monmouth.

In more modern times, the testimony of Story, the next witness, would have been disallowed on the grounds of hearsay. All he could say was that he had heard Monmouth say that he had depended on his friends in Cheshire, and they had let him down. Vaux, who followed him, was much more to the point. On 26 May Delamer had sent for him, and they had left together the next evening. Delamer insisted that Vaux should always call him Brown, and why, he knew not. Delamer had explained however that his son was ill in Cheshire and they needed to make all haste. They had met two others, but Vaux could only remember the name of Edlin.

Edlin and three others (Tracey, Pounceford and Babington) were all called to prove that Delamer was travelling under the name of Brown. Pounceford went further by saying that Monmouth's declaration was to be sent to "Mr Brown" in Cheshire, and it was widely known that he and Delamer were the same person. Then came Mr Hope, landlord of the Three Tuns in Coventry. He claimed that Lord Delamer had travelled post and stayed at his inn five times in only a few weeks, and discussed with him the political tensions caused by the Duke of Monmouth.

Thus far, none of the witnesses had been able to say anything particularly damaging to Delamer. It was widely known that he loathed Roman Catholics and therefore James, and that he was sympathetic to Monmouth's cause, but these were not treasonable offences. Even the fact that he had travelled under a false name, suspicious though it certainly was, was not a crime. To put him on the scaffold, the prosecution needed to prove that he had actively plotted with the Duke of Monmouth. And in the person of Thomas Saxon they thought they had found it. The Attorney General asked him what he knew of Lord Delamer concerning any rebellion designed by him in Cheshire.

"At the beginning of June last," replied Saxon, *"I was sent for to Mere, my Lord Delamere's house in Cheshire, where I was conveyed into a lower room, where were my Lord Delamere, Sir Robert Cotton, and Mr Crew Offley... They had sent to the Duke of Monmouth, who was in Holland, and received an answer by one Jones, and as soon as they had an answer, My Lord Delamere came away post into the country under another name... to raise ten thousand men for the Duke of Monmouth in Cheshire by the first of June."* They were not able to do so, they said, because it would have cost £40,000 to arm and equip them, even if they had been recruited. They asked Saxon if he would take a message to Monmouth and gave him generous expenses for his journey. Saxon then explained to the Attorney General how he allegedly had become acquainted with Lord Brandon, who had recommended Lord Delamer.

All this was hanging testimony if it was believed. Delamer however does not seem from the transcript to have been unduly worried. He was allowed to cross-examine through Jeffreys and established that Saxon had never mentioned the matter until he was in prison at Dorchester. Later he had retold his story under oath when he was taken to Newgate. He had never been employed by Lord Delamer and had only met him the once. As a tradesman in Middlewich, Saxon knew many people. But Saxon did not know the name of the man who had sent for him to go to Mere. He had borrowed a horse from a neighbour and arrived at Mere as it began to get dark. At that point his evidence began to falter. He did not know which door he went through or whether it was next to the stables and saw no one except Lord Delamer and his two friends.

The Attorney General had at least temporarily concluded his case *"until we see what Defence this Noble Lord will make for himself."* Lord Delamer began with a ringing declaration of his innocence and then surprisingly had Saxon recalled to face a string of witnesses all of whom testified against Saxon and his honesty. He owed Richard Hildage £6 and more; he had forged a letter about the debt; he had cheated 80 year-old Mrs Wilbraham of 25/-; he had duped Richard Shaw by forging another letter in William Pangston's name; he had borrowed £6-10-0 from Peter Hough but only signed a bond for £6; he had hired a horse from Edward Wilkinson at 12d a day for 3 days, but never returned.

Jeffreys was beginning to get restive at this stream of character witnesses, none of whom were strictly relevant to Lord Delamer's trial. *"This is the same case with the other,"* he protested. *"...this is no evidence at all."* Delamer replied that he needed to establish that Saxon was completely untrustworthy because he was the star prosecution witness. Further, Saxon had said on oath that he had met Lord Delamer in company with Sir Robert Cotton and Mr John Offley. This was impossible and he would prove that

Cotton was in London. This he did conclusively with a string of witnesses, some of them Cotton's servants and therefore of perhaps doubtful veracity, but others, such as Messrs Ashburnham and Heveningham, quite neutral and unimpeachable. Without exception they all claimed to have seen Cotton in London throughout the period April to the end of July, so he could not possibly have been in Cheshire at any time. Saxon certainly did not see him at Mere Hall. Did he in fact see anyone there? Did he even go there? These were the doubts that Delamer was trying to plant in the minds of the 27 Lords who were trying him.

Delamer then called his old friend Sir Willoughby Aston, who was able to give a day-by-day account not only of his own movements between 26 May and 5 June but also those of his friend John Offley. Two of his servants went into even greater detail, and assuming the timings they gave for various journeys were accurate, there was no possibility of Offley having called at Mere Hall. Delamer then began to explain his temporary absence from London. He admitted leaving town on 27 May, but was back by 3 June when his brother Charles saw him. Jeffreys was at his most sardonic. *"He did make a great deal of haste backward and forward, that is certain,"* he commented, and then asked for clarification about the alleged sick child. Delamer requested time for one more witness, and his friend Lord Lovelace testified to having stood by him in the House of Lords during Lord Macclesfield's case, proving he was in London throughout it.

Delamer claimed to have proved that he, Cotton and Offley were not at Mere, and he had never seen Saxon in his life. Saxon's story was ridiculous. He remembered nothing of the layout of the house, the doors, the entrances or the stables. *"I beseech your Lordships to look at him. Is this Fellow a likely Fellow to be used in such an affair? Does he look as if he were fit to be employed for the raising of 10,000 men?"* Delamer conceded that he had left London under a false name because he believed there was a warrant out against him, but he needed to arrange a very profitable lease and his mother had written to say that his son Langham was seriously ill. However no sooner did he reach Cheshire than an express letter came from his wife with news that his eldest son George was also very ill, so he had to set off back to London.

The Dowager Lady Delamer testified concerning Langham Booth's illness. He was *"more than ordinarily precious to him, in regard it was born to him at that time, when he was an innocent honest man (as he is now a Prisoner in the Tower for High Treason) above two years ago....."* While Delamer was at Mere *"it pleased God to visit his eldest son with a dangerous distemper, upon which my daughter sent for him post, if he intended to see his son alive. And thereupon I think he made what haste back again he could."*

The last in the defence case was Sir Thomas Millington, a physician, who had examined young George Booth on 28 May and found him very sick.

The Solicitor General began his summing up of the prosecution case. Saxon's statement was positive proof of Delamer plotting in Cheshire, and Lord Grey had demonstrated Monmouth's trust in him. Delamer had left London in great haste and there was plenty of evidence about his journey and his false name. Furthermore, Lord Delamer's reason for using a false name was that he thought there was a warrant out for him. There was no such thing, and he could give no very good account of his swift journeys. Before Delamer could state his case for the defence, Jeffreys interrupted. As a matter of law, he said, there must be not less than two positive witnesses before a man could be convicted of treason. Saxon was the first, and if what he said was believable, the sum of the other witnesses might be considered as a second positive.

Lord Delamer was very eloquent in his final speech. He claimed not to be master of law or rhetoric and to have had only little time to collect his defence. (The trial transcript suggests quite the opposite!) Would he have surrendered to the King's Proclamation if he were really guilty? And as for Saxon, *"Besides My Lords, this Very Fellow Saxon is but one evidence, and how far you will believe him, I must submit it to you, but surely one Witness will never be sufficient to convict a man of Treason, tho' thousands of hearsays and such trivial circumstances are tacked on to it... Would not any of your Lordships think himself in a bad condition as to his Fortune if he could produce no better evidence to prove his Title to his Estate than what has been produced against me this day.....?"*

He concluded with a direct appeal: *"Blood once spilt can never be gathered up again, and therefore unless the case be very clear against me, you I am sure will not hazard the shedding of my blood upon a doubtful evidence. God Almighty is a God of Mercy and Equity. Our Law, the Law of England, is a Law of Equity and Mercy, and both God and the Law require from your Lordships Tenderness in all cases of Life and Death, and if it should be indifferent or but doubtful to your Lordships (which upon the Proofs I have made, I cannot believe it can be) whether I am innocent or guilty, both God and the Law require you to acquit me.*

*My Lords, I leave my Self, my Cause and all the consequences of it with Your Lordships, And I pray the All-Wise the Almighty God direct you in your determination."*

When the Peers returned after an absence of only half an hour, their verdict of Not Guilty was unanimous and Jeffreys was compelled, very reluctantly one suspects, to discharge him.

What of others? Ford, Lord Grey, had been outlawed for High Treason and grovelled for pardon at the Kings Bench Bar. It was granted, but on the unspoken condition that he give evidence against his former co-conspirators. He did, of course. Lord Brandon was his chief victim. He was found guilty of treason and sentenced to death, but later pardoned.

One of the witnesses against him was Thomas Saxon, who after the Delamer trial, was charged with perjury on the same day that Delamer, Cotton and Offley were discharged of their bail bonds. Saxon pleaded not guilty, at which Chief Justice Jeffreys, not noted for lack of bias, expressed his surprise because the evidence (as yet unheard) against Saxon was so strong. Saxon said he might have mistaken the time he saw Delamer and the others, but he had witnesses to prove it. Jeffreys commented that Saxon's statement was strange, since it was widely known that Sir Robert Cotton at least was in London at the time. Eventually Saxon asked to change his plea, but Jeffreys refused and remanded him for sentencing on 23 January. The evidence against Saxon was so very full, and he himself had nothing to offer against it, that the jury, without going from the bar, brought him in guilty of wilful perjury. He was sentenced to be pilloried three times, to be whipped from Ludgate to Westminster one day and from Newgate to Tyburn the next, to be fined 500 marks; and to be imprisoned until all was carried out.

Furiously, Delamer wrote a poem in stately Latin which echoes the punishment that

Saxon received. The translation is:

> *"Brook no delay, O Retribution, most just avenger of the wicked,*
> *And repay this man his just deserts,*
> *Who, by violating faith, lying, perjurious and shameless*
> *Dared to condemn so innocent a head.*
> *But, O wicked one, may you suffer no easy death; you deserve*
> *That the evil cross and the flame of the pyre should destroy you after this,*
> *Flogged and flogged again, as though by terrible torture,*
> *And by this example be a warning to others of justice"*

The day after the trial was extremely busy for the Cheshire gentry. Sir Willoughby Aston spent the day dashing to and from their various lodgings and celebrating his brother-in-law's birthday. He went to congratulate Delamer, but the latter was not at his mother's or his wife's house. Then his sister-in-law, Anne, in a great excitement, sent a servant to tell him that two gentlemen from the King, a Mr Burton and Mr Ward, wished to speak with him. Their message was that His Majesty regretted the great inconvenience that *"so many worthy gentlemen had been put to this trouble by Saxon."* Saxon would be tried for perjury in due course, but meanwhile Sir Willoughby and his friends should take no action in case it stirred worse trouble. Aston replied that he would obey all the King's commands, and he was entirely at His Majesty's disposal. He wished merely to have the honour of kissing the royal hand.

The question remains, what was Delamer's involvement, if any, in the Rye House plot and the final Monmouth rebellion? The circumstantial evidence against him was strong, he was known to favour Monmouth and his hasty ride to Cheshire and back at the time of the rebellion was suspicious at the least, but 27 of his peers were unanimous in believing that he was not guilty of any plot against the King. But Lord Grey implicated him in complicity at least in the beginnings of the Rye House plot. According to him, Lords Macclesfield and Delamer (Henry's father) were going to advise Monmouth, whose progress to Cheshire would be *"under the shelter of some fair pretence"*, which gentlemen of the county could be entrusted with the secret. Monmouth believed that he had secured the loyalty of the Booths and the Macclesfields and when the uprising began they would join him in the West with their followers. If Grey was telling the full truth in his written confession, the court's verdict could well have gone against Delamer. At the very least it seems fairly certain that he was a party to discussions in Cheshire, even if he perhaps knew nothing of the intention to kill the King. He may have decided that if the legal attempt to exclude the Duke of York from succession to the throne were to fail, then he would take Monmouth's side in the struggle. In the event of course, the Rye House plotters wanted to wipe out York and the King at the same time and nothing implicates Henry in that.

As for Monmouth's invasion, Delamer's abrupt departure for Cheshire, taking side roads and under a false name, is very suspicious. Nevertheless he had a convincing explanation, the Court believed it even if Jefferies didn't. It is likely that Monmouth was too optimistic about the amount of help he would receive and simply chose to believe too literally in any protestations of help that Delamer may have made. As for Delamer himself, he was probably aware in general terms of Monmouth's intention to claim the throne but judged that it was too premature and was doomed to failure.

Delamer was cautious after his narrow escape from the executioner and after kissing the King's hand (one imagines with great reluctance) returned to his estates to live quietly. He remained fanatically Protestant and bided his time in case of better things. James II obstinately continued on his pro-Catholic activities. Catholics were admitted to high office for the first time in 1686; the following year the Declaration of Indulgence granted toleration to both Catholics and Protestants and the alarm of the country increased in 1688 when James's son, James Edward Stuart, was born, a Catholic heir to the throne. James ignored all the opposition to his policies. Just before the birth of his son, he issued a second Declaration of Indulgence, which largely repeated the first but was more alarming. It nominally allowed freedom of conscience, but threatened with dismissal from all public and military service all those who refused to co-operate with his policies. They were replaced with totally unqualified men. Even some Catholics were nervous when they saw *"popish clergy so busy themselves in secular affairs, no way relating to their function, that they are grievous to his Majesty's Protestant, and vexatious to his Roman Catholic, subjects."* The only possible interpretation was that total obedience to his wishes took priority over freedom of conscience.

He seemed bent on his own destruction and refused to listen to reason. Only the Queen and Catholic priests seemed to have any influence on him. He sincerely believed that his father's troubles and execution had come about by his failure to act harshly enough. *"I will make no concessions,"* he said to the Papal Nuncio. *"My father made concessions and he was beheaded."* When he insisted that the Declaration was to be read from every pulpit on successive Sundays, the bishops revolted, protesting that its measures had often been declared illegal by Parliament. Seven of the ten English bishops were promptly thrown into prison charged with sedition. This was too much. The fact that the jury predictably found them innocent in no way decreased the King's unpopularity.

Seven leading members of the House of Lords and the Church of England, hastily and in great secret, concocted an invitation to Prince William of Orange, a Protestant grandson of Charles I, and ironically son-in-law to James II, to sail for England and take the throne. This was the signal for Delamer, his hatred of the Catholic king still fierce. He realised that it would be his last chance; he must either continue to live the life of a provincial country gentleman or hazard everything including his life to openly support William. There was no choice for him. He knew that if James remained King, all Protestant hopes would disappear and England would soon in all probability become once again a Catholic land.

If Prince William failed for any reason to overthrow James II, Delamer's life would be forfeit, and he knew it. He still had some time and he spent the late summer of 1688 writing a long letter to his children, to be given to them posthumously. He had already lived through times of serious trouble, he wrote. He was only 9 years old when his father had spent seven months in the Tower for the 1659 Cheshire uprising and, he reminded his sons, he had been tried for his own life *"for adhering to the interests of my country."*

He advised his children to adopt certain principles many of which are sound advice even today. It was an essential principle of a Christian life that they should *"Let all your Dealings be measured by the golden Rules, of doing to others as you would be done by"*, and it was very sad that it was not practised as widely as it ought to be. Nevertheless, such behaviour was essential if one wanted to earn the name of an honest man. His children must at all costs be dutiful and affectionate to their country, as *"there never yet was any good Man who had not an ardent zeal for his Countrey"*. However they should not be too hasty in taking up any official post; they needed to be qualified for the job and to undertake it not for their own benefit but for the good of the country. When they had duties to perform, they should behave equally to everyone, allow easy access to all applicants, never be unjust for fear of dismissal, and be upright at all times.

Delamer outlined to them his principles of English Government. It ought to suit the general inclinations of the people. A king's power is derived from the constitution and he has no authority to rule arbitrarily. The ancient rights of the English people have priority over the monarch's prerogatives, and he must not exceed his powers. Delamer demonstrated that he had a good knowledge of the law himself, and he advised his children that Bacon's *Uniformed Government of the Laws of England* was worth its weight in gold. His eldest son would of course succeed him and sit by right in the House of Lords. There he should speak clearly, briefly and to the point; good common sense was worth far more than *"the finest Words and Phrases."*

*"Let not any thing of Pride appear in you, either towards your Equals or Inferiors"*, he advised, and *"Do not too easily credit any thing that is told you to the disadvantage of another."* As for the management of their estates, Delamer realised that his children would probably inherit grave difficulties. He advised them strongly to live within their means - which neither he nor his father had done. The more expensively one lived, the more readily would his friends help him to spend his substance, and the more they would openly despise him when it was all spent. Servants should always be treated fairly and should not be reproved for every small error. Indeed, they should usually be spoken to

in private and only if they seemed unable to correct themselves should they be admonished publicly in front of the other servants.

The children should manage their estates themselves as much as possible, because no one was too great to look after his own affairs. Tenants should be allowed 21-year leases, with 'fines' of no more than 1 year, and even then, their annual rents should be rebated accordingly. Meanwhile the farmers should do their own repairs when needed, because they would do for themselves at 6d work for which they would charge their landlord 18d!

Lastly, Delamer turned to the future of his children. All children were *"a blank paper, upon which you may write what you will."* It was therefore vital that they should have the best possible education, but without going to University. There they would receive only pedantic education, and would run a grave risk of becoming debauched. When their own children were growing up, they should provide *"convenient"* marriages for the daughters, with good but not extravagant portions; *"Giving a daughter an extraordinary Portion... has hurt many more Families than it has advantaged."*

Delamer had clearly learned much from his own life and wished to pass his experience to his children. It is however strange that in some matters he was still unable to follow his own advice. For the rest of his life, he continued to incur heavy expenditure, although it was not on himself but for what he conceived as the good of his country. But strangest of all, the marriage arrangements he negotiated for his own daughters were so extreme that they came near to bankrupting his own son!

For the time being, Delamer was in no hurry to declare his hand politically. However he was likely to have powerful support when he did, in the person of the Earl of Derby, who was restored to the position of Lord Lieutenant of Cheshire and Lancashire, posts which had been in his family for generations but which had been in abeyance for nearly four years. Derby was invited to go to London for a personal interview with the King, and the assurances of Lord Dunmore that the bishops were free and satisfied with James's promises, the Church of England was wholly trusted, and the Charter of the City of London had been restored. All was well in the land, said Lord Dunmore.

Derby duly went to London to be confirmed as Lord Lieutenant of two counties by the King who treated him very cordially, unaware that Derby was loyal to Protestantism, not to James. His friends suggested that he should at least raise the militia to preserve the peace in the north west but he might have a quiet word with Lord Delamer.

Back home at Knowsley, Derby arranged a meeting with Delamer and discussed in confidence various ways in which a rising could be managed. Delamer undertook to begin his uprising as soon as he heard of Prince William's landing, which was expected shortly. Derby had to act with great secrecy for the time being, not take any of the other Deputy Lieutenants into his confidence, and raise only those of the militia officers he was certain were reliable. When William landed and Delamer went public, Derby would quarter some of the militia near Dunham to guard it.

Derby needed to be particularly cautious because he had enormous power and influence as Lord Lieutenant, but it could be stripped from him in an instant if the King should suspect his loyalty. He summoned various men who would be his Deputy Lieutenants, who were unanimous that neither he nor they should act as lieutenants until his formal commission arrived. Until then, Derby proposed that they should establish how many of the old militia officers were still fit and able to serve. He did the same for the proposed deputy Lieutenants of Cheshire.

Meanwhile, William was in no hurry. He had been invited, but he did not arrive with his fleet and army until 15 November when his ships dropped anchor in Torbay to a hearty welcome. Delamer already knew the day of landing and was ready to raise his tenants. He was as good as his word and called his men to a meeting on Bowdon Downs on the same day. His speech was a testament to his personal convictions:

*"My very good friends and tenants.*

*The occasion of this is to give you my thoughts in the present juncture, which concerns not only you but every Protestant and free-born man of England. I am confident there are none among you but wishes well to the Protestant religion and his country, and I am also persuaded that you think both in danger and now to lie at stake. I am also persuaded that every man of you will rejoice to see religion and property properly settled. If then I am not mistaken in my conjectures concerning you, can you hope for a better occasion to root out Popery and slavery than by joining the Prince of Orange, whose proposals contain and speak man that loves his religion and liberty? And in saying this I will invite you to nothing but what I will do myself, and I will not desire any of you to go farther than I move myself, neither will I put you upon any dangers where I will not take my share in them. I propose this to you, not as you are my tenants, but as you are my friends and as you are Englishmen. No man can love fighting for its own sake, nor find any pleasure in dangers, and you may imagine I would be very glad to spend the rest of my days in peace, having had so great a share in troubles, but when I see all lies at stake, I am not to choose whether I will be a slave or a Papist, or a Protestant and a free man, and therefore the cause being just, I should think myself false to my country if I sat still at this time. I am of opinion that when the nation is delivered, it must be by force or by miracle. It would be too great a presumption to expect the latter, because God Almighty in the methods of his Providence, works by second causes, and therefore our deliverance must be by force, and I hope this is the time for it. A way is now put into our hands, and if it miscarry for want of assistance, our blood is on our own heads, and he that is passive all this time may very well expect that God will mock when the fear of that come upon him, which he thought to avoid being indifferent. If the King prevail, farewell liberty of conscience, which has hitherto been allowed, not for the sake of the Protestants, but in order serve Popery. You may see what we are to expect if he gets the better. He has lately given you of this town a taste of the methods whereby he will maintain his army, and you may see of what sort of people he intends his army to consist, and if you have the mind to serve such a master, and stand by and see your countrymen perish, when they are endeavouring to defend you, the crime will lie at your own doors. I promise, upon my word and honour, to every tenant that goes along with me, that if he falls, I will make his lease as good to his family as it was when he went from home.*

*The thing then that I desire, your country does expect from you, is this, that every man that has a tolerable horse, or can procure one, will meet me on Bowdon Downs tomorrow where I intend to rendezvous; but if any of you is rendered incapable by reason of age, or any other just excuse, that then he will send a fitter person, and put five pounds in his pocket. Those that cannot procure horses let them stay at home, and assist with*

Lord Warrington's message to his tenants. *Courtesy of The British Library*

*their purses, and send it to me, with a particular of every man's contribution. I impose*
*upon no man, but let him lay his hand upon his heart and consider what he is willing to*
*give to recover his religion and liberty, and to such I promise, and to all that go along*
*with me, that if we prevail, I will be as industrious to have him recompensed for his*
*charge and hazard, as I will be to seek for it myself. This advice I give to all that stay*
*behind, that when you hear the Papists committed any outrage, or are rising, that you*
*will get together, for it is better to meet the danger than expect it. I have no more to say*
*than that I am willing to lose my life in the cause, if God see good, for I never was*
*unwilling to die for my religion and my country, so I rest, your loving friend, Delamer."*

What Delamer refrained from saying in his speech was what, if anything, would happen to any tenant who did not join him without good excuse. At least one man, whose name has been lost, was worried when he heard that Delamer was very annoyed with him, and he made haste to write "all speed" to Sir H. Ashurst to intercede. He was *"surprised and troubled my Lord Delamer should retain any opinion of me that has soe truly loved and valued him in his adversity, be sure could not forsake him in his prosperity, especially where religion & the rights of all men are concerned."* He did not even know of the rising until it was too late to join the muster, and even then he had sent a man to catch up with Delamer at Newcastle or Uttoxeter. He *"would rather be cut in pieces than break his word."* Only a tenant terrified of his landlord's hasty temper and of the likely consequences would have written such a panic-stricken letter.

Delamer's rising in support of William of Orange was his most dangerous gamble. He was well known as a Whig, and well-known for his championing of the Duke of Monmouth some years before. He was a tainted man, in open rebellion, and if things had gone wrong, he would almost certainly have ended his life on the scaffold.

Delamer ordered a copy of this speech to be fixed to the market cross in Warrington and the news of the Prince of Orange's landing in England and Delamer's uprising spread like wildfire throughout the county. Sir Willoughby Aston was visiting Lady Sarah Haughton on 17 November when a Captain Wodham arrived with *"news of Lord Delamer being gone in."* The next day he received a letter from Sir Richard Brooke with more details. Delamer had declared for the Prince of Orange, mustered 1000 horse at Bowdon and was riding to Newcastle-under-Lyme. He would be joined there by Lord Cholmondeley, Mr Legh of Booths, one of the Leicester family of Tabley and several other of the county gentry. Aston had no idea what if anything to do. He may have remembered that less than a month before, Delamer had visited and levied a fine of some of his estates to Aston and Sir Thomas Mainwaring. If so Aston might have connected it with the uprising and realised why Delamer needed the money so urgently.

On 20 November Aston heard at last from the Earl of Derby, but only a panicky letter about rumours that companies of Papists had been raised to capture and murder him. An informant had told him that a critically ill soldier had confessed that there was a plot among the soldiers to take him prisoner if he was in league with Delamer. This may have been a false alarm, but Derby took no chances and put a strong guard on his house at Knowsley. Derby was obviously in a cleft stick. He considered that Delamer was far too impetuous and premature; the other gentry were unprepared, they would not be able to raise their militia. There was a danger that the whole enterprise would simply go off half-cock, and if Prince William abandoned his plans or was driven off, their lives would not be worth a candle in spite of Delamer's brave words. Should he abandon Delamer to his fate and openly assist James II, should he keep his word to Delamer, or would it be best to keep his options open by rousing his Deputy Lieutenants?

He decided on the latter course. He sent orders to all his Deputy Lieutenants that they were to take all measures to preserve the peace in Cheshire. Governor Shakerley of Chester was sending blank commissioning papers so that Aston and his colleagues could appoint Militia officers. Aston went to Lord Derby on 28 November, but Derby was just as confused as ever. He did not know that eight companies of foot soldiers commanded by Colonel Gage had reached Chester, armed and spoiling for a fight. They had tried to call out the Militia Guards who had sensibly refused rather than run the risk of open violence and had eventually been billeted in the Town Hall to avoid disorder. Governor Shakerley was desperate. He had no idea what to do and appealed to Whitehall. *"I do suppose... that it is His Majesty's pleasure they come hither and therefore I admitted them into the garrison and assigned them quarters as though they were of the garrison, but I pray you let me receive HM's orders concerning them for I am told... that Lord Forbes will be here suddenly with his whole regiment, and also that several troops of dragoons are to come hither from Ireland.... The public houses within the city will not be able to receive all these and the King's Declaration ties me up from quartering any upon private houses. Therefore if more forces are to come over, I presume you will send me orders that these march out before those come or otherwise so as there may be quarters in the public houses for those HM designs to stay... I pray you let me receive a letter from you per next post..."*

The shortage of reliable news was creating more and more confusion in Cheshire. Lord Derby had kept his dealings with Delamer completely secret, so he could -and did - still pretend to be loyal to James II. Now making up his mind, he sent out his instructions to the Deputy Lieutenants, and on 30 November Sir Willoughby Aston convened a meeting at Northwich with Sir Thomas Grosvenor, Sir Philip Egerton, Sir Richard Brooke and Thomas Cholmondeley. They were alarmed at the rumours that were spreading, some of which had grains of truth - army regiments were rampaging around virtually out of control and threatening to burn the houses of people who refused to support Catholics. It had *"given the City and the County great disquiet."* Faced with such dangers, the Deputy Lieutenants filled in the blank commissions from Lord Derby to call out the County Militia to join the City forces. Their declared aim was to preserve the City and more importantly the Castle for the King's service.

The news of Delamer's uprising was breeding its own rumours. A Lieutenant Godman's report had at least the advantage of being first hand. Shortly before the Bowdon meeting, Delamer rode into Manchester at the head of fifty horsemen wearing blue. Delamer and his senior officers went into the King's Arms, leaving the men outside drinking on their knees the health of the Prince of Orange and confusion to the King. Inside, Captain Lees, a neighbour and acquaintance of Delamer, questioned him. He answered scornfully that he was going to fight for the Prince and if he wished, all Lees' company could leave Lees and follow him. Godman also witnessed the Bowdon Downs meeting and heard Delamer claim that the Prince of Orange was come *"to vindicate the Church of England and that they could do no better than to joyne with him, whereat they huzzaed and threw up their hats and promised to follow him wherever he went."*

Captain Lees suffered more humiliation in Newcastle-under-Lyme a day or two later, when Delamer with about 500 men confiscated a consignment of arms and ammunition destined for Lees' company. The crowd cheered him and seized the Collectors of the Excise and Hearth taxes and took the money *"for the preservation of the Protestant religion and the good of the Kingdom."* The revolt was spreading fast. In Stafford, Lord Aston summoned his militia, but many of them refused. When he dismissed them they promptly joined Delamer. In despair he reported the facts to Lord Preston in London, saying that the county militia were completely unreliable and that Delamer and his men were on their way to Derby and Nottingham.

Other parts of the country were equally confused. Reports began to flood in to Philip Froude, the man in charge of the King's Letter Office in London. He received a running commentary of varying degrees of accuracy about Delamer's advance. John Francys in Derby sent an express ('Haste, haste!') that five troops had arrived at 4 am. They were on their way to Nottingham - Lords Delamer and Cholmondeley were on their way, demanding a petition for a free Parliament. Delamer reached Nottingham the day after his advance guard with five hundred horse, all well armed, and a wagon load of arms. A meeting was being arranged to petition for a free Parliament. Moreover, Delamer had met Lord Stamford and the Earl of Devonshire, and between them they would command 5,000 men before the meeting would take place.

Sir John Reresby among many others in York wanted a free Parliament, but wished to assure the King of their basic loyalty. No sooner had they begun to compile a draft letter to the King but there was an alarm of a Catholic uprising in the city. The Earl of Danby and his son Lord Dunblaine, with Deputy Lieutenants of Yorkshire, grabbed the opportunity and rode out to the four militia troops, calling out for a free Parliament, the Protestant religion and no popery, *"and all the rabble shouted."* Known Catholics in the city had their houses plundered and their horses stolen. Even Reresby lost provisions that he had laid in for the city garrison. Large numbers of the local gentry openly declared for redress in Parliament and guarantees that Catholicism would never become the official religion of England.

Only then did the news arrive of Delamer's rising, followed by the defection of numerous grandees such as the Dukes of Grafton and Ormonde. Reresby estimated in his Memoirs that *"The number of those that revolted were not 1000 in all as yet, but everyone was so jealous of one another that they knew not who to trust... there was scarce an hour but his Majesty received, like Job, some message of some revolt or misfortune or other"*. When most of the tumult was over he gave an account to Lord Halifax that summed up the feeling in England. *"My Lord, we are all surprized with this great and generall revolution... I should be glad to receive some light in this obscure matter..."* Froude received this bad news from Roger Hardcastle in York.

The Prince of Orange advanced very slowly from the west, just as James's army headed very slowly towards them, neither side being anxious to give battle. Lord

Delamer clearly expected fighting and was bringing some 500 men with him, from his own estates and from other gentry who had joined him. On 1 December he wrote to Prince William from Gloucester, *"I with some of my Cheshire friends came to this place last night.... We intend to be at Bristol tomorrow and there to expect your commands; for my design of taking up arms is to serve God, your Highness and my country, and to act as your Highness shall be pleased to command me. I hope my zeal for your (service) and difficulty of circumstances I was under will plead my excuse that I came no sooner and in no stronger a posture, but if your Highness shall think fit to command me any further service, I doubt not to give undoubted proof of my affection to your Highness."*

The country was in a ferment and the wildest and most fanciful rumours spread unchecked. Lord Delamer claimed allegedly that James was preparing to pour French and Irish soldiers into England to carry out wholesale massacres of Protestants; heavy artillery was being mounted on the walls of the Tower of London, and the city was being provisioned to withstand a siege; a certain *"Squire Mullinax"* would have burned Dunham Massey Hall, but it was guarded by over 4000 men so he turned back; Delamer's forces had fought a battle near Lancaster and killed sixty or eighty Papists; he was leading an extravagantly large army of up to 10,000 men; he was disarming all Catholics and any of the King's troopers he met; he was equipping his men with their arms ....and so on. In fact Clarendon was probably more realistic when he remarked that Delamer only had 200 - 300 men and they were poorly equipped and horsed.

The King began to panic - there was too much opposition to Catholicism in England and on 26 November he caved in to popular demands and agreed to call Parliament. Meanwhile Delamer continued his advance, but Lord Derby remained suspiciously quiet. He agreed to protect Lady Delamer against any mob, but otherwise gave no hint of his agreement with Delamer. Delamer was furious and wrote insultingly to Derby:

*"My Lord,*

*Had I foreseen how backward your Lordship is in doing your part, I should have told your Lordship that it was not worth the while to mention your name to the Prince; for you cannot forget you promised to raise the militia immediately, and to quarter Bucklow Hundred at Altrincham, and that if, in case the Papists committed any outrage, or rose in arms, that then you would fall upon them and leave neither root nor branch. How far you have made this good, your Lordship can best tell; but I hear, that on the 3rd instant, no militia of Buckley Hundred was up, and, though the Papists made an attempt to burn my house, yet I don't hear of any resentment your Lordship has expressed against it... But God be praised, we need none of your help, or, if we be distressed, we shall not seek to you for succour.....*

*Just now I hear you have suffered the Papists to possess themselves of Chester.."*

This bad-tempered letter was grossly unfair to Lord Derby. No Catholics went near Dunham and no harm of any kind came to the house. However Derby had taken sensible precautions against the rumours that his own house was in some danger and he had alerted his servants to guard it. Nothing happened, but only two days later Derby was warned not to go to Winstanley or Knowsley because there was a plot to assassinate him.

In the event there was no Catholic uprising, although a few troops had been raised before the militia were summoned. As for taking Chester, Colonel Gage's men began to calm down and after being billeted there for a few days they were disarmed peacefully by the city militia and townsfolk.

Prince William advanced cautiously to Salisbury, and there he was joined by Delamer and Lord Stamford from the north. Almost daily his support grew. *"Bath, York, Hull, Bristol, Hull and all the eminent nobility and persons of quality through England, declare for the Protestant religion and laws, and go to meet the Prince, who every day sets forth new Declarations against the Papists. The great favourites at Court, Priests and Jesuits, fly or abscond."*

Demands and counter-demands flew backwards and forwards between James and William. Nothing was going right for the King. He knew he was deeply disliked and distrusted by most of his subjects, but that was perhaps not too important in his eyes. However when he was faced with a powerful and potentially hostile contender for his throne, when he realised that he could not count on the loyalty of his own army, and when he saw trusted friends and supporters deserting his cause, he lost heart. Early in the morning of 11 December 1688 he surreptitiously left Whitehall aiming for France, throwing the Great Seal of England into the Thames as he fled. For the next few days, England was a kingdom without a king.

Sir Willoughby Aston learned of these startling happenings within three days, as did Governor Shakerley, who began to realise that James II's cause was lost. The main danger therefore was that his Catholic supporters would rise in revolt, so he sent out orders that all Catholics were to be disarmed. The next day even more terrifying rumours spread that a huge body of cavalry were advancing towards Cheshire looting, killing and burning as they came. As soon as he heard this, Aston hastily sent his servants to warn all his friends. They were greatly relieved the following day when the *"great body of horse"* turned out to be no more than a few straggling deserters. But on the same day reliable information arrived from London. The King had unofficially abdicated, the Lord Chancellor was in prison and the House of Lords as a body had declared for the Prince of Orange. The Lord Lieutenant of Cheshire and his deputies had been slightly too quick in supporting James II, but at last they had firm intelligence and as adherents to the Church of England could with clear consciences accept the arrival of the Protestant Prince of Orange.

There was still no official government of any kind in London. The Earl of Rochester, a High Tory and Stuart supporter, was quick to perceive the vacuum and to fill it urgently with a provisional council. He contacted as many members of the House of Lords as he could, and by 11 am on 11 December, a committee comprising both Archbishops, 4 Bishops, 10 earls, 2 viscounts and 9 barons had assumed temporary power. The London militia was ordered into readiness to put down any civil disorder; the commanders of the army and navy (Lords Feversham and Dartmouth respectively) were instructed not to give battle against William's forces; Lord Lucas was appointed Chief Governor of the Tower of London, with orders to disarm any Catholics; and finally and most important, the committee issued a declaration that they would *"assist His Highness* (Prince

William) *in the obtaining such a free Parliament."*

William could continue his advance without fear of opposition, and politically the throne appeared to be vacant, so he could not be accused of usurping it. He still had to be careful however, because he could not know exactly where James was and what he was doing. In fact, he had got no further than Faversham in Kent, where he was recognised and detained. Firm news of his whereabouts caused consternation in the Council of Peers, composed as it was of both Loyalists and Williamites. After much discussion, they sent a loyalist delegation to James, who began to return unchallenged to London on 16 December. Recovering his spirits a little, he insisted that he be served ceremonially on bended knee, received foreign ambassadors and proposed a meeting the next day with William for *"a personal conference to settle the distracted nation."* William ignored the invitation, but with the whiff of compromise in the air, the normal machinery of government began to revive.

William meanwhile was considering his next move. He called a meeting of the English peers. Eleven of them who had thrown their hats into the ring and joined him answered the summons, including of course Delamer, with five other convinced Williamites, Lords Shrewsbury, Mordaunt, Macclesfield, Wiltshire and Stamford. He asked just one question; what was their advice, now that James had gone back to Whitehall? He then left the room, leaving the peers to their discussion. Delamer, supported by Stamford and Macclesfield, proposed immediately that James should be sent to the Tower. He had already fled the capital once, which amounted to a dissolution of the government, and he could no longer claim to be king. Lord Churchill and the Duke of Grafton were more moderate, and eventually a compromise was reached that James should be advised to leave Whitehall and go to Ham House, a villa belonging to the Duchess of Lauderdale, on the rather spurious grounds that he would not be safe at Whitehall.

The Earl of Clarendon asked mildly why it would be unsafe for James to stay at Whitehall with his own guards, and why might he not be at liberty to go where he pleased? Delamer's temper, always fragile, snapped. Notoriously anti-Tory, puritanically nonconformist, he had been one of James's most outspoken critics since he had first entered Parliament in 1678. Now, at the last throw of the dice, he was in no mood to make concessions: *"...Lord Delamer very angrily (a little thing puts him into a passion) said, he did not look upon him as his King, and would never more pay him obedience; and that he ought not to be like a King in one of his own houses, and earnestly pressed that he might be directed to go to them."*

Prince William stopped the heated debate by instructing that James would be advised to leave. Not surprisingly there were no volunteers to deliver the message. If things went wrong, trials for High Treason and shameful deaths on the scaffold would be certain. William realised the dangers inherent in any delay and nominated the Marquis of Halifax, the Earl of Shrewsbury and Lord Delamer, who would be protected by three battalions of foot guards and a cavalry escort. His written instruction was the essential act of deposing the King and led to his second and enforced removal from London.

*"We do desire you, the Lord Marquis of Halifax, the Earl of Shrewsbury, and the Lord Delamer, to tell the King that it is thought convenient, for the greater quiet of the City*

*and for the greater safety of his person, that he do remove to Ham, where he shall be attended by guards, who will be ready to preserve him from any disturbance.*

*Given at Windsor, the 17th day of December 1688.          G. Prince d'Orange"*

Delamer and his colleagues marched into London late that evening. Their troops secured St James palace peacefully and continued to Whitehall. James was told of it just before going to bed, but thought it was only Prince William getting ready for the meeting proposed for the following morning, 18 December. On being told by the Dutch commander of the escort that it was nothing of the kind, he was nonplussed. Moreover, he was out-manoeuvred. The Dutch troops, in some force, were in full battle order, and his own were definitely not.  Also he had specifically ordered them not to offer resistance. Rather than countermand his orders and start a blood bath, he ordered his troops to stand down, and went passively to bed.

Halifax, Shrewsbury and Delamer had gone to the latter's lodgings (commandeered from the Marquis of Powys), and were planning exactly how to present William's message to James. Just after midnight, they returned to Whitehall and demanded immediate admittance. The Earl of Middleton, James's Gentleman in Waiting, made a token protest, but then woke the King at about 1 a.m. Even then James did not bother to get out of bed, but had the delegation admitted to his bedside.

Halifax, Shrewsbury and Delamer must have felt at least slightly nervous, but in a united front they presented the King with William's paper. James read it carefully and phlegmatically. If he was surprised at being woken at dead of night to be confronted with an ultimatum from a royal usurper, he showed no sign of it. Instead he calmly agreed with William's "request" to leave and asked just two questions. Could he choose his own servants? This reasonable request had been foreseen and the delegation agreed. But just as they turned to leave, James asked if he might go to Rochester rather than Ham House. this was outside their terms of reference, so Lord Halifax dashed off a hasty letter to William by express messenger. It was William's turn to be woken, to consider his uncle's request. He granted it, with the proviso that he would supply the guards.

James, with no room to bargain, left London for the last time at 11 am, just as Prince William was preparing to enter the city. However he felt no particular ill-will towards Delamer and according to the Dictionary of National Biography declared that Delamer had *"treated him with much more regard than the other two lords to whom he had been kind, and from whom he might better have expected it."*

Thus far everything was going right for William, but he was unsure how to become the lawful King with the full majesty of government behind him.  The provisional government had very properly ceased to function on 15 December pending James's return the next day. The Loyalists had resumed their functions and the revolutionaries had either stayed with William or prudently retired from public notice.

William's lawyers had advised him to declare himself king by right of conquest and to issue writs for a Parliament in his own name. He rejected this, deciding instead to seek the advice of the House of Lords, and called a meeting of all the 65 peers who were in or near London.  They met in the Queen's Presence Chamber on 21 December to consider the best way for William to call a Parliament, but they disagreed on almost everything.  All they could agree on was to thank William for his Solemn Declaration *"for the securing and maintenance of the Protestant religion."*

As for considering how to summon a parliament, which was their prime purpose, they did nothing whatsoever.  It was Delamer who proposed the motion of thanks, with the rider that the peers would stand by Prince William with their lives and fortunes.  But he had no support.  Backing down a little, he proposed that it should be left to individual discretion whether or not to sign the Declaration of Association to the Williamite cause.  However he wanted it put to the vote whether the Association should be tendered to be signed.  Lord Wharton was sceptical. He had signed so many declarations he could not remember them all and never found any that signified much.  Besides not everyone necessarily agreed with the text of the Association, so the Lords might consider something all could agree to.  Delamer, hot-headed as ever, wanted real action and quickly.  He replied curtly that several people had already signed the Association and to try to think of something else would certainly cause dissension.

Eventually the Association was laid on the table and several peers signed it.  Delamer had won his point and decided to strike his Protestant blow while his iron was hot.  Those Catholics who held office under James still did so, and they were anathema to his soul. He therefore moved that, as a matter of urgency, all remaining Papists be removed.  But before he could elaborate on this, from the country or just from office? - the other peers were less sure and wanted advice on how it could legally be done - they pacified the indignant Delamer by saying that everything should be done in accordance with the due process of law. They would deliberate the question of lawyers the next day with.

When the Lords met in the Chamber of the House of Lords the next morning, they first had to decide on those lawyers best qualified to advise on constitutional law, and several names were suggested.  The Marquess of Halifax took the Chair and proposed that Heneage Finch and Sir George Trevy, the Recorder of London, should be their advisers. Immediately Delamer, difficult as ever, leapt to his feet and objected to them; they should not be named again, otherwise *"there would be objections made on them."* In fact, Delamer was objecting on principle, because Halifax was a known moderate and he wanted chiefly to reduce his influence.

Eventually however, a list of four lawyers was agreed and they were called in. Halifax told them that the principal business of the day was to consider a way of calling a Parliament, but first it was necessary to find the easiest and most effective way of removing the Catholics from office.  The problem was to define Catholics, and three of the lawyers said without thinking that it should be quite easy.  Halifax then demonstrated his moderate opinions by saying that Catholics who had taken military commands and the Irish officers should be exempted, and the Bishop of London widened the net still further by proposing that those who had taken the various oaths and tests be also included.  Tradesmen, foreign ambassadors and their servants were sticking points.

Delamer listened with growing impatience to the discussions, wanting to move from the general to the particular, and leapt to his feet at the first opportunity.  He had an old grudge to settle.  Bitterly he reminded his colleagues that he well remembered what it was to be held a close prisoner in the Tower of London.  That building was then holding no less an august personage than the ex-king's Lord Chancellor and erstwhile Lord Chief Justice, George Jeffreys of Bloody Assizes fame. Panicking, he had fled in disguise when James left first, but he had been recognised and clapped in the Tower. Delamer commented that opinions seemed to have changed during the last few days, and the main reason, he believed, was that too many people had unrestricted access to Jeffreys. Jeffreys did not deserve more favour than he had shown to Delamer. He should be under closer restraint with only one servant. Moreover, no one should be permitted to speak to him other than in the presence of a warder or without express permission from the Lords.

Halifax had reservations, stating that Jeffreys was a member of the Lords and was confined without charge. The confinement, he said, should be legalised and Lord Lucas, Chief Governor of the Tower, duly received his written orders from the Lords' overworked secretary, Francis Gwyn, that Jeffreys should speak to no one except in Lucas's presence, and a list of them be given to the Lords each day.

The most important task of the Council that day was to draft and agree an order that all Catholics were to leave the City of London and return to their homes without delay. Even important Catholic landowners were to register with the nearest Justice of the Peace. Only certain named diplomatic foreigners were exempted and merchants who had traded in London for more than three years.

Francis Gwyn compiled the various exemption certificates and the Committee was about to break for their well-deserved Sunday rest when Lord Pagett reminded them that their business on Monday ought to be to consider a free Parliament. Delamer grabbed the opportunity and went further, demanding that the state of the government should be their first and most important business, leading to the consideration of a free parliament, and wearily their Lordships agreed.

It was not quite so, however, because a flood of personal applications had to be dealt with first. Five warrants for treason were issued, several applications to be excused from banishment were heard. Warham Horsemanden, a deputy Lieutenant of Essex, was not in fact a Catholic, and so on. Some time elapsed before the matter of a free parliament was even mentioned by Lord Cornwallis. Various peers talked round the question rather irrelevantly, until the Earl of Abingdon mentioned that writs had already gone out to call a Parliament. Should they be proceeded with? Delamer took up the point. Had all the writs gone out? He was actually arguing against himself, because he had already claimed that the late King's actions had no force in law, but he was so anxious for a new Parliament that he was overlooking this in his impatience. Lord Culpeper replied that there was no government and no Sheriffs; otherwise they would not be meeting there. The writs had of course been sent out by Royal command, but as there was no longer a king, they had no legal standing.

Delamer, slightly embarrassed, shifted his ground. Yes, of course the writs were invalid, because of the Oath of Allegiance. But the most important thing was that the country should have a free Parliament as soon as possible.

It was left to Halifax to take the bull by the horns. Prince William, he said, still had no official standing, and as far as the strict letter of the law was concerned, was only a usurper. The House of Lords should resolve the problem by inviting him to shoulder the administration of Government until a free parliament settled it, and a small subcommittee of legally qualified peers (including of course Delamer) should draft the request.

Being Christmas, the Lords did not reassemble until the afternoon of 25th December, and Delamer was absent from the first roll call, perhaps catching up on lost sleep. The proposed draft of the subcommittee was prepared, *"writ fair on vellum"*, but the Council noted a small omission, so the whole address had to be rewritten and Delamer arrived in time to sign the final version. Prince William formally accepted the invitation and agreed to protect the Protestant religion. Six weeks later, at a dignified ceremony in the Banqueting House, Whitehall, the Marquis of Halifax formally tendered the Crown to him and he became William III.

Delamer's rewards were soon coming. On 28 March 1689 he was appointed Under-Treasurer of the Exchequer and on the same day Chancellor of the Exchequer, to be held during the King's pleasure. Soon afterwards he was made Custos Rotulorum of Cheshire and at this Lord Derby's patience broke. He had done his best for William III. In the Orange interest he had commissioned 29 Deputy Lieutenants, all loyal Protestants; he had recruited many militia officers, and made certain of Chester; and he had formed *"four good and great regiments of foot and five troops of horse, all which, in convenient time, did unanimously declare for his Highness the Prince of Orange"* and had received nothing but snubs for his exertions, while honours were being heaped on Delamer. And to find that Delamer was also being made Lord Lieutenant of Cheshire, which Derby regarded as his private fiefdom, was too much for him. His aggrieved petition is very bitter about the way Delamer double-crossed him by arranging to advance together from Cheshire to Prince William and then leaving without waiting for Derby, and worse still by accusing Derby of being dilatory. Many of Derby's actions were more deserving of praise than criticism, and to be thus treated by Lord Delamer, to be stripped of the offices of Lord Lieutenant of Cheshire and Custos Rotulorum, which Derby actually held at William III's accession, *"to be given to the other, it must be endured with humblest submission to his Majestie....."*

William III was not quite firmly settled on the throne. In March 1689 Sir Willoughby Aston commented to Sir John Crewe that there were undercurrents. *"Things are not here* (London) *as you may imagine"* but he dared not be precise. All he could write in another letter was that Lord Delamer would be travelling back to Cheshire and *"you may hear all mysteries revealed, which cannot be written but I fear will appear too soon if not timely prevented."* Peter Shakerley was to be Governor of Chester Castle and this would surprise Delamer when he heard of it, because, Aston hinted, he (Delamer) had expectations of it himself. Delamer was at least temporarily the darling of the London hotheads, and when he returned to London in July, he was conducted in to the City by a guard of honour of 500 horsemen and many more on foot. There he had a request from the Cheshire gentry to have quashed all the outstanding presentments against them outstanding from when James was rocking on the throne.

Lord Delamer did not stay long in William III's favour. He was too prickly and confident that his opinions were always correct for that. Anyone who dared to contradict him or disagree with him was certain to earn his displeasure at the least or his enmity at the most.  Delamer's family traditions caused him to believe firmly in close restrictions to the Royal prerogative, and in this he did no more than follow his father and great grandfather.  William however failed to see any logic in having been summoned to take the throne, only to have his sovereignty circumscribed by law by the proposed Bill of Rights, which Delamer enthusiastically supported.

The direct cause of his break with the King was the latter's policy towards Ireland and towards Catholics.  The ex-king, James, had recovered his nerve to some extent, and looked to the Irish Catholics for help in recovering his throne.  He landed there in March 1689.  At first William was content to leave the problem in the hands of Count Schomberg, his trusted commander, but when Schomberg proved defeatist and incompetent, William decided to take personal command, planning to defeat the Irish Catholics as a means of ridding himself of any danger from James.

Lord Delamer fervently opposed William's plans to quash the Irish Catholics.  It may seem strange that Delamer with his hatred of Catholicism did not support William, but he believed that William's brief acquaintance with England could not have given him a detailed understanding of the country and it could have been calamitous to leave it so soon after his arrival.  Moreover Delamer's pride, dogmatic character and certainty of being always right meant that he simply could not understand why the King rejected his advice. He genuinely thought that his distinguished services to William made his counsel vital. Hurt and baffled, he summed up his reasons in a long letter to the Marquis of Carmarthen (Sir Thomas Osborne, Earl of Danby), the President of the Council:

*"You will be surprised that I, who have daily opportunity of discourse, should address you in writing: it is the nature of the thing that induces me to communicate my thoughts by this paper.  The small regard which the King has given to my advice and opinion, as to persons and things, shews that I ought to be silent rather than, unasked, to offer him my sentiments upon his going to Ireland."*

Delamer complained that the King was showing preference to people who had previously been opposed to him, whereas he, Delamer, who had dared so much for William, was distrusted.  Therefore he would not speak to William about the Irish business.  His sense of duty however would not let him be completely silent, so he was relying on Carmarthen to relay his thoughts to the king.  For a man to argue against a king whose mind was made up was difficult, especially when Schomberg, a man of high reputation, had failed, but *"everything considered, I cannot be persuaded to consent the King's going out of England.  Should another, in his absence, step into the throne, I fear he must, for ever, bid farewell to it.  It has always bin the policy of Princes to be more careful to secure themselves in the throne than to consider how they got into it.  Out of sight, out of mind, is an English proverb that is applicable to kings as other men; for absence has lost many kings their crowns... there is too great cause to believe that numbers want to shut the door upon King William, who has no majority either in the Lords or Commons and who has not as many friends as when Prince of Orange"*

Delamer thought that the danger was too great.  Was the expedition worth being hazarded on *"the caprice of the multitude?"*  Was it even certain that the army was completely dependable?  Although William was on the throne, ex-king James was not without support and if the Irish adventure ended in tragedy, he would certainly return to England, with predictable results for his opponents. That is the reason why Delamer, a fanatical Whig, broached the subject to Carmarthen, a high Tory, politically poles apart.

Carmarthen did decide to show Delamer's letter to the King, who predictably took no notice of it. It marked the beginning of the final break between him and Delamer. In the spring of 1690, the King needed more than £6,000,000 for the army in Ireland and only £3,000,000 was available from the revenue. There are indications that Delamer objected. Finally in March he was dismissed from his posts of Under-Treasurer and Chancellor of the Exchequer and ordered to hand his seals of office to Richard Hampden. He had been in office just less than a year. Immediately £200,000 was granted for the army in Ireland.

As for Catholics in England, Delamer had shown his hand as early as January 1693/4. A small quantity of arms had been found at the house of Sir James Poole, and Delamer as Lord Lieutenant of Cheshire had been ordered to disarm the Catholics in the county as soon as possible. He objected to this and wrote to Sir Willoughby Aston saying that the Deputy Lieutenants should agree unanimously before taking action. It was a very small matter and it was not in his opinion worth searching all known Catholic homes.

William was not ungrateful for Delamer's work and as a consolation advanced him in the peerage from Baron to Viscount Delamer and Earl of Warrington. He also granted him a generous pension of £2000 a year from the income of the Duchy of Cornwall, but little of it was ever paid before it was suspended. Two years later Delamer was pleading for the pension to be restored, but it seems that he never received an answer.

Bitterly hurt at having been so pointedly snubbed by William, Delamer (Lord Warrington we should now call him) retreated to Dunham Massey, to adopt it as his permanent home for the first time. The hall was his mother's residence from 1684 (the death of his father, George, 1st Lord Delamer) until her own death a few years later, and Warrington had been living in Mere Hall when he was in the area.

His enforced retirement allowed him to collect the speeches he had made and the articles he had written with a view to publication. Unfortunately the health of his wife Mary began to give cause for concern and after a long illness she died. She was buried in the family vault in Bowdon Church on 6 April 1691, with an immensely long sermon by Richard Wroe, the Warden of Christ's College in Manchester. He described her as even-tempered, but quite capable of controlled anger if aroused. And as befitted a good and dutiful wife, she managed the household well and taught her children to read and write.

Warrington was grief-stricken. Rather unusually for those days of arranged marriages, he seems to have deeply loved Mary and she certainly supported him through thick and thin. When he had recovered a little, he composed a long poem in her praise:

> "Thus, in one moment have I lost
> That which of earthly things I valued most
> For with one fatal stroke Death does destroy
> The greatest Blessing Man did e'er enjoy.

Her virtue was above Temptation sure,
As chaste as Ice, no Mixture would endure.
Safely I might my Honour with her trust
Who was in that and all things else so just.

What Wisdom and Affection she did show
When the rough Storms full in my face did blow?
With how much Pleasure she her part did bear
Or rather say, did take the bigger share,

And always forward still to interpose
'Twixt me and any Storm when it arose?"

Warrington had suffered for his beliefs and he was at pains to explain, mainly for his children, his political and religious principles. He explained his political principles in many of his speeches and writings and summed them up in his *Essay upon Government* and in his speech to the Grand Jury of Chester on 13 April 1692. These works could in themselves serve as a Bible for the Whig party, although even the name 'Whig' had only been coined in about 1680. Certainly in his beliefs and principles, Warrington could be described as one of the founders of the party, although there was of course no party organisation as such. The Whigs however were united in believing that the powers of the monarchy should be strictly limited, and that there should be no distinction between the different factions of Protestantism. These were the very foundations of Warrington's political and religious philosophy.

Having a literal belief in God, there was no doubt in his mind that a government of some sort was essential. Various types of government had existed, and their mere existence was sufficient demonstration of God's wisdom. It was up to each country to choose its own constitution by natural instinct, and that of England was the best in the world, because it was founded on just statutes and avoided all extremes of tyranny and liberty. England's constitution was ideal, that of a monarch acting with a parliament. Parliament was the means of representing the king in a true light to his people, and there was no better foundation than the great principles of Magna Carta. Parliament was responsible for money supply, the repeal of obsolete laws, the creation of new statutes, and appeals to justice. Failing these, there was only despotism *"and that King of England who is uneasie with the Ancient way of governing will never be pleased with any, but what gives all into his hands."*

Warrington maintained that the English monarchy was not necessarily hereditary. In fact until the conquest of England by William I, succession had been by election, and William I had no right to the crown by inheritance or descent. However on becoming king, he took an oath to maintain the laws and properties of the country, *"although some little irregularities must be admitted."* After him, the crown did not always pass to the nearest by blood - William II and Henry I both became king during the lifetime of Duke Robert, William I's eldest son, and several other instances of kings being chosen occurred during mediaeval times. In fact, Warrington had a theory that succession by popular acclaim implies that election of the sovereign is preferable, and that, conscious of the honour conferred upon him, the King should use his royal prerogative for the general good and advantage of his people.

A king needs advice and therefore a Privy Council is essential to advise him, but when it becomes a self-serving cabinet, it becomes evil, because its members tell the king only what they think he wants to hear. The consequence is the neglect of Parliament, and without this, true government cannot continue. This was a point that Warrington particularly stressed when Charles II began to reign without a Parliament. The whole country, he said in a speech, desired a Parliament. A king without a Parliament who relied on the advice of favourites was powerless, because many of his advisers were selfish men with no great fortunes or estates who thought only of their own benefit. For the sake of the country they must be removed from positions of power and influence. Warrington was scornful of these *"caterpillars, his Favourites, their care is not how to serve him, but to make their own Fortunes."*

All advice tendered to the king must be open and plain, so that his people can see for themselves that he is acting in their best interests. *"When he is shy of being seen, the People in a short time will as little value the sight of him, as he is willing to expose himself to view."* He should listen to advice from whatever quarter it comes in order to distinguish between good men and selfish place-men. *"When he... values every Man according to the rate that the Nation sets upon him, he then at once bows the hearts of all the People as one Man, and thereby becomes as safe and great... as the Wisdom, Blood and Treasure of the land can make him."* However, if he ignores them *"then as Naturally as Corruption succeeds Death, their Rooms must be supply'd by others, who have neither Interest, Principle, nor Morality, but are compounded of Knave and Fool, the very Scum of the land...."*

Freedom and liberty were essential planks of English law, and Warrington quoted seven separate statutes of Henry III and Edward III, all of which had been infringed from time to time by various Privy Councils. No accusations and punishments without due process of law; false and malicious charges punishable; all trials to begin before Justices otherwise they were void in law. All these Warrington referred to in a great speech.

The king must acknowledge that all the various parties are equal and have equal rights before him. He must not act so as to cause jealousy. To judge between them is not easy, because distinctions will always exist. There will be good and bad, *"For as long as there are either Fools or Knaves, there will be difference in the size and strength of parties, and there will be Fools and Knaves until Christ's Kingdom comes... How great a Blessing or a Burden then is a King to the Land, and how ought a good one to be valued and a bad one to be dreaded, since there is no Medium betwixt those two."*

Every government and every king should aim at order and peace for the country. Magna Carta laid down that every man has a clear right to his lawful possessions, which cannot be taken from him without his consent. This is an essential principle for an honest stable government, failing which the country will be plunged into chaos and disorder. The king must also recognise his prerogative as being *"to help and relieve the People when the edge of the law is too sharp and keen."* His greatest virtue is in being restrained by the law, and if he attempts to act outside legal authority with absolute power, he will inevitably oppress his people. Indeed, if he, Warrington, had criticised the monarchy in such a way in the two previous reigns, he would have risked losing his head. As it was, the exercise of arbitrary power had caused the death of Charles I, shaken Charles II, and brought about the downfall of James II.

The king will certainly make mistakes, but as long as they are honest mistakes, they can be corrected. If however he imposes them deliberately, refusing to admit the error, they are evil and he will be judged to be a bad character; on the other hand if he does correct them, he will be seen to be wise and just. All people are fallible, and *"....he that always keeps in the right road is a fortunate Prince."*

Clearly the institution of kingship came after the commencement of the existence of the people, so in that respect he is to some extent subservient to his people. He owes them protection and they in turn are subject to him and owe him obedience. This mutual trust creates a bond between the king and his people, and only the king can break this bond. However the king must acknowledge the will of the people and them in turn. If the king destroys the government by acting outside the established law, he is breaking the bond with his people, and this is precisely what happens if the king is a Catholic, because his allegiance is chiefly to papal authority.

Even Charles II, recalled by popular demand, had a concealed wish to surrender his people's religion and liberties. His reign was marked by moral looseness and debauchery, disguised as loyalty to himself and the Church, and by sham plots by Protestants against him. He exacted penal laws against dissenters, while acknowledged Catholics walked free.

Attempts had been made to demonstrate that the monarch made the laws and therefore could dispense with them if he wished. The laws of the land were in fact made by Parliament and therefore by the people and only thereafter were they referred to as the King's Laws. It followed that his powers were strictly limited and even Charles II had expressly disclaimed any powers of dispensation. Only if the king acted within the established laws of the land could his actions be always legal, and he could not change them at his pleasure or to suit his own objectives.

By this logic, Warrington considered that the deposition of James II was justified in law, just as Papal authority was not justified. If the king did not or could not protect his subjects, their obligation to him was discharged and they owed him no loyalty. It was safer to have a Protestant king whose morality was suspect. *"When the King forsakes the Law, he ceases to be king, and makes room for another who is more righteous than himself: and therefore, because he endeavoured to set his will above the Law, was the late King James set aside, and I am perswaded with all the Justice in the world."*

As for the rashly impetuous Duke of Monmouth, Warrington had never made any secret for his support, on the grounds that James II was an avowed Catholic, and that the Mosaic law of inheritance (the next of blood) was irrelevant. Monmouth was the nearest alternative and the Bill of Attainder against him was badly flawed. It had passed both Houses of Parliament in a single day, and Monmouth had been judged with no opportunity to state his case. Did Parliament even have all the evidence? In Warrington's opinion, there was a strong case for reversing the Bill of Attainder passed against Monmouth.  Before his elevation in the peerage Warrington had stated publicly that we should fight or burn and that the then Duke of York ought to be legally excluded from the throne.  It was better to risk loyal lives to defend the law rather than to let him inherit, because any opponents would be doomed by the Pope to death.

In Warrington's mind, politics and religion were inseparable, and for the same reasons that he detested the idea of absolute monarchy, he detested absolutism in religion and was entirely inflexible in his attitude to Catholicism.  Having been brought up in the tolerant Presbyterian faith, he also distrusted and disliked the more extreme Protestants. There was no need for laws against Dissenters, which punished many people who led worthy godly lives in their own ways.  *"True religion needs no such methods to support it,"* he proclaimed. Too much effort was put into punishing people for nonconformity, and too little into reforming their lives and manners.  Those who did not or could not go to all Church services as the law adjoined were automatically criticised as rogues and villains, even if they led upright and blameless lives.  On the other hand, men who led lives of wickedness and debauchery and rarely attended church but railed against dissenters were hailed as good honest sons of the true church.

Sadly, Warrington did not live long after arranging for his various speeches and writings.  While in London late in 1693, he contracted some feverish infection.  He died on 2 January 1694.

He was interred in the family vault in Bowdon Church during the night of 15 January and once again Richard Wroe gave the funeral sermon. George Malbon described the catafalque:  *"...much like a bed, the top something sharp every way upon a flatt supported by four pillars and rails like bedsteads, all covered with black cloth and open, that is to the pillars from the rails to the canopy or top over it, and strip of black hanging down round about the top like bed vallance, and so likewise from the rails to the ground, all adorned with scutcheons and pennants.  At the top... the crest - perle and diamond, a lion passant perle.  Upon the capitals of the pillars, his hon'rs arms and supporters, that is - perle, three boars heads erected and erased diamond lingued ruby and tusked topaz, supported by two boars diamond... within the herse a great coffin... with a flat top covered with pure black cloth.  Upon the lid or top a black velvet cushion with knobs and tassels and thereon a coronet gilt...."*

This magnificent funeral must have strained the finances of the family even more.

Warrington's death may not have caused too much distress to some in the court or in the House of Lords.  Macaulay said of him:

> *"A restless malcontent even when preferred....*
> *His boding looks a mind distracted show*
> *And envy sits engraved upon his brow."*

But at least two others wrote tributes. The following anonymous verse appears in John Broston's *Vale Royal of England:*

> *"A brave asserter of his country's right,*
> *A noble but ungovernable fire*
> *(Such as the Heros) did his breast inspire,*

*Fit to assist to pull a Tyrant down,*
*But not to please a Prince that mounts the throne,*
*Impatient of oppression still he stood,*
*His country's mound against th'invading flood"*

John Dunton, a *"citizen of London"*, was effusive in his praise:*"Lord Delamer, a very great man, and one that deserved well of his Country. He asserted the English Liberties with a noble zeal; and never carried his point by noise and tumult, but by prudence and the strength of argument. He was a Christian as well as a politician, though he made no bustle in the Church; for his principles had nothing in them but moderation and peace. His "Posthumous Works" give a better character of him than I can do. They shew he was well acquainted with the World, and how little he expected from it; and they discover a very generous concern for Posterity, and the great interest of religion."*

Much of what Dunton said was certainly true. Warrington did uphold the ancient English liberties, and his Christianity was beyond doubt. However he made his points with a great deal of *"noise and tumult";* tact was not his strong point. He was arrogant, obstinate, intolerant, bad-tempered, fanatical in his beliefs, and even worried his friends. Aston seems to refer to him as *"your crasie friend"* in another letter to Crewe and decided not to invite Crewe to dine when Warrington announced his intention of visiting. On another occasion, Aston politely asked for a lift in Warrington's coach during a rainstorm. Warrington refused and Aston got soaked and caught a bad cold, but remarked philosophically that *"great Lords will have their little ways."*

Only a man dogmatic to the point of stupidity would risk upsetting even one king. Warrington succeeded in upsetting three kings, at great risk to his life. However, whatever his faults of character, he cannot be accused of failing to stick to his principles.

Nowadays he is usually no more than a footnote or at best merely a brief mention in any history of the time. But his influence at the time was far greater than history has credited him. Perhaps it is not too far-fetched to speculate that had it not been for Warrington's courage and decisiveness, we might today be living in a Catholic country?

Sources

CSPD has many references for the progress through Cheshire of the Duke of Monmouth, and Volume 18 of the Chester & North Wales Architectural, Archaeological and Historic Society has Katherine Howard's diary and reminiscences of his visit to Dunham. The trial for high treason of Henry, first Earl of Warrington, was transcribed and printed in 1686, and was consulted in the City of Manchester's Social Sciences Library, as were *His Lordship's Advice to his Children* and his *Collected Works.* HMC Fleming and Kenyon flesh out the story of Warrington's support for William of Orange, and many reports of his progress to join William are in British Library ADD MSS 41805. The Earl of Clarendon's Correspondence throws unflattering light on Warrington's character. The complete proceedings of the House of Lords Council are given in Robert Beddard's *A Kingdom without a King.* Warrington's philosophy and politics are well expressed in his own *Collected Works.*

George Booth Second Earl of Warrington, 1675-1758,
with his daughter, Lady Mary Booth.

Dunham Massey Hall in the 19th century.

# Chapter Four
## George Booth, Second Earl of Warrington

Immediately on the death of Henry, first Earl of Warrington, his eldest son George succeeded to the title and great estates. To inherit such huge responsibilities at the age of only 19 would have been a daunting prospect to anyone, but the young George also knew that his inheritance had been in a shambles for many years. An estate that had been rich when old Sir George had died 42 years before was now bankrupt and every part of it was mortgaged to the hilt. An earldom needed a profitable and wealthy estate with contented tenants, but the new earl inherited nothing but financial ruin.

He could remember only hardship since his earliest youth. His father had been in the habit of celebrating the anniversary of his acquittal by holding a 'public day' on which poor people were fed and clothed, but his finances had deteriorated to such an extent that he had been forced to abandon even this practice.

Some years later, Warrington wrote a paper sombrely recalling their financial straits and explaining to his younger brother Henry just what the situation had been at his inheritance:

*"When we lay at our grandfather Langham's house the winter before the Revolution, my mother was sometimes so streighten'd for money that she borrow'd of some of the servants, and even of what little pocket-money my sister and I had. And at the same time of being in Town she was forced to borrow £60 for housekeeping there, which was not repaid until after my father's death.*

*"While my father lived, they could never spare money for any sort of furniture, not even for her own chamber when we came to live at Dunham, so that there was only the little Dining Room with old moath-eaten Turkey-work chairs for company to dine in, and when a great deal of company came, were forced to dine in the Hall. And so few rooms furnish'd to lodge strangers that when only a little company lay here, I was often removed out of my chamber, tho' very meanly furnished. When my father furnisht the Great Dining Room and Drawing Room after my mother's death, there was above £200 unpaid for that furniture when he dyed. And always during his life soe streighten'd for money that they could scarce spare any for necessary bed or table linnen for the house. My mother had but £400 for her own pin money and £10 per an apiece for us children to find herself and us with cloaths and all necessaries.*

*I have seen my father several times the year before the Revolution fall aweeping at the greatness of his debts: and they were increased at the Revolution. When my mother dyed, my father took that opportunity to leave off keeping a publicke day in the house, and dined on the Bowling Day at the Ale House in Dunham Town, to save charges."*

The estate was also effectively bankrupt. Its income was £2685, but unavoidable expenses totalled over £3500. Only fines for renewing leases and heriots kept it solvent, with about £600 remaining *"for all repairs at Dunham House, out-houses, mill, park and demesne: and at Sinderland and Bowdon: and for all furniture, smith's work, day-*

*labourers, coopers, carpenters, wheelwrights, coachmaker, saddlers, husbandry tools, carriage of goods, law charges, and all other incident charges whatsoever."*

How had a great estate fallen into such hard times? Warrington was in no doubt, blaming all the problems on extravagant lifestyles and the expenditure caused by taking leading roles in the political troubles:

*"That all this taken together is a very strong proof that our family has served the publick to a greater degree and made a greater figure than the estate at its best could hold out to do; and consequently, that now the estate is lessen'd thereby, the getting or keeping up an interest and sway and making ourselves popular... must necessarily be the absolute ruin of our family.*

*That it is very unreasonable for the world to expect me to live as great and serve the publick as much as my family before me has done, when the reason they expect it of me is the very reason why I can't do it; by which I mean that people, having seen what my family has done formerly at their own expense, do therefore think my estate can still do the like."*

He had put his finger on a problem that has bedevilled some people since a man wanted a better cave. In the 17th century there were very clear demarcation lines between the different ranks of the aristocracy. A baron was greater than a baronet and an earl was two steps up from the mere baron. Moreover each peer was supposed to live in a manner befitting his rank, even if his estate could not support the extra expenditure necessitated by promotion within the peerage.

This was precisely what had happened to his father and grandfather, and a study of the family papers reveals a sorry catalogue of increasing expenditure on a static estate. Old Sir George Booth could not be blamed. He had lived within his means. His costs had been very high during the Civil War, but he remained rich in Cheshire. In 1649 he was easily able to afford to arrange portions for his daughters Mary, Frances, Katherine and Elizabeth merely by arranging trusts on Thornton le Moors, the rectory of Bowdon Church and the Dunham salt works, none of which were essential parts of the core estate. Even arranging a trust for lands in Sale for his grandson shortly before his own death was a matter of small importance.

Unfortunately Young Sir George seems to have been less wise than his grandfather. Even in 1649 he wanted to inflate the portions available to his daughters, using the property old Sir George had made available to him. If there was only one daughter, she would receive £4000, if two, £3000 each, and if more than two, £2000 each, and for this, Young Sir George used the Thornton le Moors lands, Stayley, Ashton under Lyne and Saddleworth, under a 60-year trust. Even before his disastrous 1659 attempt to overthrow the Protectorate, he was in need of ready cash and converted the Thornton le Moors and Stayley trust into a straight mortgage for £3000. More seriously, he included the home lands of the manor and barony of Dunham Massey, together with the surrounding properties in Timperley, Hale, Altrincham, Bowdon. Then when he desperately needed money to equip his forces in 1659, he even took out a second mortgage on the Thornton properties, but after the Restoration of Charles II (although he proudly only accepted half of the £20,000 offered) he was able to pay off the mortgages.

After the Restoration, the now Lord Delamer seems to have spent an increasing amount of time in London, since his chaplain's stipend went from £40 to £15 in the normal year as we have seen.  Moreover living in London, taking part in extravagant court life, was a heavy drain on his finances, with no guarantee of profit.  Quite the reverse in fact, as Warrington commented. *"How long did either of them (his father and grandfather) continue in favour when they would not be servile courtiers?"*

It is hardly surprising therefore that by 1671 Delamer could not increase the portions of his daughters except by putting more of his lands in trust.  He presumably felt that their existing settlements were not in keeping with the dignity of his peerage and he wanted also to make adequate arrangements for his son Henry.  Nothing else could explain the extravagant expenditure. Four years later the Bollin and Wilmslow properties went into trust to make £2000 available for his eldest daughter Vere.

Even this was not enough.  Four years later, he revoked the trusts and made new ones, in order to provide settlements of no less than £5000 each for Elizabeth and Diana, provided that he consented to their marriages when they took place.  He then had to mortgage Thornton le Moors again, Stayley, Saddleworth, Hattersley, Bollin and Bollin Hall and Norcliffe when Diana was marrying the Earl of Conway.  He was still short of money and even had to borrow £2500 from Richard Mulys and Roger Jackson of St Martin in the Fields.  So Carrington, Ashton on Mersey, Partington and Sinderland all went as security on the loans.

The estates therefore were heavily charged even when the first Lord Delamer died and his son Henry succeeded.  But they soon became worse.  Almost immediately Henry discovered that Diana had not actually received her £5000 portion and the late Delamer had died in debt.  He was forced to re-assign the existing mortgage to Messrs John Swynfen and Horsey, in return for £5000 due to Diana and an extra £1200 to discharge Delamer's various debts.  Henry had to re-mortgage (again) Thornton le Moors and messuages, farms, cottages, etc. in the area surrounding Dunham Massey.

Even the core of the estate followed in 1691.  Henry wished to outdo the generosity of his late father in providing sumptuous portions for his own daughters, and he needed to raise the huge sum of £10,000 for each of them.  *"The manor and barony of Dunham Massey with all appurtenant messuages, lands and tenements in Dunham Massey, Sinderland, Bollington, Bowdon, Hale, Altrincham, Sale, Timperley, Partington and Ashton upon Mersey, and capital messuages called Carrington Hall in Carrington and Bottoms Hall in Hattersley"* were put in trust for that purpose.

So the 19 year old second Earl of Warrington had every right to be horrified and at a loss as what to do.  All the estate was charged.  Ashton-under-Lyne, Warrington and part of Hattersley were part of his mother's jointure; Carrington and Sinderland were mortgaged  for £5,000; Stayley and the rest of Hattersley were mortgaged to the hilt for £6,200; Thornton le Moors had two mortgages, one to the mortgagees of Stayley and Hattersley, the remainder to Warrington's Aunt Diana; Wilmslow was mortgaged to his spinster Aunt Vere; even Dunham Massey was charged with his grandmother's jointure.

And that was not all.  Where was Henry's will, if indeed he had ever written one?  Young Warrington knew nothing of it, nor did any of his relatives in the house, his Uncle George, Aunt Vere and sister Elizabeth.  They decided for security to lock up the room where Henry kept all his papers and to wrap the key in paper sealed by them all, but when they all opened the room the following afternoon, they were surprised and disappointed to find nothing.

Warrington wrote urgently to John Edmonds, the estate steward in Cheshire, informing him of the death of the first Earl and instructing him, with his deputies, Thomas Hunt and Richard Drinkwater, to search every possible place where any will might have been put, including the *'Evidence Closet'* where all the property deeds etc. were kept. He found nothing, nor did Warrington's Uncle Cecil, who was also asked to search. However, some two weeks later, Edmonds was looking for another document, happened to come across what appeared to be Henry's will, and wrote to Warrington accordingly. He was ordered to keep it secret until Warrington came back from London in the middle of March. Then Warrington read the will, written in his father's handwriting, signed, sealed and witnessed and for the first time realised the full horror of his situation. It was impossibly generous, he realised, and his father's assets simply could not support it. By any standards, he was bankrupt. Henry's daughters Elizabeth and Mary each received the interest of 5% on £5000; the two younger sons Langham and Henry Booth each received an annuity of £200; and there were minor bequests to other relatives.

He found it hard to believe that his father had meant it to stand as his last will and testament. Firstly, there were the circumstances of its discovery. Edmonds said he had found it in *"...a large old Deal Box with a broken Lidd without Lock or Key to it, which seem'd to be placed there purely for a Receptacle for cast-away papers, being full of old useless dusty papers confusedly tumbled together, it being his common practice, when he found no further use for a paper, to throw it carelessly away, without further thought of it, or considering it needfull to destroy it."*

Secondly, as we have seen, the terms of the will could not possibly be met, given the circumstances of the estate. Henry's financial state, which he must have been aware of, was so disastrous that there could have been no possible chance of finding the money to pay the bequests. But that was not all. Even if there had been enough money, young Warrington should have inherited the bulk of the estate. He was the next head of the family and on his 21st birthday could be the master of 11,000 fertile Cheshire acres, but he was not even mentioned in the will except as executor. It was grossly unfair to him.

Thirdly, there was the date of the will, made on 16 October 1688. The more Warrington thought about it, the more crucial the date seemed to him, just two weeks before Prince William of Orange landed at Torbay with his army. Henry's decision to side with William had, of course, long been made, and he must have known that his life was in grave danger, either by facing death in the likely battle, or perhaps at the hands of the executioner if William failed or changed his mind. *"He did not take time to consider in what posture his affairs then stood, but made his will in a great hurry... a fortnight before the then Prince of Orange landed in England."* His *"thoughts were then soe much employed and taken up in that business that he could not consider the Condition of his owne private Estate or Affaires... the Joyntures, Debts and other Incumbrances wherewith* (his) *Estate was then charged, together with what was charg'd thereon and given away... were more than the profits of the whole Estate was sufficient to discharge, without any provision for this Respondent"* wrote Warrington in answer to questions put to him two years later, *"and (what is still more astonishing) all this, without any provision whatsoever made for the Education, Maintenance, or even buying bread for me, his eldest son, on whom his Honours were to descend."*

Warrington was so anxious to believe that there was no valid will that he even began to think the servants could have foisted a forgery on him. His father and grandfather had both left the servants to their own devices in the running of the estates and Warrington had long suspected that the head servants at least were not entirely honest. After all, John Edmonds, the steward, did not even look after the key to the Evidence Room himself; that was left to a junior maid, obviously an unsatisfactory state of affairs.

Lastly, according to Warrington, his father had always put his mind at rest about the relative poverty by telling him *"he should not be troubled thereat, for he would order his affairs soe that he would make it up to him."* Henry may have been thinking of expectations from the Duchess of Somerset, who had told him that she would leave him all her landed property, on condition that he would not reduce the portions that he was thinking of for his daughters. (Henry's wife, the daughter of Sir James Langham, had been until her death the Heir-at-Law of the Duchess.) He was therefore in honour bound to arrange those portions but the hoped-for wealth did not in the event come to him. The legacies finally went to his daughters: Elizabeth and Mary both received substantial legacies, but this of course was of no help to Henry and even less to his son George.

The more Warrington examined his father's will and other papers, the more it seemed that Henry's affairs had been so chaotic that he had shut everything out of his mind and ignored it. He had even drawn up a list of his debts and expenditures, so he must have known that what had once been a rich estate was in a shambles of debt and there was no apparent way out. His gross debts totalled £24,315, including his Coronation expenses, even a guess that his various stays in the Tower had cost not less than £2000. Then there were the sums set aside for family annuities, making £1183 and a grand total of £25498.

Against this his assets were quite small. His personal estate was valued at £5000, the only considerable sum and the remainder was only £1287. Warrington studied this 'Will' and began to convince himself that his father had never intended it to be his Last Will & Testament. What then, was he to do about it? If he made it public to his family, he stood to ruin himself, having no inheritance and no means of satisfying their justifiable hopes. On the other hand, he stood little chance of keeping the matter quiet, because his relations simply would not believe that Henry had made no will, they could not know the true parlous state of the estate or that Henry had effectively disinherited his eldest son, and in any case several people already knew that there was indeed a will. The unfortunate young Warrington was damned if he did and damned if he didn't.

He finally persuaded himself that his father's will was invalid, so there was nothing to be gained by admitting its existence. He even solemnly denied to Elizabeth in the presence of witnesses that no will had been found. Secretly he copied out its main provisions but over a year later began to take legal advice, not on the original (carefully lost) but on the partial transcript. Perhaps his conscience was beginning to prick him, and also his Aunt Vere was harbouring grave suspicions, not particularly about her brother but about John Edmonds. She accused him of embezzling her inheritance. The poor fellow protested his innocence vehemently, as well he might: *"I wish all the curses in divine writt may light upon me if I directly or indirectly know more than this..."* Lord Warrington had ordered Edmonds to keep the will secret. *"This considering how I was involved - by acting for a Minor without a Guardian, I know not what I could have done more or less, that and the hope of having some profitts by the Leases to advance my narrow fortune, made me willing to venture my little all for my Lord...."*

So the secret was really out and the pressures began. Warrington's sister Elizabeth was already harrying him, because she had taken responsibility for maintaining her younger brothers, Langham and Henry, who were both minors. He offered to pay her £250 on each of three Quarter Days and £200 on the fourth, but she refused point-blank, telling her trustee Sir John Mainwaring that she was losing interest on the promised money because of her brother's delaying tactics. *"If you have any respect to the memory of him that is gone, noe longer to delay, there has credit enough bin shewed my brother."* Sir Willoughby Aston agreed with her, thinking *"her proposals being so reasonable and honourable that I doubt not but they will be accepted by my Lord."*

They were not. Warrington arranged for a rental of the home estates, proving that Dunham, Sinderland, Altrincham and Carrington only produced £828 net per annum, so his proposals were more than generous in the circumstances. Elizabeth persisted in her refusal and wrote to Sir John Crewe, asking him if he could remember any of the contents of the first Lord Warrington's will, which he had witnessed but he had only been asked to witness Henry's signature. Even his own servants began to take Elizabeth's side. Grace Walley and William Legh, a retained servant to Warrington, both gave evidence that Elizabeth wanted to be the official Guardian to her younger brothers and would bear the expenses from her own resources as long as she remained unmarried, and would be sparing in her own expenses, suiting her own standard of living to maintain them out of her own resources. Then when she accepted Thomas Delves' proposal of marriage, she insisted that a sufficient sum be set aside from her dowry whenever her brother paid up. Delves decently agreed, and when Elizabeth sadly died, he also refused to take back over-payments of the schooling and maintenance for Henry and Langham.

Warrington told her that he *"was not such a fool as to produce the Will... for that it was as prejudicial to him as if he had been disinherited."* When she taunted him that he had come of age, he replied untruthfully and with a hint of increasing desperation that *"he could dye with a safe conscience without producing it... and that it was the weakest action of his father's life."* Elizabeth arranged for *"a Person of Honour to mediate the Matter, informing the Earl, that his Sister would be obliged to take some publicke Course for the discovering of the Will."*

She duly did so, with a petition to the Lords in Parliament. Warrington began to waver and admitted to Elizabeth that he was taking legal advice. His whole future depended on it, he claimed, so surely she could not blame him for doing everything possible to ensure that he was in the right? He had done absolutely nothing dishonourable and would answer her letters fully as soon as he had advised with his lawyers.

So by May 1696, more than two years after his father's death, Warrington's attempt to conceal the will had failed, and although he had won himself some breathing space, he was in no better position.  Elizabeth unhappily died before her petition was heard, but Cecil Booth, uncle to her and to Warrington, took it up.  It was heard on 30th March 1697, and in it Cecil said that Warrington had asked him to take out Letters of Administration because the first Earl of Warrington seemed to have died intestate.  Warrington had accepted almost all the cash of his father's personal estate, but had then referred all the creditors to Cecil and tried to get the Letters of Administration revoked, which would obviously have been very expensive for Cecil.  Moreover, Cecil alleged that his nephew had concealed the existence of a deed which secured a small annuity to his uncle.

Warrington predictably had answers to these allegations, and they were dated 7th April.  As a minor, he could not take out Letters of Administration and had agreed that Cecil should do so on his behalf, *"but not with any intent that he should meddle with the personal estate."*  In fact he had tried to get the administration discharged because he was worried that Cecil would break open his father's closet in his absence.  Virtually all of Henry's liquid assets had been spent, some by the stewards Edwards and Harrington and some by himself, all to discharge debts or on funeral expenses.  Only about £200 was left.  However he had satisfied his sisters of the legacies left them by the Duchess of Somerset, so his conscience was clear in that respect, and as for the alleged annuity deed, he had searched exhaustively but found nothing.

Cecil Booth's reply was dated three days later.  Cecil denied any attempt to break open Henry's closet, but claimed that Warrington's behaviour in concealing what was due to Elizabeth made him suspicious about his, Cecil's, alleged annuity and he would have felt justified in doing so. He had taken legal advice with a view to getting an amicable agreement, but his nephew had done nothing but delay.  He had been very forbearing, otherwise he would have taken possession of Henry's personal estate to protect himself against importunate creditors.  In summary, Warrington had *"for two years stopped the payment of the small provision made for Cecil by his father, refused to pay his brother the remainder of the money for which he had sold his annuity to the late Earl, endeavoured to deprive his sister of part of her portion, and turned his two brothers for three years together to live on the charity of relations, although provided for by their father.  The alleged search for the deed is a pretence;* (Warrington) *concealed for two years his father's will, and, after protesting solemnly that it could not be found, sent notice... that it had been discovered about three weeks after his father's death."*

By 1700 Warrington was even further in debt and was writing to Mr Edward Lloyd in Kensington.  He was expecting to receive the remainder of the debt from Sir James Langham in a few months, but even then it would be entailed, so he needed cash urgently.  *"Sir,*

*I am highly obliged to you for enquiring out the Money for me, and the time you mention, viz: Michaelmas will be soone enough for me, because I must give notice to my Creditor that I shall discharge their Debts, which they will expect some little time to looke out for some other security for their money.*

*"...my £6,050 is to be paid off of that Security in N'shire about a year and a half hence and then to be layd out by my Lady Langham, two Trustees and two for me upon*

*some other Security, as we can find it out; and soe to remaine till six months after her death: but neither her Trustees nor mine can dispose of it on any Security without consent of all four besides her consent and mine... But these trustees need not be... bettering the Security that yr Friend will have for her Money. As soon as I heare from you again I will send up my Deeds by the Courier..."*

A large and guaranteed supply of money was more essential then ever, but he was no nearer a solution to the problem. The only answer was to marry some rich heiress, love being an irrelevance to any proposed match. However, there was of course a distinct shortage of eligible daughters of rich peers who were prepared to bail out a colleague probably known or suspected to be desperate for money. Moreover, he would be expected to marry into his own class if at all possible, since to marry into trade would be unusual to say the least. There had already been rumours about a possible match between him and a Madam Thomas, a Welsh girl, said to be worth £3000 or £4000 a year, who had *"been courted by, and has rejected, some of the greatest men of the Kingdom"*, but unfortunately for Warrington, these rumours came to nothing.

But in 1701, Mary Oldbury came to his rescue.

## John Oldbury and his daughters

Mary Oldbury was the elder of the two daughters of John Oldbury, a merchant, who lived in Broad Street, London. Oldbury was rich by 17th century standards, reputedly worth not less than £100,000. He owned property in Finchley, Hornsea and Lambeth in London, at Witham in Essex, and the rectory of Sittingbourne in Kent. But as well as being a landowner, he also traded with the British East India Company, established by Queen Elizabeth's charter in 1600, as had his uncle (also John Oldbury) before him, and he had risen to a position of trust in the company.

John Oldbury senior was trading as early as the 1660s. He and Henry Stanley owned *The Paul*, of a type known as a 'pink', a shallow-draught, wide-beamed vessel, ideally suited to the shallow North Sea, but which also sailed on a voyage to Cadiz, Bordeaux, Malaga and Gallipoli. A few years later, Stanley was being sued by one Robert Edwards and Oldbury guaranteed bail for him. To show their mutual concern, Henry and Robert Stanley both gave their word that Oldbury would suffer no damages for his favour.

There are indications that he died late in December 1674, leaving his nephew as his heir, and in 1678, John Oldbury junior was trading with one George Potts. Potts went bankrupt and was imprisoned in the Marshalsea Debtors' Prison. Oldbury issued a warrant to Joseph Coling, the Marshal of the prison, to have him released, on the signed guarantee that Potts released to him all his interest and title on two ships, *The Whiting Dogger* and *The Comfort*. Two years later, he had a bond of £149 for the return of *The Hope of London*, on a voyage to the coast of Africa with trading cargo, and from there to Nevis and Barbados. In 1683, the *Hope* was the subject of a dispute between Oldbury, on one hand, and Henry Whistler and Robert Whittingham, on the other, concerning a debt of £100 owed to Oldbury.

In 1680 he is noted as the factor for the Company of Merchants Trading in the East Indies. In the original Charter, a factor was the third class of Company servants, entitled to buy and sell on behalf of a Company merchant, to act as a mercantile agent and as a commission agent from the Company offices in Leadenhall Street. However, factors could and did trade on their own accounts, depending on the availability of space in the trading ships and this is how they made fortunes. Oldbury preferred to stay largely independent from the Company, dealing and trading with the individual masters of ships, venturing a proportion of the ship's cargo on a signed guarantee to buy that proportion on its return and buying from the Company at their annual sales. Shrewdly he also invested his capital by lending it out on interest. In modern terms he was a banker and mortgage supplier in addition to his trading activities.

John Oldbury would trade in any commodity, whether from the East Indies, or to and from the American and West Indian colonies, which were just opening up for trade. The most profitable trade was in spices, in which the Dutch had virtually cornered the market. It was said that one pound's weight of nutmegs could be sold for their weight in gold, such was their desirability, although they could only be bought from the Low Countries, imported from the Spice Islands in the East Indies. At that time the nutmeg tree grew only on one small island and was said to have medicinal properties in the treatment of fever, asthma and heart and kidney disease. As with many rare commodities, it was also popularly supposed to maintain and increase sexual vigour!

During the 17th century, trade had increased dramatically. The East India Company opened stations in Madras in 1637, Bombay in 1644 and Calcutta in 1696, giving access to far more opportunities. By 1711 Joseph Addison could write: *"Our ships are laden with the Harvest of every Climate. Our Tables are stored with Spices, and Oils, and Wines. Our Rooms are filled with Pyramids of China, and adorned with the workmanship of Japan. Our morning's Draught comes to us from the remotest corner of the Earth. We repair our Bodies by the drugs of America, and repose ourselves under Indian canopies."*

John Oldbury and his fellow traders could deal in cottons, calicoes, muslins, chintzes, pepper and other spices, chinaware, silks and teas. They were importing and re-exporting all these and other commodities to the American Colonies and the West Indies. He also traded in other far less savoury cargoes.

In order to carry his cargoes, he also owned ships, sometimes the whole ship, sometimes sharing ownership, and always on a temporary basis. *The Paul* was a shallow draught vessel. Many other ships are mentioned, *The Speedwell* of which he owned one eighth, *The Providence* which sailed between London and Havre de Grace with cargoes of wine and raisins, *The Aleppo Merchant*, trading from the Mediterranean, *The Hope of London*, sailing from the coast of Africa to Barbados and Nevis, and *The Lisbon Merchant*, to name but a few of the more than thirty ships listed in his papers.

*The Providence* had a chequered career. In 1682, captained by George Nanton, she was off the coast of Nevis in the West Indies when she infringed the rights of Vice Admiral Sir William Stapleton, the Governor, who seems to have suspected her of piracy. *HMS Deptford*, under Captain Billop gave chase, put a shot across her bows and he was amazed when the fire was returned, killing one man and wounding another. Eventually he boarded *The Providence*, but instead of returning to Nevis, sailed with his prize to St Christophers. There the cargo was unloaded. By rights, it belonged to the Crown, if indeed *The Providence* was breaking any laws, but that aspect of the case was never considered. Captain Billop ignored the laws of capture and embezzled most of it. When he was called to account, he answered insolently that he was being questioned merely because he had been *"plundering a captured interloper."* Governor Stapleton reported that he was *"one of the worse men we ever saw in the King's service, and the most unfit to continue in it."* Billop showed the accuracy of this comment when he resumed command of his ship and flaunted his contempt of Stapleton by remaining in plain sight from the shore. Stapleton was furious, *"His ill-behaviour cannot be paralleled. I never saw such contempt of a subaltern officer to his superior,"* he reported angrily to London. *"Since he came out here Billop has acted more like a merchant, and sometimes more like a piratical one, than a man-of-war or one that holds the King's commission."*

Billop was court-martialled three months later, but was amazingly acquitted. The Attorney-General of Nevis complained that he should have been given notice of the trial and that therefore the verdict was to be set aside for Billop to face an Admiralty court. Stapleton's final report was very bitter. "(Billop) *has taken upon himself to relinquish seizures, detaining his own share without any trial ....to compound with some for inconsiderable sums, and to break open chests and take money from them. He has so frightened the people here that they durst not go about their lawful avocations in ships and sloops while he remained here. He has run away from the King's colours, and I thought it was felony by common and statute law....."*

What about John Oldbury? The cargo was a dead loss to him, and it was a particularly valuable one. The ship was carrying over a ton of elephant ivory, 1680 lbs of copper, 1544 lbs of redwood, 107 lbs of wax and 215 Negroes to be sold into slavery. Even worse, smallpox was raging among the unfortunate slaves, and several of them had been killed when Billop captured *The Providence*. Then *"Billop and his men have conveyed away all but eighty-four of the worst and twelve infected with small-pox, besides eight or nine killed......"*

The *Providence* remained an unlucky ship. With another master, Captain John Strong, she sailed to Africa again in the autumn of 1683 to collect another cargo. She arrived off the coast of Guinea in January 1684 and stayed there until April, collecting and loading her cargo, before leaving for the Virginia colonies. She must have been becalmed in the doldrums, because she began to run short of water and food and was forced to put in to St Thomas. She refilled her water barrels and resumed her interrupted voyage. Hugh Palmer, a merchant travelling on her, takes up the story: *"....meeting with contrary currents the ship touched at Cape Lopus from thence put to sea towards Virginia but finding the ship leaky & having more water then the ship cld hoard we putt back for the River Gaboone in order to stop leaks & having stopt our leaks from thence we sayled again towards Virginia & having beene at Allowance of water for about a month the ship touched at New Providence and from thence... for Virginia (our desired port) but meeting with Extraordinary fowle Weather & the tayle of a Hurricane the ship sprung leaks whereupon* (we) *putt back for New Providence where being viewed by Captain Phipps commander of the Rose Frigott his officers & carpenter and they judged insufficient to proceed her said voyage to Virginia impossible to be in that place repair'd & amended whereupon the Master & ship's company left said ship providence in the port of New Providence & took passage in other vessels for Jamaica."*

Facing such hazards it was no wonder that high rates of up to 14% assurance were commonly charged. Large amounts of money passed through Oldbury's hands. On 14 May 1688 for example a Bill of Exchange passed to Ambrose Canham, a merchant in San Lucar, for one thousand pieces of eight in solid gold for his account, to be paid within 30 days of the arrival of the frigate *Fryston*, it being quite normal for Royal Naval ships to indulge in a little mercantile moon-lighting when on foreign stations.

Oldbury was very shrewd in the management of his finances. His cash-book for the period 1696-1701 shows that he calculated his income carefully each quarter and never invested more than he had received. Invariably he retained a percentage, having estimated what income he was likely to receive.

His wife had died in about 1690 and he wanted to prepare his daughters for advantageous marriages, so great risks were unwise, despite the possibility of enormous profits. In the three months April to June 1696, his income was a mere £427, and in the four months to July he invested out £375. In the next quarter to August, he received £1395, including £329 for the mortgage of Moulton Park to one Lisle Hackett. This gave him extra investment potential, so he loaned out just less than £1000, including a £500 mortgage to Thomas Kerridge for a house in Broad Street London.

August and September brought in £467, so he loaned out £459. October 1696 was a good month, with income of £746. Again his investments were almost exact at £744, including *"Thos Bennet, master of Roward of London on adventure £300 for the repayment of which he hath entered into bond to me in penalty of £800 conditional to pay £450 on return from Smirna or at 16 months end with £10 per month for all time above 14 months if ship be lost in voyage within 16 months proceeding with convoy, bond void and to service payment."*

The last two months of 1696 brought in the huge sum of £4158, which included a long-standing involvement with a naval officer soon to become posthumously notoriously for wrecking his fleet on the rocks of Scilly. *"To money rec'd of Sir Cloudely (sic) Shovell for interest of £2000 from 15th March 1692/3 at 5/5d % per annum to this day £150-7-11d in which is included £3-6-6d for interest of £73-6-8d, being my proportion of the cost of suite allowed me in Chancery, & is in part of money due from Creswell Draper esq. dec'd to my dtrs for which lands in Kent were mortgaged."*

He was able to loan out £3266, including £2586-1-4d *"left in the hands of Mr George Newlands and Simon Bockley, scriveners in Smithfield, for which I have their note to pay on demand."*

By 1700 John Oldbury was very rich and wanted to find husbands for his daughters, whose mother had died several years before. He kept them at a house in Greenwich while he attended to his business in London, but he pampered them, and carefully kept account books detailing exactly how much he spent on them from at least 1690 onwards, when Mary can have been no more than six years old. (She had come of age by 1705). Dorothy was even younger of course. Whatever he thought they needed he bought for them, but on examining his accounts, it is clear that he thought of them not as little girls, but as people who would grow up to be ladies to be trained in the marriageable arts many years before they actually came on to the marriage market.  Most of the entries are for clothes much in advance of their ages, and only one entry mentions toys.

| | |
|---|---:|
| White gloves, Muslin for bibs and Apron, | |
| 2 yards of Broad Poynt for peake for Mary. | £1 - 19 - 4d |
| Two yards of narrow poynt for Mary | 14 - 6d |
| Fifteen yards of silk for coats for them. | 4 - 2 - 6d |
| To making their coats and petticoats | 1 - - -d |
| Gloves, 2 pr shoes, 5 pr stockings | 11 - 4d |
| Playthings & washing quilt | 3 - 6d |

The girls had their own governess, Mrs Creswell, and Oldbury paid her out-of-pocket expenses of £1-13-4d *"for things she bought for them"*.  They also had their own maid servant, who could also buy small things for them, and Oldbury repaid her £1-12s.  To make sure their education fitted them to be eligible ladies for the highest society, Mr Crouch was engaged as their dancing master, at a fee of £1 per quarter and 17/- at the end of each term.  Altogether, Oldbury spent £136-9-4d in the year ending December 1691.

Naturally the girls needed more as time passed.  By the end of November 1692, Oldbury calculated that his expenditure had risen to over £210.  In that year Mr Crouch was replaced by Mr Holt, also at £1 per quarter, plus 2/6d per visit, and the living expenses of the girls, excluding food, totalled £290 for the six months to mid-June 1693. Food seems to have been only a small part of their expenses, at only £2 per week for them and two servants for 16 weeks at Greenwich in 1693.

Unfortunately, Dorothy was taken ill with smallpox in 1694 and had to be separated from Mary while she recovered.  Her doctor's bill came to £4-10s, the apothecary's, Thomas Cawthorne £3-8s, the full-time nurse only £1-10s!  Mary stayed with a Mrs Stanley at Greenwich meanwhile at an extra cost to John Oldbury of £30-10s. Altogether, John paid out £495 for his daughters that year, including £3 for black cloth as mourning for the death of Queen Mary.

The year 1695 cost John Oldbury £384.  By 1696, they needed even more gentle accomplishments and a writing master was engaged, together with a new singing master, a Mr Goodson.  He was also careful to note down commodity prices in his household accounts.  A leg of mutton 2/6d, shoulder of pork 1/10d, shoulder of lamb 1/9d, a chicken 1/4d, carrots and turnips 3d, rabbits 1/-, pigeons 1/6d, ducks 2/3d, a pheasant 2/-, woodcocks 2/-, 2 pounds of  bacon 1/6d, larks 10d, and a great rarity in those days when sugar was scarcely a known delicacy, double refined sugar for 2/10d.

They had inheritances in their own right, being entitled to parts of the estates of their grandfather, Thomas Boone, their uncles Charles and Thomas Boone and their aunt Dame Jane Foche.  They were therefore very eligible young ladies.  John Oldbury put out feelers to trace some equally eligible gentlemen and in August 1701 he received a letter from Henry Tate who had connections in Cheshire and had learned of Lord Warrington.  His account of the Earl was calculated to make John Oldbury's mouth water, and of course neither Tate nor Oldbury could have known that Warrington's finances were much exaggerated to say the least.

*"Sir,*

*I am desired by a relation of mine in Cheshire to name the Erle of Warrington for your eldest daughter, his estate is now £4000.  If ye lives all fall, then its £10,000 per Annum, hee gaines great Esteeme amongst all peeple by his genteel carriage & honest temper..."*

*4 Aug 1701*

Tate mentioned a possible competitor, a Mr Oglin of Middlesex, whose disadvantage was that the estate of £3800 was about £12000 in debt. He failed to mention the enormous debts owed by Warrington. Warrington's motive for marrying a rich heiress were obvious, Oldbury's motive for bartering his daughters perhaps less so. Warrington's circumstances were so desperate that he could not afford to wait until a girl of his own landed class came along, even if such a girl had a father who was prepared to help Warrington to such a great extent.  Oldbury on the other hand must have been a great snob, anxious for his daughters to marry into the peerage and thereby enhance his own social status.  He knew that it would cost him a great deal of money and it seems he was willing to pay almost anything.

Warrington asked his uncle George Booth to be his intermediary in the marriage negotiations.  However tragedy struck when John Oldbury died suddenly on 19 August 1701 without having definitely agreed any settlement, and what was worse, without leaving a will.  Mary and Dorothy had been staying with their uncle, Doctor John Castle, who was married to John Oldbury's sister and they were actually on the road to London when they learned the terrible news of their father's death.  The orphaned girls were only teenagers, and begged Castle to help them.  He went to their father's house with them and agreed to take out Letters of Administration on their behalf until they came of age.

Uncle George Booth continued the negotiations with John Castle.  Warrington had been given unduly optimistic accounts of the sisters' fortunes and was hoping for a dowry that would relieve him of all his troubles.  Less than a month after Oldbury's death he wrote to Uncle George.

*"Their Fortunes are so great, that if I can attain them I should think no Trouble or Expense ill employ'd; and if their be any great hopes for me, I should be glad to dispose of my reversion of Lady Langham's Money, that I may have money ready for Occasion; because the Interest-Money that I pay constantly makes me that I can never have any great Sum by me.*

*I should think my self Happy to get into such easy Circumstances not only for my own Sake, but also that I could then shew that Kindness to all my friends, which, were I in a Condition to do, I should take to be one of the greatest Pleasures of my Life to be doing."*

Love, for the propertied gentry, could not be allowed to get in the way of advantageous family alliances.  If love followed, that was all to the good, but it was far less important than the acquisition of power, influence and riches.  This was particularly so in Warrington's case.  He had not seen his intended bride and his hopes for her were based solely on what her dowry would bring him.  In fact, he was not troubled which of the girls he was to marry; there were two sisters who were to be apportioned between him and a Francis Herbert - and that was all he cared about.  Even the fact that Dorothy had suffered from smallpox and might be marked did not deter him.  Two weeks after the letter above, he wrote again to his uncle George.

*"Dear Uncle,*

*I hope the Success of this Affair will be such, as that I shall be capable of Shewing the Sense I have of my Obligations to You and Yours.  Mr Leigh* [Warrington's London solicitor] *has no further thoughts of my pursuing this Matter; for he has a Notion of them, that they are not such Fortunes as talk'd of.  He told me, when he spoke to me last of them, That tho' the Younger is Sickly, yet she is in no way Disfigured with her Illness; if so, I should take her rather than none...  I should be extreamly glad, if possible, to dispose of my Reversion of Lady Langham's Money, for Money is scarcer in these parts than was ever yet known; and my Interest-Money is so great that it makes me mighty uneasy...."*

On 13 October he wrote again, making his mercenary feelings even plainer.  He would happily pay 1000 guineas down as a guarantee of his good faith and wanted it to take place as soon as possible.  He still did not know exactly what his future wife's portion would be - nor indeed who she would be.  He drafted proposed Articles of Agreement, which would expedite the process rather than wait for the formal Settlement.  He wanted £4000 to be paid on the marriage day.  In return he would guarantee that if he should die within six months of the marriage, his estate would be subject to a rent charge of £400 until the remainder of the portion was paid. If the girl was unlucky enough to die within six months, the portion would still be paid.  If all went well, however, the rest of the portion would be paid before the six months were up *"...if the Ladies Fortunes be certain £24,000 each (tho' that's less than I believ'd). Yet I shall be glad to get the Youngest.. as to the 1000 Guineas which are to be given, I am very well content to give it.*

*But I desire to be inform'd in what Posture their Fortunes are, and if you can guess what Settlement will be required..."*

George Booth could not give his nephew a firm answer about the girls' portions, but Warrington remained optimistic although matters were advancing too slowly for his liking, and when a great storm broke several windows, he wrote *"but no other Damage, which I am always afraid for this poor old House in bad Weather."*

Uncle George placed Warrington's goodwill bond for £1,000 and reported to Warrington accordingly.  If the latter was disappointed with the letter, he did not show it, but still demanded to know exactly how much the unfortunate girl would bring to the marriage consummation.

*"Dunham, Octob. 11, 1701*

*I receiv'd your Letter of the 7th, which tells me that the Ladies Fortunes are not above £24000 each, and if they be certainly that, I think it very well worth my while to get the Youngest, if I can, and not the Eldest, as your Opinion is...  But I beg the Favour to be inform'd in what Posture their Fortunes lye, and if you have had any Discourse, or can guess what sort of Bargain will be required for the Lady's Fortune,,,,,"*

There is no record of his feeling when he discovered that the dowry, on which he so much counted, was not the initially rumoured £50,000, nor even the £24,000 which his uncle had guaranteed, but barely £20,000.  However the marriage duly took place on 9

April 1702. It may have been the first time that Warrington and Mary saw each other.

Unfortunately, there was no sign of the £20,000 portion that Warrington was due to receive. Neither he nor Francis Herbert could get a penny from the reluctant hands of Dr John Castle, not even the £4000 they should have received on the day of the marriage, and it was becoming obvious that Castle was not interested in collecting the money due to Oldbury's estate. Four months after the marriage, on 29 May 1702, Warrington and Herbert went to court before the Lord Keeper of the Great Seal. It marked the start of many years of litigation for Warrington.

They had already been before the Prerogative Court of the Archbishop of Canterbury, which had declared that Castle's Letters of Administration for Oldbury's estate were null and void during the minorities of Mary and Dorothy, because of his inactivity on their behalves. Through their solicitors, John Leigh and William Morgan, they were now seeking to force him to give up all the securities and other writings that he held, so that they could ascertain how much the estate was worth. They were concerned that several debtors had expressed their readiness to repay their debts to the estate but if Castle was not prepared to receive that money, they would not continue to pay the interest due. In response, Castle acknowledged he had been granted Letters of Administration and that he was entitled to reasonable costs out of the income he collected. The Courts had given leave for the marriages to take place and approved the settlements, with the proviso that any surpluses above the £20,000 each would be for the exclusive use of the girls.

The Court heard both sides and ordered that Castle should surrender all the documents into the care of Richard Hoare, the famous banker soon to be knighted, who was to take steps to collect all the money due on the securities. Warrington and Herbert were to be permitted to consult his accounts at any time, as was Castle. At last Warrington and Herbert could rely on receiving the settlements so important to them.

Sir Richard Hoare wasted no time and by July 1704 he had collected all the capital debts due and paid most of them to Warrington and Herbert, but was hanging on to the remainder. The news was not good. The settlements were much less than either of them had been promised. *"Pursuant to the said Order there has been paid in to the said Sir Richard Hoare £37,122 -1-8d, of which he has discharged himself as paid to the said Earl and his Countess £18, 377-8-11d, and to Mr Herbert and his wife £17, 462-18-5d, and according to an equal dividend there will be owing to the said Earl and his Countess £183-11-11d, and to the said Mr Herbert and his wife £1098-2-5d. And the said Mr Herbert and his wife have often required the payment thereof from Sir Richard Hoare... but* (he) *insists on a reward for his care in the Trust, though he has been a considerable gainer by having such great sums of money in his hands."*

The situation was complicated by the fact that Herbert was refusing to discharge Hoare from his responsibility until he had been paid his full settlement. The Court took the sensible view and ordered that Herbert was to give a discharge for all the money he had received from Hoare, who was to pay him the remaining £1098-2-5d, when Hoare would be fully discharged.

Some individuals had been hugely in debt to John Oldbury, whose interests spread far and wide. Mr Nathaniel Horne paid £3000 principal on 16 July 1702, and £270 interest for 18 months. Only four months later he paid another £1100-10-0d in full repayment of his bond. The largest single sum was of nearly £10,000, owed by Thomas Phipps; Sir Edmund Wiseman paid £5000 in one amount in January 1703, and Lysle Hackett £4000 two months later. Francis Herbert took the precaution of having Hoare's accounts independently audited, but the Court said that if there were any small and insignificant errors, they were due to Hoare not having quite all the information. They should be disregarded and Sir Richard Hoare fully discharged from his responsibility.

This still left the problem of John Oldbury's real estate, which had not been successfully divided between Warrington and Herbert, so in 1705 Warrington and Herbert found themselves in Court again. They had agreed on at least a temporary division of the property until Dorothy came of age; Warrington's share was bringing in profits of £300-17-2d and Herbert's share £307-11-4d, so the purpose of the Court case was to indemnify each other against any proceedings in respect of the small amounts which would give each other precisely equal shares. The Court was in agreement.

Warrington was still owed over £2,000 out of the original £20,000 marriage settlement and the only way to get the capital was to sell Oldbury's property in Finchley, Hornsea, Lambeth and Witham, together with the Rectory of Sittingbourne, but Francis and Dorothy Herbert perhaps did not have the same financial problems as Warrington and were in no great hurry to agree. Eventually (with many background negotiations), they came to Court yet again in May 1707 to obtain official agreement for the sale of the property to the best possible purchaser and for the proceeds to be used according to the original marriage settlements.

But that was not quite all. Mary and Dorothy had been left property by her Boone grandfather and uncles, which the Court also took into account, but it also included some for Alexander and Dorothy Pitfield. Mary and Dorothy each received one quarter and the Pitfields the rest. Warrington managed to get the Court to agree that he should have priority: *"out of the first money that shall be raised by and out of the parties' proportion of the said estates, the sum of £2700 be applied to discharge the incumbrances remaining on the Earl's settled estate pursuant to the said Marriage Settlement"*.

So, five years after the marriage, Warrington had at last managed to get the dowry. Not the £50,000 share he had first hoped for, nor even the £24,000 his Uncle George had half promised, but slightly more than the £20,000 guaranteed.

One last twist remained. His uncle had arranged with Warrington to take out a bond for £2,150 with one James Isaacson. From this Warrington duly paid his uncle £1,075 plus £15 interest, as a gratuity to him for his work as a marriage broker. For some years Warrington claimed to be satisfied with the arrangements, *"upon Belief that the Appellant (Booth) had behaved himself herein with Sincerity."* However in 1711 he made further enquiries and found that Dr Castle had not in fact received his £1,075 to which he was entitled by virtue of having been the other broker.

Warrington, litigious as ever, reported the whole matter to the Court of Chancery. Booth, not surprisingly, disputed the details. He claimed that Castle might well have been the girls' uncle, but he did not remember that he was their guardian or that he was solely responsible for them and their fortunes. He had gone to Castle, but Castle had then suggested he should use Isaacson and one Towers as intermediaries. He had done so, and they had assured him they could effect the marriage treaty. The security had been deposited with Samuel Jackson of Holborn, had been given to James Isaacson, and the money had been paid to the mysterious Towers. In any case, he said, the whole matter was irrelevant, because of the Statute of Limitations.

Warrington answered that Castle had been appointed guardian of the girls by the Court of Chancery and Booth could not possibly be ignorant of this. He must have known that *"the young ladies were never out of the Company of the Doctor and his Wife ...for years before and after the death of Mr Oldbury, until the Match..."* Moreover Castle was the sole person with whom Booth had dealt. Warrington had all the documentation to prove it.

The Lord Chancellor listened to both sides and announced that he was not entirely satisfied that the agreement had existed, nor that there were such persons as Isaacson, Jackson and Towers. He referred the case to a Master of the Court to establish the existence or otherwise of the three men and whether any money had actually changed hands. Booth could not produce the bond but found a Philip Oddy who stated that he had witnessed its signing although he could not say anything as to its contents. The Master reported *"that it did not appear to him to whom the said Bond was delivered, or by whom it was taken away after the Execution thereof; or that there were any such Persons as Isaacson and Towers at the time of the entring into such Bond... or that any Money was really and bona fide paid to any Person whatsoever upon the said Bond."*

The Chancery Court gave a very severe judgement on Uncle George Booth. It found that there had not been any transaction between him and Isaacson and Towers, and that the payment of the £1,000 guineas and £15 was *"a mere fiction and fraud in the Appellant* (Booth) *and therefore Decreed the Appellant to pay to the Respondent* (Warrington) *£1,000 guineas and 15 Pound, with Interest from the Time of Filing the Respondents Bill, with Costs of Suit."*

## Warrington's Marriage

At first Warrington, realising that Mary was young and inexperienced, indulged her to some extent, although he did not always approve of the friends she made. More seriously she took no responsibility in the running of the household, which she would have been expected to do, leaving her husband to look after the estates and his duties in the House of Lords. Moreover she showed no willingness to learn. Warrington wrote to his uncle:

*"Dunham, Aug 29, 1702.*
*Dear Uncle*
*    The Weather being so hot, as it must needs be with you, when it is so here, I am glad you continue out of Town for some Time... It is for my Wife's Ease, as much as my own, that I don't care to be in Town sooner than needs, it being less Shocking to be thus Separated from her old Acquaintance, than to have it deny'd her if in Town; and the Respect my Relations shew her ought to give them the Preferrence in her esteem of them and her own, which I hope Time will do; and she can't be uneasy to be here as long as she don't take the Trouble of the House, or any other Business on her Hands; which, tho' it be so much more Burthensome to me, I am willing to undergo for a Time, that she take*

*a liking to be from such Company as is unfit to come near her; which when we come to Town there musty be some Pains on my Part to alter. Pardon this Impertinency: But 'tis a pleasure to open one's Mind to a Friend; ands as such you must ever be Esteem'd by*
*Your Obedient Nephew and Obliged Servant Warrington"*

Unfortunately for them both, Mary flatly refused to take any part in the running of the household and before long Warrington's patience wore out. Even the birth of his daughter Mary the year after the marriage, did nothing to improve his relationship with his wife. They were to spend 38 years of marriage in barely disguised mutual hostility.

By 1711 he no longer bothered to conceal his dislike of and contempt for her. She was lazy, idle, bad-tempered, intolerant, and sometimes drank too much. A letter surviving in the Beaufort papers to his uncle George gives details. Warrington does not wish to come to London and will arrange a proxy for Parliament until after Christmas, because London is *"not a suitable Place fore one to make a long stay in, with One's Family, when a Wife is so far from taking Care, or ordering any Thing; that I believe she never bestowed one thought towards Management of any Thing that's mine: What is within her own Circle, that, according to her Notion, is her own, distinct from me; she can manage to such Nicety, that she'd not trust a Servant with a Key to fetch but a Pin or a bit of Thread, yet is insensible to every Thing belonging to me; and if I should run out of all, I'm confident she'd never once think of it; I am endeavouring to prevent it; I have no hopes of an Amendment; especially when the only commendable Quality, viz. That she seemed Good-natur'd and easy in being Advis'd, is turn'd to a sower dogged Temper, whenever she's told any Thing that could make her appear like other Ladies, yet can learn and imitate every childish and insignificant Thing of her own accord; it's a black view, to consider One's whole Life must be worn out with One of no Conversation nor any good Quality, but being Vertuous, in the narrow Sense, that comprehensive Word is us'd, tho' sometimes she'll have such Discourse, where she's free, as don't become a Vertuous Woman: And a little matter would bring on strong Liquors, for she's often for a good dose of Cordial, under colour, that something she has eaten lies on her stomach..."*

Mary's behaviour could not be kept secret and came to be notorious among society. In 1722, Peggy Bradshaw wrote to the Countess of Suffolk from Gawsworth: *"We dined last week at your fellow-servants, Mr Booth's* (Langham Booth, Warrington's younger brother) *Earl and Countess of Warrington met us, which to me spoiled the feast; she is a limber dirty fool, and her consort the stiffest of all stiff things, so that instead of an agreeable freedom which one always expects at a bachelor's house, it was as solemn as a funeral, and I was chief mourner."*

In fact Warrington made no effort to keep his distaste for his wife a secret. As late as 1738 he wrote to Peter Legh of Lyme, hoping that Legh's nephew and his wife would visit him at Dunham: *"In the meanwhile, must intreat most earnestly that from what I told you of the situation of my Domestick affairs, you will be so good as to prepare her for such unusual reception as I fear she'll meet with, for I yet perceive no likelyhood of change in a temper that has ever been stubborn and obstinate for above 36 years."*

For many years Warrington brooded about the malign fate that had condemned him to spend half a lifetime with a woman he hated and who hated him. The fact that he had married her simply for her dowry, were quite irrelevant.  Such arranged marriages were normal in his sphere of society.  Love without financial security was an expensive emotion.  If it developed after marriage, so much the better, but if it did not, mutual tolerance was acceptable. For Warrington, his wife had not attempted at all to make the marriage a success, even on the surface.

It was quite unsupportable, he thought.  Why should the law of the land be so narrow as to compel a man and a woman who were married to, but hated each other, to remain living together in a sham of a marriage, without any hope of release?  The only possible ground for legal separation was infidelity, and even then, only an Act of Parliament could bring this about.  Eventually he wrote down his thoughts and had them published under the title *Considerations Upon the Institution of Marriage*.  Marriage, he considered, had three purposes, the creation and education of children, the avoidance of immoral fornication and the provision of mutual support, help and comfort between husband and wife.  It was the mother who was chiefly responsible for the care and upbringing of the children.  She was by nature better fitted for the task, and in any case, the father *"of what Rank soever he be, has such Duties incumbent upon him, with regard either to the Publick, or his own ...Concerns, as must necessarily employ his Time."*

Sex within marriage was of course important, because it helped to avoid infidelity, provided that the partners could satisfy each others' carnal appetites. Sometimes, however, a woman might be incapable or find the sexual act distasteful.  Similarly, a man might find that he disliked the woman, so that sex with her became unpleasant.  In that case, he might, in order to become a father, have to *"bring himself to a capacity of performing his duty."*  However, the most noble aim of marriage was mutual society. Pleasures of mind and soul were more important than mere bodily appetites, or procreation: *"...after a very little carnal Converse with the most exquisitely framed Body, the future Course of his Satisfaction therein, lies chiefly from something he finds pleasing in the Mind and Conversation, more than meerly in the Body."*

Warrington had made implied criticisms of Mary. He spelt them out in unmistakable terms: *"Now supposing a Wife, who after all possible endeavours of her Husband to teach and infuse into her the Obligations of that Relation, is of such a natural Defect of Reason as to be totally incapable of being, either any Conversation, or any ways assistant or useful to her husband, intirely negligent of, and indifferent towards all his Affairs; totally insensible of any Subjection or Duty she owes him, and contemning all Advice or Instruction therein; excessively hasty and passionate, extremely stubborn, surly and ill-natured; Guilty of Freedoms which only want of Sense can excuse from Indecency and Immodesty, yet angry when admonished thereof; very unjustly reflective on her Husband's Good-Name; perfectly remiss in any care of her Children, and through Indiscretion, or Malice, infusing Notions into them, tending to create in the a Contempt and Hatred of their father, and to corrupt their Morals; and who, through the whole course of many Years Marriage, never did an Action that could look, either like a Desire of gaining the Affections of her Husband, or a Regard to her Marriage Vows..."* Nothing, wrote Warrington, was worse than being linked to *"such an unsociable, helpless, uncomfortable companion."*

It was more miserable than to be alone. Such a wife was incapable of bringing up children. She was the absolute opposite of pleasant society, help and comfort, and to cohabit with her was a positive encouragement to unlawful desires and fornication outside marriage. Surely it could never have been God's purpose to make such marriages indissoluble? It was not consistent with divine justice to frame laws which could not be obeyed, and the laws that govern marriage were of course framed by man. Such laws should always conform to man's natural and God-given abilities. Marriage had not always been bound by present laws. Before the laws of God were written down, even polygamy was allowed under God and could not therefore be sinful in His eyes. When the Jews first received His laws, it was generally acknowledged that an unsatisfactory wife could be legally sent away, and adultery and desertion were just causes. Remarriage was permitted if the first marriage was declared void. In the reign of Edward VI, laws were drafted, but not implemented, that would allow divorce and a second marriage.

Warrington recognised limitations on both parties; women could not be forced always to submit to the sexual demands of their husbands, they could temporarily withhold consent; husbands always had a duty to love their wives as they did themselves, in spite of any defects he might see in her. They were duty bound to be patient with troubles that did not amount to grounds for separation. However, *"if ....upon the most intimate cognizance that several Years Marriage can give, we find ourselves linked to a meer animated vegetable, is it possible to exercise that true Conjugal Rational Love which in its Nature can receive complacency from a Rational Object only?"* If the wife has *"some unalterable Cause or Nature, or ....a more criminal Perverseness of Mind";* if she is *"made up of unalterable, innate distasteful Qualities"*, *"a sort of Non-entity, a Privation of all that makes Conjugal Society comfortable";* if there are *"such extream Degrees and Excesses .....as may be above the present Frame of our Souls to bear,"* her husband is no longer compelled to love her.

Warrington felt very strongly about sex in marriage. It is almost certain that his morals were very strict and that he did not countenance the idea of any adulterous relationship, even though it would have given not only mental but also physical relief: *"And although it is our Duty to exercise our Patience under such kind of Crosses and Troubles we meet withal in Wedlock, as we do not find to be justifiable Grounds for Separation, rather than separate for every trifling Cause of Distaste ....yet as in the Body there are such Diseases and Infections as will unavoidably destroy it ....so there may be such extream Degrees and Excesses of those Passions and Affections to which the Mind of Man is liable, as may be above the present Frame of our Souls to bear...."*

Warrington summarised his arguments.

A wife, he wrote, is understood to be a good wife as far as possible, and therefore an evil wife was no wife at all *"....as far as she is naturally incapable to act as a Wife, so far she ceases to be such, and if totally incapable, the Husband seems in such Case, from the Nature of the Person, to be released; or if, by an habitual undutiful Deportment, and Perverseness of Will, she omits every Duty of a Wife, has no regard to her Marriage Vows, she seems, in such Case, virtually, if not expressly to desert or depart, and thereby release her Husband, who is then, according to the Apostle, not under Bondage.*

*Where then, a Man who enters into Marriage upon a full and deliberate Consideration of the Duties he is thereby to take upon himself ....yet meets with One, whose both Temper of Mind and Weakness of Capacity, are such, as with whom, after many Years Tryal, he finds every End of Marriage, is so far from being in any degree attainable, that the Reverse of them all is inevitable, viz. First that she is not only totally incapable of bringing up her Children in the Fear and Nurture of the Lord, and to the Praise of his Holy Name, or of taking care of them in every Temporal Respect; but endeavours, or at least endangers the Corruption of their Morals, by the evil Notions she infuses into them, to the Hurt both of their Souls and their Bodies. Secondly, that she has such odious innate Qualities, as check all complacent Desire towards her; and are rather a Snare and Temptation to lead a Man into some Irregularity of Mind, in compelling himself to frequent Cohabitation with her, than any Remedy against Fornication in the true Gospel Sense thereof. And, Thirdly, that she is so far from endeavouring to be any Society, Help, or Comfort to him, as that she makes herself the direct contrary to each and every of them: By all Rules of Reason it must of consequence follow, that such Woman cannot deserve the Honourable Appellation of a Wife."*

Even in English law, desertion was sufficient reason to permit a second marriage after a certain time. Taking all these into consideration, Warrington concluded: "*....that a Marriage cannot be esteemed to exist, when none of its Ends are attainable; and that the Duties of that State cannot be obligatory on a Person under a moral Impossibility of paying them, that Impossibility arising not from any fault of the Party himself: And that therefore, altho' ...a Man cannot be separated from the most intolerable Wife, by obtaining a Legal Dissolution of the Bond, yet that in good Conscience he may in such Case separate himself, so far as that can be without incurring any Legal Penalties: And that, when from incurable Weakness of Mind a Woman cannot, and from perverse Stubbornness of Spirit she will not pay any of that Subjection, Submission, Obedience or Reverence which is enjoined her, and which by her Marriage Vows she has bound herself to; When the Love commanded the Husband, cannot (through some invincible Impediment in the Wife) be wrought in him; when the Benevolence required of him, cannot (for the like Cause) in the true Sense thereof be paid: That then a Man may piously believe, that as to him those Duties are not obligatory .....and that if by continuing with such a Wife, we cannot attend upon the Lord without Distraction, that then ....it will be rather to the Glory of his Mercy and Goodness to live chaste, pure, and separate....*"

## Warrington's Legal Battles

While Warrington was brooding over his malign fate, he was also involved in complex legal battles going back to the Duchess of Somerset, who had so disappointed his expectations many years before. When she died in 1692, she left a Will and Codicil in which she bequeathed £2,000 to be used to buy Lands of Inheritance to be settled on young Langham Booth and his heirs. Her executor, Sir William Gregory, proved the Will and Codicil. However he died before buying any land, so Langham was granted powers of administration when he became twenty-one years old. Altogether he was able to retain

£3,604, including interest on the original £2,000.

It will be remembered that Elizabeth had looked after Langham and Henry Booth during their minorities after their father's death. Warrington had owed £3,000 to his late sister Elizabeth and had secured it by conveying the Manor of Thornton to Thomas Delves (effectively to Elizabeth) and Elizabeth had given each of her younger brothers £1,500 as they came of age. With it, in 1705, Langham bought Thornton Manor from Warrington, but half of it belonged to Henry. Henry Booth agreed to accept the security given by Langham and not to demand it of Warrington. However he fell into debt to a broker and in 1719 Warrington settled the debt for him.

On 12 May 1724, Langham died, leaving the real estate to his brother Henry for life, with remainder to Lord Warrington if Henry died with no direct heirs. After Lord Warrington, the next heir was George Legh of Lyme. All his personal estate without exception was left to Henry, who, living then in Holland, renounced his executorship to Warrington. Less than two years later, Henry himself died unmarried, so Warrington took possession of the estates, with all deeds and papers relating to the matter. He was advised that by the deaths of his younger brothers he was entitled to the £2,000 real estate (i.e. the monies mentioned in the Duchess of Somerset's Will and Codicil) with interest accrued from Langham's death. He also claimed the £1,500 that Langham Booth had loaned Henry by a mortgage in 1705, and as administrator, he was a creditor for this money plus interest at 4%.

However the situation was even more complicated. Henry had been friendly with one Mary Saxon, and his Will left her £100 a year out of the Thornton lands, and George Legh, Henry Legh and Sir Henry Mainwaring had been looking after her affairs. Warrington could not therefore get his hands on the income from Thornton Manor and the other lands, and Henry's personal estate was not enough. In fact, Warrington claimed it was less than £100 in total, if the alleged debt of £2,000 was taken into account.

In 1727 the case of Legh versus Warrington came to Court, thirty-five years after the death of the Duchess! Legh began by alleging that she had actually devised the Manor of Chirton in Wiltshire to Langham, but he dropped this particular matter in the later proceedings on learning that it had been revoked in the codicil. Warrington claimed that because the £2,000 had not been laid out precisely in the original terms of the Will, Langham had in fact defaulted. As Langham's only remaining heir, he was entitled to it and therefore was a creditor against the real estate.

The case rested on how much the real and personal estates were actually worth. He was certain that the personal estate was not enough to cover the debt to him, so asked the Court to grant him the balance out of the real estate. Legh claimed the same, to which Warrington replied that he was a creditor against the estates of his deceased brothers, but the personal estates would not cover the debt to him.

Four years passed before the case next came before the Master of the Rolls in July 1731. For Warrington it was good and bad news. The Master dismissed his claim that he could charge £2,000 plus interest on Langham Booth's real estate. Further, he had to account to the Court for all Langham's personal estate and produce all the relevant books, papers and vouchers. The good news was that the Master would then compute what was actually due to Warrington for principal and interest from Langham's personal estate.

However Warrington was still determined to get the money from the real estate, and in May 1732 appealed to the Lord Chancellor, on the grounds that the debts owed to him were not covered by the personal estate in his hands, and should therefore be settled out of the real estate. The Lord Chancellor determined that the £2,000 was in fact chargeable against Langham's real estate, having regard to the wording of his will. Accordingly, Warrington was to account to the Master of the Rolls for the personal estate he held. If it was not enough to satisfy the debt or debts, enough of the real estate was to be sold to make good the deficiency.

It was now George Legh's turn to appeal, this time to the House of Lords. His case was that there was no precedent of a Will charging real estate with debt by contract. Langham did not believe that the £2,000 could in fact be considered as a debt. He could have settled his land in strict accordance with the Duchess' will and either barred them from any future settlement or indeed disposed of them in any way he chose. This would have defeated Warrington's pretensions to the money even as a debt against the personal estate. He therefore requested the House of Lords to overturn the Lord Chancellor and re-affirm the first decree.

Warrington countered by repeating the fact that Langham had not obeyed the terms of the Duchess' will. If he had done so, there would have been no doubt that Warrington would have inherited an estate in absolute title, and in consequence he was justly entitled to receive money in lieu of the land. Also, Langham's will directed that all his debts be paid from his worldly estate, making no distinction between real and personal. As they could not be discharged in full from the personal estate, common justice demanded that they should be settled from the real estate as well. He, as Respondent, asked the House of Lords to bear in mind that Legh was no relation to the Booth family or to the late Duchess. He would *"in Effect have the Benefit of the said Duchess's Legacy, and the Respondent and his Family be deprived thereof, contrary to the express Words of her Codicil, and contrary to the Intent at least of Mr Langham Booth's Will, for it cannot be presumed that Mr Langham Booth could intend the Benefit of his Real Estate to a Stranger, exclusive of paying a Just debt to his own Brother."*

The House of Lords heard counsel from both sides and made their decision on 12 April 1733. It dismissed Legh's petition and appeal and ordered that the part of the original decree that Legh complained of be affirmed. Victory therefore for Warrington.

Brief mention has already been made of Henry Booth falling into debt to a broker and having to be bailed out by Warrington. It was a serious business and took up a great deal of Warrington's time and energy even while the trouble over the Duchess of Somerset's will was being sorted out. It all began in about 1710, when Henry was twenty three years old, when the country was heavily in debt through the French wars. The South Sea Company was formed with a view to exploiting the hoped-for wealth of the islands and countries in the Pacific, and distributed huge bribes to the Government with a plan to absorb the whole of the national debt of £30,000,000. Even John Aislabie, the Whig Chancellor of the Exchequer, bought £27,000 of stock before introducing the project to the House of Commons in April 1720. Only Robert Walpole stood out firmly against it, despite having a modest investment himself. *"...it held out a dangerous lure for decoying the unwary to their ruin by a false prospect of gain, and to part with the gradual profits of their labour for imaginary wealth.... The great principle of the project was an evil of the first magnitude; it was to raise artificially the value of the stock, by exciting and keeping up a general infatuation and by promising dividends out of funds which would not be adequate for the purpose."*

The bill secured an easy passage through Parliament and a feeding frenzy broke out for the stock. In little over a year, it had risen from 128 to 1050, and large numbers of companies, some genuine, some entirely bogus, were floated on the back of the South Sea Company. One proposition to desalinate sea water was centuries ahead of its time, but it is hard to imagine anyone falling for the chance to invest in *"a company for carrying on an undertaking of Great Advantage, but no one to know what it is"*; the artful swindler took £2,000 in cash before prudently disappearing .

It could not last. The fraudsters were prompt to vanish without trace, and the Government, alarmed, began to suppress the smaller honest companies. Speculators took fright and began to sell to cut their losses. By October 1721 the South Sea stock had slumped to 150. Those who failed to sell in time were ruined. Savings vanished overnight, and the gullible crowds wanted revenge on the Government. The Postmaster-General was only one of many who committed suicide. Stanhope, the Chief Minister died of strain, and the directors of the Company were arrested and their estates forfeited to repay some of their army of creditors.

It is hard to see how easy it was for intelligent men to be tricked so easily. Henry Booth however was one such. He was entirely ignorant of stocks and shares and in 1719 fell like a ripe plum for the sales patter of one Thomas Warren, who had been a broker in the City of London. Warren began by persuading Booth to allow him to act as his broker in buying and selling stocks, and promising him *"he would always act and do for him, the said Mr Booth, as for himself."*

In a few weeks, Warren had fleeced Booth of all his ready cash and was after the big prize. Pretending to be optimistic, he convinced Booth that not only would the first investments yield vast profits, but also that there would be huge gains in the future. Booth, still unsuspecting, gave Warren four Bonds, one for £13,270, with a penalty of twice that amount for failure to pay up on the expiry of the Bond. The other three totalled £15,490, and again with a penalty of twice that amount, £30,980 for failure. He assured Booth that he had safely entered into contracts for investing the bonds, but in fact was in no position to do so, being nominally confined in the Fleet Debtors Prison!

It goes without saying that according to Warrington some years later, *"Neither, in Fact, did the said Warren ever make any Contract for Mr Booth, not one Entry appearing in the said Warren's Books that he had bought any Stock for Mr Booth of any Person, or sold for Mr Booth for any Person, or ever paid to the Value of a single Shilling for Mr Booth to any Person whatsoever, nor ever named to Mr Booth any one Person he made any Contract with on his Account."* All this despite the fact that Warren was obliged by oath and bond to keep registers of all his dealings, contracts and agreements.

Warren deliberately made matters more complicated by conspiring with William

Hodgson to assign to him the three £15,490 Bonds. Hodgson pretended that he paid Warren the full amount, but actually only agreed to pay two promissory notes of £500 each when and if Booth finally paid up.

Meanwhile Booth realised that he had been well and truly duped, and took refuge in Holland, safe from Warren and Hodgson. At least he was out of reach of the tricksters, so he hastily wrote to his brother Warrington to tell him the whole sad story. Warrington made sure not to approach Warren and Hodgson personally, but through a trusted agent, who eventually agreed with Warren that Warrington would buy the £13,270 Bond, the various mortgages that Henry had deposited with him, the two £500 promissory notes, and another £500 note of Hodgson's payable in two months. Warren realised that he had little chance of getting any more money from Henry, so accepted £1,310 instead of the actual face value of £14,770, a good bargain for Warrington.

By 1724 Warrington had received £2,266 for the mortgages and also received judgement in the sum of £700 against Hodgson for the £500 brokerage bond. The following year, Henry Booth put in a Bill in the High Court of Chancery, calling on Warren to account for the moneys and to be relieved against the three bonds of 1719 for £15,490. Warren obviously put in an objection, but the Lord Chancellor deemed it insufficient and ordered him to explain how the Bonds became due to him. However matters became even more confused because Warren died before he could do this! Meanwhile Hodgson had put in an answer to Booth's Bill, claiming to have bought from Warren the Bonds, paying him the full purchase price plus interest.

Then Henry Booth himself died intestate in February 1726, so two of the principals in the matter were dead. Warrington, as next of kin to Henry, scented large sums of money and took out Letters of Administration reviving Henry's suit against Warren and Hodgson. In reply, Hodgson petitioned to have Henry's assets fully disclosed, to have the bonds paid to him out of those assets, to cancel the previous judgement relating to the 500 guineas given by him to Warren, and claiming that Warrington's purchase thereof was with Henry's own money and therefore in trust for him. Warrington claimed that the three bonds assigned to Hodgson were obtained by fraud, and that Warren and Hodgson were colluding fraudulently against Henry and himself.

The hearings took place before the Lord Chancellor in February and March 1729/30. At first things did not go well for Hodgson when it was proved that he had not paid Warren (as he had claimed) for the bonds, except for a token five shillings. And when his books were examined, it became obvious that he had neither bought nor sold anything on Henry's behalf. Also, it was proved that Warrington had in fact paid over the £1,310. Warrington's Counsel argued therefore that the whole transaction was flawed and fraudulent, and should be dismissed out of hand. On the face of it, Warrington must have thought he had a good case, but the Lord Chancellor decreed otherwise. Mr Bennet was to calculate what was due to Hodgson, both principal and interest, on the three bonds, and Warrington was to pay him out of whatever money he held of Henry's estate. If anything was left, Warrington was to deduct the sums of £1,766 and £500 he had received during Henry's lifetime. Warrington's claim against Warren was dismissed, as was the setting aside of the bonds assigned by Warren to Hodgson.

Hodgson, however, was greedy, and petitioned that Warrington should produce a formal release of the 1st August 1719 Bond. When this petition was dismissed, he appealed to the Courts against the decree allowing Warrington to retain whatever was left out of Henry's estate. Warrington, with nothing to lose, repeated his previous arguments, that Warren obtained the Bonds by fraud; that Hodgson and Warren were in collusion; and that he flatly denied buying the Bonds with Henry's money.

When the case came before the House of Lords the following year, it was extremely complex. Hodgson was appealing against the part of the decision in favour of Lord Warrington, who was therefore the respondent in that matter. But at the same time, Warrington was appealing against those parts of the decree in Hodgson's favour, so Hodgson was the respondent in that. The hearing began by a recapitulation of the previous hearings, in which Hodgson had claimed that Henry Booth had promised that he was good for the Bonds. Hodgson thought it was a safe investment and paid Warren the £15,540 of their value. As for Warren he was in debt to Hodgson over another matter, so it was a neat way of cancelling the debt. Hodgson had been let down by Henry Booth, and now was seeking to prove that Warrington had destroyed at least one of the Bonds, for £6,500, together with other important papers. Warrington admitted that he had found a cancelled Bond among Henry's papers and had destroyed it as useless.

Warrington's prospects were not looking good. Hodgson's case was based on the burning of the Bond and that Warrington had been acting as a Trustee for Henry; he had paid only £1,310 to Warren and had then repaid himself out of Henry's money. The £1,310 was actually part of Henry's assets and should be at Hodgson's demand. Moreover Warrington's solicitor admitted under examination as a witness that he had personally arranged with Warren to release the £1,310 Bond to Lord Warrington, and he was able to produce the Release.

Warrington had no new evidence. He relied on his claim that the Bonds *"were obtained by the said Warren by gross Fraud, Imposition and Misrepresentation, under a false pretence of Payments by Warren for Mr Booth"*, that Warren and Hodgson were acting in collusion with each other and that he, Warrington, had not bought the Bonds and notes in trust for his brother or with his brother's money.

The House of Lords did not take long about their deliberations. They had already spent a day and a half hearing the cases of the opposing sides, and they made their judgement on the second afternoon. Warrington, to his relief, was completely vindicated. The dismission by the Court of Chancery of Warrington's first bill was reversed; the three Bonds entered into by Henry were to be delivered to him to be cancelled; he was not obliged to produce his accounts; Hodgson's bill was dismissed with all costs against him, and he was to pay £200 to Warrington *"for his costs in respect of bringing this vexatious Appeal."* Lastly a perpetual Injunction was awarded against Hodgson to prevent him attempting any further litigation in the matter. The judgement could not have been better.

## Warrington's Finances

For many years Warrington pleaded poverty, but when he died he was very rich, and it is interesting to examine how he managed such success against the odds. He owed much to the premature deaths of his relations, beginning with his sister Elizabeth in 1697, which saved him at least £5,000, thanks to the generosity of Sir Thomas Delves in forgoing the marriage portion at her untimely death.

This still left Warrington with the mortgage on Thornton le Moors, and this was finally extinguished in January 1706, so the estate passed to Langham, his younger brother, saving Warrington the expense of the annuities for Langham and George. Soon after came his payment of Mary Oldbury's £20,000, followed by the favourable judgement of the House of Lords in the matter of the alleged £1,000 bond of security.

He was still owed money dating back to the lifetime of his father Henry. Henry's wife Mary was the daughter of Sir James Langham of Northamptonshire, who had agreed a dowry of £10,000, payable within six months of his death. Warrington was forced to take out a bill in Chancery to enforce the agreement, and in May 1699 agreed that the Langham property in Northamptonshire was to be sold. Langham died a few months later and Warrington leapt into action again. By an agreement dated 17 February 1699/1700, it was discovered that the sale of the land had produced over £20,000. Lady Langham was to get £15,500 and Warrington the surplus of £6,050.

His next real chance of making serious money came in 1713. The Earl of Oxford, the Lord Treasurer, was in trouble over the Malt Tax Bill and wanted to be sure of enough votes in the Lords. He could not guarantee enough support from the Tories, so he had to use somewhat unconventional means to drum up just enough support from Whig peers. Warrington was of course far from wealthy by comparison with some other peers, but in spite of that, had been a conscientious attender at the House of Lords since coming of age in 1696. He was not one of the 'poor lords' but attendance in London was certainly an unwelcome drain on his finances. In 1732 for example, *"the expense of Housekeeping and Stables at London in this year amounted to about £240-7-8d"* and *"journeys to and from London in this year, exclusive of the Carriage of Goods £68-0-4d."* In 1736, it cost £319, the next year £285 and in 1739 £138.

Lord Oxford was well aware of all this of course, and he also had other useful knowledge. Critically he knew that Warrington had an outstanding grudge. His father Henry, when he was promoted to the Earldom, had been awarded a pension of £2,000 a year, but only £1000 of this had been paid by his death. Warrington considered that at least the balance of £6,500 was an outstanding debt, but there was little likelihood of it ever being paid. Oxford was too shrewd to propose a straightforward bribe for Warrington's support. Warrington was too stiff-backed and basically honest and sternly Presbyterian for that. In a letter to Oxford he told him *"I have never tied myself to any sort of persons... it has always been my desire as I knew it my duty to do whatever were in my way as I thought for her Majesties Service."*

Oxford cunningly enticed Warrington with a promise of the arrears on his father's pension provided that Warrington voted in favour of the Malt Tax bill. Warrington could assuage his conscience with the thought that he would receive only that which had been a debt to his father and to himself for over twenty years. Not surprisingly, Oxford decided that Warrington could not be trusted too far and kept the promise of the money hanging over his head. However as a sweetener he paid £1,000 to Warrington in

December 1713. When Warrington demanded £4,000 of the outstanding amount, Oxford promised to pay it as soon as possible. Warrington compromised at £2,000 down and reminded Oxford that he might need his vote again. However, neither event occurred. Oxford did not need Warrington's help, and did not pay Warrington any more.

Eventually Warrington decided to apply for a pension in his own right, and was granted £1,000 a year as from March 1715. He received the first instalment in January 1716 and two months later the pension was increased to £1,500 a year. Unfortunately the payments soon became chaotic and Warrington wrote to Walpole to get matters clarified, claiming that he was already £1,000 in arrears. Nothing happened. Warrington wrote again in April 1717, asking Walpole asking *"to have desired the favour of you (Walpole) to have what is due this last Lady Day as soon as you can conveniently, for it will be of very great service to me at this time to have it quickly..."* It came only intermittently, and by 1720 was a whole year in arrears, prompting Warrington to refuse to attend Parliament until it was paid! Finally the pension was terminated in 1730 after a very bad-tempered letter from Warrington to Walpole.

*"Sir, Now that Parliament is up and people gone out of town, that you are more at leisure, I take liberty to remind you of your late promise to me, and the manner of it, which, when you sedately review, I'm perswaded you'll not only allow me to think, but will yrself believe you're engaged to keep your Word so given. At least if you please to pay me the Arrears which in such strong and express terms you assur'd me I might depend on, I can more easily believe you were disappointed in continuing your endeavours for continuing my pension. I am very unwilling to make the conjectures which would naturally occur, if you conclude your transaction with me in the manner you seem at present to have closed it; having more Inclination to be, what you have yet in your power to make me, Sir, your most humble servant*

The pension was still probably in arrears at that time. However, in1747 Warrington decided that he was getting rather too old to make the tedious, difficult and sometimes dangerous journey down to London for sittings of the House of Lords. He seems to have attended during 1746 and then in 1747 for the trial of Lord Lovat for his involvement in the 1745 Jacobite rising. This coincided nicely with the fiftieth anniversary of Warrington's coming of age, but his declining health would probably prevent him taking part in many more sittings of the House. It seemed a convenient time for him to apply for another pension or perhaps a reinstatement of the previous one, and the great Thomas Pelham-Holles, Duke of Newcastle, Secretary of State for the Southern Department and later First Commissioner of the Treasury, agreed that he deserved it. As from 1747 Warrington gratefully received a pension from the Royal Bounty of George II. Sometimes it was as much as £1,500 a year, at others only £750, and Warrington was put to some little bother to claim it. It was always entered rather coyly in his account book as *"a present"!* Regularly he used to write to Newcastle in suitably grovelling terms, reminding him politely that the monthly amount was due and if His Grace agreed, Mr. John Jackson, Warrington's legal and financial adviser in London, would wait upon His Grace's convenience to collect it. The following letter gives a flavour of his correspondence with Newcastle:

*"The Honour of your Grace's letter obliges me rather to be a little troublesome in intruding again on your Grace's valuable time than in being defective in paying my most thankful acknowledgements for the repeated condescension your Grace is pleased to shew me, and I beg leave to assure you they are an unalterable tie on me...."*

The Duke of Newcastle retired from the Exchequer briefly in 1756 in favour of the Duke of Devonshire, but was restored only six months later, much to Warrington's delight. However, Warrington himself was coming to the end of his long life. He was wealthy and no longer needed the pension, and he wrote to Newcastle accordingly.

*"My Lord Duke*

*My years and growing infirmities making me little capable of being in any ways serviceable to His Majesty, I ought not to be a burthen to him, that if Your Grace please to clear my affair to last Michaelmas, it will be the last I shall either ask or expect."*

The year 1732 gave Warrington much satisfaction when William Hodgson was compelled to repay him at least some of the money he had cheated Henry Booth out of. He paid £600 in that year, £176 the next year, and £122 in 1734. By then Warrington's finances had improved so much that he was able to begin the great rebuilding of Dunham Massey. The stable block had been the first major building project in 1721, but the house itself was over a hundred years old and had had no major expenditure since young Sir George Booth had added the south wing in the 1650s. By the 1730s Warrington felt able to tackle the great house itself, but rather than just renovating its rather flamboyant Jacobean architecture, he decided to rebuild in the simpler 18th century style which was much more to his unbending Presbyterian taste. The Jacobean mansion was to become an 18th century gentleman's country residence.

Dunham Massey Hall in the 19th century.

# Appendix
## Warrington's Estates

What follows is taken largely from three sources. First and most important, come the transcripts made by Joyce Littler of an estate survey of 1701 and rentals of 1704 and 1709 onwards. Any analysis is bound to owe a great debt to her work and to her *The Protector of Dunham Massey* published in 1993. Second is an account book covering the period 1732 to 1750, which is still held at the Hall, and third is a rough draft account book used by Lord Warrington from which to transcribe into his fair copy. It covers only part of 1758, but is more detailed than the 1732-50 account book. It is catalogued in the Dunham Massey Papers.

No records survive of any building or reconstruction works prior to 1732. In that year Warrington spent £17 on roofing slates and laying them, which indicates that work was already well in progress. Brick-makers cost £121, the brick layers £15 and lime for mortar £10 19s. Carpenters and joiners cost £79 and timber £185. Stone cost over £20, and another £23 went to pay the masons. Some walls were ready to be plastered and painted, and Warrington carefully noted £6 15s for plasterers and painters, laths £6 10s, hair 15s and oils and colours 7/4d.

He incurred heavy costs the next year, spending nearly £400 on woodwork, timber and joinery in the house and £676 on bricks and brick layers. Even lime for mortar cost £129, so one can assume that the main house was being built. Surprisingly, Mr. Norris the supervisor was paid only £28 5s, *"for timber work at new building"*, which casts doubt on the assumption that he was the main architect. In 1735 the woodwork costs rose to over £600, while brickwork, including labour and mortar, dropped to less than £500. Much of the building work seems to have finished, allowing interior panelling to go ahead. Mr. Norris only received £2 2s.

Expenditure in 1736 however showed a sharp increase to a total of £1,551, including £27 to Mr. Norris, but £379 for boards. Presumably flooring and panelling was the main activity. By the next year, most of the work was finished, and only £644 was spent. In 1738 Warrington paid out bills for over £1,200; the glazier and the plumber made their first appearance, receiving £217, and Mr. Norris received £50. Costs dropped in 1739 to only about £524 (Norris £5) and then to £299 in 1740. By 1742, all building expenses dropped from the accounts, leaving no more than routine maintenance.

There was of course normal inescapable expenditure. Land Tax, Poor Lays, Constable Lays, Church Lays, Window Tax (he did not resort to blocking up windows as many people did) and Highways totalled £121-4-11¾d in 1732. He was always meticulous in his accounting!

At least half of these taxes were assessed charges for the parish maintenance of the poor, but every year he also willingly agreed extra payments for individual cases he considered deserving. Clothes for twelve poor people at Christmas, schooling and clothing poor children (£55 in 1732), sent to Miss Guy, very poor, five guineas; to the poor in Ashton parish ten guineas; to loss by a fire in Plumley one guinea; to Sarah Shrigley, a poor woman of Cheadle and a poor man in Altrincham one guinea each; to a boy in Altrincham breaking his arm 10/6d (January 1750); to a poor woman for loss of cattle five shillings (April 1750); *"Old Dr Bridge's son"* five shillings; children of a late school master two guineas (May 1750); and in June 10/6d to *"a poor travelling woman"*; to Mary Wilcocke, a poor woman of Altrincham the same; and a guinea to another poor woman of Altrincham *"near lying in"*, are typical examples.

It seems that no genuine pauper who begged at the back door of the house was turned away empty handed. But with this apparent generosity, it should still be noted that every year he gave his detested wife £300 "pin money."

Attendance at the House of Lords was an expensive duty he could well have done without.

He never bought a house in London, leasing a house whenever necessary at about £37 a time, but although Parliament did not sit every year, it was still an expense he rather begrudged. He attended fourteen sessions in the 19 years of the main account book at a total cost of £2,678, with a maximum cost in any one year of £329 in 1733.

Although Warrington grumbled to his brothers about the expense of maintaining his position in society and lectured them about the need for keeping it to a decent minimum, his own household expenditure was quite considerable, and he did not stint himself or his guests. It was never less than about £1,250, and in 1741 was £1,806. His accounting system costed provisions from the estate farms as loss of money he would otherwise have made and if one takes actual costs into consideration the household expenses reduce to about 40% of the sums he admitted to. But the amounts are perhaps less interesting than the commodities themselves. Without doubt Warrington kept a good table and enjoyed life's luxuries. His dairy produced 229 pounds of butter and 158 cheeses in 1732, but he also had to buy 2,089 pounds of butter. Raisins, currants and many different spices were common purchases, as were tea, coffee and chocolate. Tea was a particularly expensive luxury at £12-15s that year. Other imports from overseas were lemons and oranges, £2-9-6d, mangoes, 7/4d and even morellos and truffles, at 13/s.

Nor did he economise on his drinks bill, since he needed to entertain in order to maintain his social position in the County, although he begrudged having to do so. That year saw the purchase of 248 quarts of red wine, 102 quarts of white wine, 54 quarts of French claret, 22 pints of Frontignac, 8 quarts of champagne and 3 quarts of sherry. That large quantity of drink cost £53-5- 8d! Nor does it include the beer and ale, which were after all the staple drink of the times, water being often contaminated and unreliable.

Warrington's most important purchases were silver. Year after year he spent huge amounts on his collection of Huguenot silver which so enriches his house even today. It is not easy to establish just how much he spent, because in his account books he lumped together the plate with horse and furniture. In some years he spent nothing, but in other years it was as much as £950. This indulgence was primarily for the house and must be distinguished from personal items. In this he was remarkably careful, spending perhaps £200-£300 a year on *"My cloathes and pocket, including money given at Gentlemen's Houses and presents I made."* Oddly enough, he spent less in 1735, when he broke his arm, which cost a £50 doctor's bill. Perhaps the injury prevented him from entertaining or being entertained for a long time.

In fact he was far more generous to his beloved daughter Mary than to himself. In 1732 for example he spent £695 on her, and this was dwarfed in 1736 when he sold some capital in order to provide her with a £20,000 dowry on her marriage to the Earl of Stamford. Even then he continued to be generous, regularly spending over £100 a year for her and later for her children.

As for his servants, Warrington seems to have treated them with kindliness. In 1758 he employed 19 maids, each of whom received free clothing as well as free food and lodging. The wage bill for servants was always in the area of £300 a year, inclusive of pay and presents. Moreover Warrington paid for medical treatment for them if they were sick and when his coachman died, Warrington paid all the funeral expenses. So he does not seem to have been a mean or grasping employer, but naturally there is no record of what the servants thought of him.

With no help from the Countess in running the household, Warrington also had to manage his estates, which he did with his habitual pedantic attention to detail. His income varied considerably, with the variations depending not so much on the rents but on the feudal dues of 'fines'. These were payable chiefly when a tenancy was transferred on the death or retirement of the existing tenant. The rents paid also varied, and Warrington carefully noted in the rentals when he bought or sold a property, which obviously affected the overall rent he received from that manor. Generally the manors of Dunham and Ashton under Lyne were the most productive; Carrington, Hattersley, Stayley and Wilmslow rents tended to stay static, indicating that Warrington left these manors entirely in the hands of agents.

Individual rents paid varied widely of course. Mary Robartes of Dunham Massey was assessed to pay £2-14s in the 1701 survey, and it did not increase in 1704. She of course was Warrington's sister and presumably did not farm the land herself but rented it out to a sub-tenant. Several others did the same, for example Thomas Walton, who had at least three tenancies. William Millington, gentleman, was another. He paid slightly less than Mary Robartes (£2-1-9) and it did not increase until 1748 when his successor, George Massey, was paying £3-17-3d. In Bollington, Henry Hesketh's rent was £2-10-6d, increasing to £3-5-2d by 1728 when Thomas Pickering was the tenant. At the other end of the scale, many tenants, such as William Bagulegh, William Newall, and Widow Atkinson, all of Dunham Massey, paid only 1/-. Warrington was content to receive the rents, the tenants were content to make a profit from their sub-tenants, and it can be assumed that even the latter made a living.

The rents from the Dunham estate tended to increase over the 19 years of the estate survey and rentals. 1732 was the lowest at £372. There was a big jump to £442 in 1733, and thereafter a gentle increase, reaching over £500 by 1739. Another large increase took it to £644 in 1745, and it hovered at about that level until 1750, when there was a large unexplained drop back down to £493. The rental income of Carrington remained static at £317 until 1741, and Hattersley and Stayley changed only by the odd pound or two in the whole period. Lord Warrington's total income tended to vary quite considerably from year to year, from a minimum of only £3,091 in 1734 to a maximum of £4,647 in 1748, with an average of £3,857. These variations are accounted for by the feudal 'fines', payable on tenancy changes or when a life had expired and the tenant wished to make it back to three lives. Rents could be predicted within limits, but deaths and the resulting fines could not. In Dunham 1743 brought him only £118, but 1739 produced £807. Only Ashton-under-Lyne was more productive in fines over the whole period. On average, the fines brought Warrington £1,167 a year, a welcome addition to his average rental income of £2,700.

So the fines were about 30% of Warrington's total estate income. It is also important to examine these feudal dues from the tenants' point of view. Again there are variations of course, which depended on two variables, firstly the unpredictability of tenancy changes forced by death or retirement, and secondly the fine payable by the individual tenant. A tenant with a small farm and low rent could not possibly pay the sort of fine that might be thought reasonable when the tenancy of a much larger and more profitable farm changed hands. The fine for one farm in Hattersley was only £6, and another £7, and two together in Stayley were only £4, but at the other end of the scale, the largest, also in Hattersley, was £64! In 1738, ten tenancies in Dunham paid a total of only £158 in fines, but the following year, twelve fines totalled £807.

Examination shows a clear connection between the assessed yearly value and the fine paid by the new tenant. In Lord Warrington's great 1704 rental, he carefully noted the individual fines paid or payable in Stayley, where there were seventy tenancies. John Brockley's tenement had the highest annual value at £30, with a fine of £32-10s payable, and John Kenworthy, whose farm was valued at £25 would have been 'fined' £21 on the death of one of the three lives. In other cases, such as John Beswick's, the fine and the value were exactly the same. The notional annual value of the Stalybridge estate was £557-19-10d, and if all fines had fallen due in the same year, they would have generated only £20 more, at £577-9s.

Warrington had scarcely started to grapple with his situation by 1701, even after seven years.

Only five tenants have notes against their names; John Lawrenson of Carrington was to add another life within six months, Mr. John Taylor of Ashton on Mersey was to do the same within a year for £30, and the fine of Eliezer Birch of Deane Row was settled at half a guinea at the death of each life. By the 1704 rental Warrington was beginning to know his tenants as individuals rather than an amorphous mass. One would like to know, for example, why Mr Newton of Deane Row was refused an extension of his lease, and what was Henry Hough's *"ill carriage to my family"* that meant he was never to have his lease renewed? We do know why Lord Warrington disliked John Worrall, who leased two tenancies in Styal - not only had the lives expired fifteen years before without renewal, but a rent of only £1 for a property valued at £80 a year was ridiculously generous. Worrall was clearly making a fat profit from his sub-tenants at Warrington's expense. *"An over-reaching bargain"* and *"a great piece of knavery"* he called it.

Warrington recognised Thomas Orrell of Deane Row as a man of sturdy independence of mind, who dared to vote against the Booth faction of Warrington's brother Henry and their friend Mr Offley in the 1705 General Election. Warrington carefully noted the fact but took no action. Jacob Taylor of Hartshead had different problems. He wanted to add a third life to his tenancy but was *"obstructed by his sister and her husband Edmund Lees, who have some assignment they can't produce."* Warrington had also studied the history of the estates. Thomas Heath and William Saunders had tenancies in Bowdon. *"This is one of the tenements Mrs Asheton inveigled to paying 4d rent to Ashley when my father was in the Tower."*

Warrington could be generous when necessary. Henry Pierce was only charged £12 to add two lives and £3 renewal fee, *"he being very old, and the lease being very old."*

If one compares the rent paid with the fine payable, the latter may seem very dear, but a study of the rent, the fine, the yearly value and the sale prices tells a different story. There are several examples of leases being bought and sold in and out of Lord Warrington's estates. In 1745 Warrington enlarged his Dunham estate by buying in Jacob Hoult's lease for £440. The yearly value of the land was only £30 (only 7% of the cost) and the rent was a mere £2-5-8d.

There are problems in assessing the fairness of the rents paid. Firstly there is the difficulty in establishing whether the tenant named actually farmed the land him or herself, or whether he was merely the named tenant but actually used sub-tenants to do the work, charged them rent in turn, and made a profit. Lady Mary Robartes was obviously one such and Thomas Walton, Warrington's friend, another. Secondly, it is clear comparing the three rentals and surveys that Warrington tinkered a great deal with the boundaries of the various plots of land, sometimes splitting a tenancy into two smaller areas, sometimes adding land to a plot, and often allowing a tenant the use of a warren. The Dickenson tenancy was an example that changed, when an enclosure was added and the rent increased from 3/6d to 6/8d. As the yearly value was only £2, it is assumed that the Dickensons farmed it themselves; they were doing so in 1701 and continued to do so well after 1740. In contrast, the plot tenanted by the Leathers of Altrincham was divided, Robert Leather continuing to farm a part and one Burgess the other part. Even more extreme was the tenancy of Thomas Clayton. When he gave up in 1717 the land was split into four separate holdings.

The same names keep recurring in the rentals. Ogden, Nield, Haslehurst, Cotterill, Warburton, Bagulegh, Holt, Drinkwater are all common, as indeed some still are. But this is not necessarily a clue as to how they regarded Warrington. Was he liked and respected as a landlord, or was he at best tolerated as their feudal lord and master, whose will was to be obeyed? It would be surprising if any definite evidence of the tenants' opinions had survived, and indeed it hasn't. There are only tenuous clues, made more difficult to track by the changes of tenancy boundaries noted above - the splits, the amalgamations, the enlargements, the allowance of waste, etc. But of the 76 tenancies in Dunham, 33 remain more or less unchanged in area in the three rentals and surveys, and of these, fourteen show either no increase in rent or only a small increase of a matter of pence. All were subject to revaluations post 1704, but many of the actual tenancies dated back to 1696, so any rent increase was measurable over a period of up to 60 years or so. Moreover, the 1704 rental was compiled just when Warrington's finances were at their worst. He was still faced with huge debts and responsibilities, his house was by his own account crumbling about his ears, and the marriage which he hoped would rescue him was socially and financially a disaster.

Although he had every opportunity and excuse to increase his rental income, he did not do so to any extent. Indeed, of the 76 Dunham tenancies, only nine were raised between 1701 and 1704, and about three were actually reduced. There was only one rise in Bollington, five in Bowdon, one in Sale, none in Timperley, one in Hale and four in Altrincham, counterbalanced by three reductions. Even when Warrington noted that a tenancy was more valuable than had been thought, he took into account when necessary the state of the tenant, as in the case of Thomas Royle of Altrincham. Royle was very ill at the time of the 1704 rental, and Warrington, knowing this, noted that it would be re-surveyed only when he recovered.

So was Warrington liked by his tenants? Almost certainly not, and the question is irrelevant. Firstly, stern and unbending, he was not a likeable man as his colleagues found out. Secondly, the class distinction gulf between him and his tenants was simply too vast for them to know him as a person rather than as their landlord and master. They could not have known what it was like to have an income of £3,000 a year, any more than he could have tried to live on an income of a small fraction of that. So probably he was neither liked nor disliked. He was the landlord and master, who lived in the great house. It was a microcosm of the social structure of the country.

But there were masters who lived up to and beyond the hilt of their incomes, who wasted their inheritances, who demanded more and more from their tenants. Warrington, whatever his faults, was certainly not one of these. Rather, he was at pains throughout his life, to live as frugally as possible, given that he was a great peer of the realm with a position to maintain, but he wanted to pass a rich and healthy estate to his daughter Mary.

At worst, he was a fair man. His expenditure was lavish, but not on himself. He kept a good table, but that was his duty in society. He spent hugely on his collection of silver, but many of his contemporaries saw fortunes live and die at the turn of a card. He lived within his income and he did not seek to improve his standards of living at the expense of his tenants.

Sources

The young Lord Warrington's own recollections of his youth, sad finances, and advice to his brothers are in the Dunham Massey Papers, chiefly 1/8 and 3/6 series. John Oldbury's papers are among the Powis papers in the National Library of Wales and include not only his financial records but also the early negotiations for the marriages of Lord Warrington and Mary, and Francis Herbert and Mary' sister Dorothy. Previously unknown details of Warrington's unhappy relationship with his Countess are taken from the papers of His Grace the Duke of Beaufort, to whom and his archivist my grateful thanks. More of Warrington's marriage and his views on the desirability of divorce can be deduced from his book *Considerations upon the Institution of Marriage* by a Gentleman. His legal battles are in the Oldbury/Powis papers, the Journals of the House of Lords and the Cheshire CRO. His struggles to get restitution of the pension awarded but not paid to his father were thoroughly researched by Beckett and Jones (Financial Improvidence and Political Independence in the 18th Century, JRUL M, 1982) and other details are in the Cholmondeley MSS in the University of Cambridge Library. All Dunham Massey researchers owe great debts of gratitude to Mrs Joyce Littler for her transcription of the three vast estate surveys and rentals. Warrington's personal and estate finances from 1732 are revealed in his account book, still held at Dunham Massey Hall.

# Bibliography

Manuscript Sources:

Beaufort Papers
Bodleian Library: Tanner papers
British Library: Add MSS 41805
Cheshire County Record Office:
    Diary of Sir Thomas Mainwaring;
    Earwaker Papers;
    Sir William Brereton's Letter Book
Chester City Record Office (now amalgamated with Cheshire CRO): Arderne Papers
Clark, J. Kent. *Goodwin Wharton*, Cardinal Press 1984.
Dunham Massey Hall:
    Booth, Henry. (2nd Lord Delamer, 1st Earl of Warrington.) *An Elegy on the Right Honourable George, Lord Delamer, who deceased August 8th 1684.*
    George. Earl of Warrington. *An Account of the Disbursements out of my Estate beginning with the Year of our Lord 1732 and ending with the year 1750*
John Rylands University Library of Manchester
    Dunham Massey Papers
    Legh of Lyme Correspondence
    Tatton of Wythenshawe Papers.
National Library of Wales: Powis Papers and Archive
University of Cambridge Library: Cholmondeley MSS


Published Sources:

*A Dialogue betwixt Sir George Booth and Sir John Presbyter at their Meeting near Chester*, London, printed for William Wilde 1659.
Beckett J.V. and Jones C. *Financial Improvidence and Political Independence in the Early Eighteenth Century* (JRULM 1982)
Beddard, Robert. *A Kingdom Without a King,* (Phaidon Press 1988)
R. Bellet, (ed) *Memorials of the Civil War*, Fairfax Correspondence.
Bevan, Brian *James, Duke of Monmouth* (Hale, 1979)
Blackwood, B.G. *The Cavalier and Roundhead Gentry of Lancashire.* Reprinted from the Transactions of the Lancashire & Cheshire Antiquarian Society (ThCAS) 1974.
Briscoe, A. Daly. *A Stuart Benefactress, Sarah, Duchess of Somerset.* T. Dalton, 1973.
Booth, Henry. (2nd Lord Delamer, 1st Earl of Warrington.) *A Speech on the Corruption of Judges His Lordship's Advice to his Children* (Collected Works, printed for John Lawrence at the Peacock, St Paul's Churchyard.) *The Late Lord Russell's Case, with Observations upon it.*
Broston, John. *Vale Royal of England* 1797.
Calendar of Clarendon State Papers; Calendar of the Committee for Compounding; Calendar of State Papers Colonial, America & West Indies; Calendar of State Papers Domestic; Calendar of State Papers Venetian; Calendar of Treasury Books.
Camden Society.
    *Hatton Family Correspondence* 1878.
    *The Clarke Papers,* C.H. Firth ed, 1894, reissued 1994.
    Letter Book of John, Viscount Mordaunt 1945.
    *Diurnal of Thomas Rugge* 1961.
    *Edmund Ludlow, a Voice from the Watch Tower* 1978.
Carlton, Charles. *Going to the Wars,* Routledge 1995
Cheshire Sheaf - all series, but badly indexed.

Chetham Society

   Vol.4 (Old Series) Life of Adam Martindale.   Vol.18 (OS) Diary of Henry Newcome.

   Vol.26 (0.5) Autobiography of Henry Newcome.  Vol.50, Lancashire Lieutenancy under the Stuarts.

   Vol.57 (Chetham Miscellanies 3).  Vol. 62, A Discourse of the War in Lancashire.

   Vol. 65, Civil War Tracts of Cheshire.

   Vol. 84 Cheshire Inquisitions Second Series Vol. 2, Civil War Tracts of Lancashire.

*Considerations upon the Institution of Marriage. By a Gentleman.* (2nd Earl of Warrington.)

Churchill, Sir Winston *History of the English Speaking Peoples* (Cassell)

Davies, Godfrey. *The Early Stuarts* and *The Later Stuarts* Oxford University Press 1959.

Dore, R.N. (ed) *The Cheshire Rising of 1659.* (TLCAS)

Dore, R.N. *A History of Hale, Cheshire* John Sherratt & Son Ltd 1972.

Earwaker, J.P. *East Cheshire Past and Present* 1877.

Evelyn, John. *Diary,* (J.M. Dent, 1966.)

Fiennes, Celia. *The Illustrated Journeys, c. 1682-1712* C. Morris ed, Macdonald 1982.

Ford, Lord Grey *A Secret History of the Rye House Plot and of the Monmouth Rebellion* (London 1754)

Higson, P.J.W. *Some Leading Promoters of Nonconformity* Reprinted from TLCAS 1969.

Historic Manuscripts Commission, 4th Report, 6th Report, 7th Report, 11th Report, 15th Report.

Bath Mss. Coke Mss, Fleming MSS. House of Lords MSS, Portland MSS. Leybume-Popham MSS.

House of Lords Journals

Ingham, Alfred. *History of Altrincham and Bowdon* 1879.

Jones, J.R. *The First Whigs, the Politics of the Exclusion Crisis 1678-83.* Oxford University Press 1961.

Journal of the Chester and N. Wales Architectural, Archaeological and Historic Society Vol 18.

                              (Diary of George Booth and Katherine Howard)

Kenyon, John & Ohlmeyer. Jane. *The Civil Wars, a Military History.* Oxford University Press 1998.

Luttrell, N. *A Brief Historical Relation of State Affairs from September 1678 to April 1714* London 1857.

*Life and Errors of John Dunton, Citizen of London.* (London 1818)

Mainwaring, Sir Thomas, *Diary* (Cheshire CRO)

Morrill, J. S. *Cheshire 1630 to 1660* Oxford University Press 1974.

Morrill J.S. and Dore, R.N. *The Allegiance of the Cheshire Gentry in the Great Civil War.* Rep 1974.

Morris, R.H. and Lawson, P.H. *The Siege of Chester.* 1924.

Newton, Lady. *Lyme Letters 1660-1760* 1925.

Ormerod, George. *History of the County Palatine of Chester* 1882.

Pepys, Samuel. *Diary,* (R.C. Latham and W. Matthews ed)

Record Society of Lancashire and Cheshire (RSLC). Vol. 94 (1940) Cheshire Quarter Sessions Papers.

                         Vols. 123 and 128, The Letter Books of Sir William Brereton.

Reresby, Sir John. *Memoirs.* (Andrew Browning ed, Jackson & son, 1936.)

Richards, Jeff. *Aristocrat and Regicide, the Life and Times of Thomas, Lord Grey of Groby.*

                              (New Millennium Pres, 2000)

Ridley, Jasper. *Elizabeth I.* Guild Publishing, London 1987

Rushworth, John. *Historical Recollections* Part 3, Vol. 2.

Scott, A.F. *Everyone a Witness, the Stuart Age.* White Lion Publishers 1974.

*Seventeenth Century England, a Chanting Culture* (Ann Hughes ed, Open University)

Sir George Booth's Letter of the 2nd August 1659, shewing the Reasons of his Present Engagement.
       Together with an Answer to the said Letter, Invalidating the Said Reasons. London 1659.

Snewin, Caroline. *The Civil War & Siege of Chester.* Barnardos North West 1989.

Surtees Society, Second Series, Sir William Brereton's Journal 1635.

The Tryal of Henry Baron Delamer for High Treason in Westminster Hall the 14th day of January
       1685/6.  Printed for Dorman Newman at the Kings Arms in the Poultry, London, 1686.

Thurloe State Papers.

Verney, Margaret. *Memoirs of the Verney Family during the Commonwealth* Longmans Green, 1894.